"This combination of practical guidebook and skiing history will enrich any backcountry skier's experience. I love the concept of *Powder Ghost Towns*, and can't wait for winter to check out the lost ski areas—with Peter's fascinating and useful book hired as my guide."

—*Louis Dawson, WildSnow.com*

"*Powder Ghost Towns* offers a tremendous review of Colorado's rich ski history. Peter's blending of story-telling and extremely thorough route information will land *Powder Ghost Towns* at the front of my guidebook shelf. *Powder Ghost Towns* is a must-read for anyone searching for new places to play in Colorado's winter backcountry."

—*Brian Holcombe, Executive Director,*
Backcountry Snowsports Alliance

"*Powder Ghost Towns* is right-on for any skier looking for a guided introduction to the backcountry. It's all here: route choices and maps. Even more experienced Colorado backcountry skiers will be fascinated by learning what was here in the beginning—and how many "new" areas of the state are waiting to be skied! The majority of the routes described here are safe and accessible for most of the winter and spring—I'd feel good about new backcountry skiers heading out with this book."

—*Pete Swenson, founder,*
Colorado Ski Mountaineering Cup

T0165963

Powder

GHOST
TOWNS

Epic Backcountry
Runs in Colorado's
Lost Ski Resorts

Peter Bronski

 WILDERNESS PRESS ... *on the trail since 1967*

To Tom and Andrew, for their inspiration, motivation,
and, oftentimes, perspiration

**Powder Ghost Towns: Epic Backcountry Runs
in Colorado's Lost Ski Resorts**

1st EDITION 2008
Copyright © 2008 by Peter Bronski

Front and back cover photos copyright © 2008 by Peter Bronski
Interior photos by Peter Bronski, except for the following by Kelli
Bronski: pp. 6, 139, 178, 234, and 244.
Maps: Peter Bronski
Cover and book design: Lisa Pletka
Book editor: Marc Lecard

ISBN 978-0-89997-466-8 (paperback); ISBN 978-0-89997-518-4 (ebook)
ISBN 978-1-64359-002-8 (hardcover)

Manufactured in the United States of America

Published by: **Wilderness Press**
              An imprint of AdventureKEEN
              2204 First Avenue South, Suite 102
              Birmingham, AL 35233
              (800) 443-7227
              www.wildernesspress.com

Visit our website for a complete listing of our books and for
ordering information.

Distributed by Publishers Group West

Cover photos: A skier's solitary tracks in the main bowl at Little Annie
                   (front, main); the author, taking another lap at Little Annie
                   (front, top inset); buildings lay dormant at the base of
                   Cuchara Mountain Resort, while the ski runs beckon on
                   the mountain beyond *(front, center inset)*; looking back
                   into the Ragged Mountain Wilderness from the slopes of
                   Mount Daly above the Marble Ski Area *(front, bottom inset)*

Frontispiece: Looking down a run at Mesa Creek, on the north slopes of
                   the Grand Mesa

SAFETY NOTICE: Although Wilderness Press and the author have made every
attempt to ensure that the information in this book is accurate at press time, they
are not responsible for any loss, damage, injury, or inconvenience that may occur
to anyone while using this book. You are responsible for your own safety and
health while in the wilderness. The fact that a route is described in this book does
not mean that it will be safe for you. Be aware that route conditions can change
from day to day. Always check local conditions and know your own limitations.

ACKNOWLEDGMENTS

As with any book, *Powder Ghost Towns* was the result of so much more than my individual effort. It was possible only through the support and assistance of many people.

First, my thanks go out to my editors, Roslyn Bullas, Marc Lecard, and Eva Dienel, and everyone at Wilderness Press, who believed in *Powder Ghost Towns* and its potential.

I'm also indebted to my friends and family who willingly and happily joined me in the backcountry for research, work, fun, powder days, and whatever else you'd like to call it, and who were infinitely patient as I photographed them skiing: Sara Anderson, Jeff Braucher, Kelli Bronski, Tom Hudson, Andrew Jones, Karla Terry, and Josh Wilkin.

I am also grateful to the many people and organizations who contributed in ways big and small to the historical research of the ski areas: Arapaho and Roosevelt national forests (especially Nicole Branton), the Backcountry Snowsports Alliance (especially Brian Holcombe), Sue Brandl, George Brodin, the Colorado Mountain Club (especially Nina Johnson, Doug Skiba, and Jan Robertson), Colorado Ski History (especially Brad Chamberlain), the Colorado Ski Museum (especially Fred Brewer, Justin Henderson, Lynn Link, and Pat Pfeiffer), the Diamond Peaks Ski Patrol, Bill Fetcher, Huerfano County, Los Animas County, Medicine Bow and Routt national forests (especially John Baumchen, Tom Florich, Kacey Hull, and Vern Bentley), Michael Miner, the Moose River Visitor Center (Colorado State Forest), Chris Roth, White River National Forest, and Bill Whittaker.

Most of all, thank you to my wife, Kelli. You have continued to show unconditional love and support for me and my writing career. When I needed to research yet another lost ski area, you without hesitation grabbed your skis and asked, "Where to next?" As manuscript deadlines approached, you ensured that I was able to focus on nothing more than the writing. As ever, I couldn't have done this without you. Thank you, and I love you.

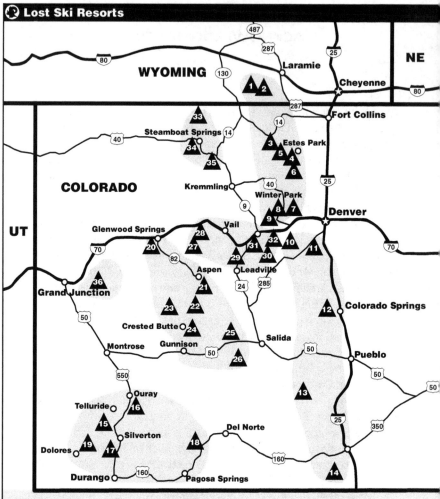

Lost Ski Resorts

Northern Front Range
1. Barrett Ridge
2. Libby Creek
3. Seven Utes
4. Fern Lake
5. Hidden Valley
6. Rock Creek
7. Saint Mary's Glacier
8. Berthoud Pass
9. Jones Pass

Southern Front Range
10. Geneva Basin
11. Mount Lugo
12. Pikes Peak/Glen Cove
13. Conquistador
14. Cuchara

San Juan Mountains
15. Lizard Head Pass
16. Ironton Park
17. Coal Bank Pass
18. Wolf Creek Pass
19. Stoner

Central Mountains
20. Red Mountain
21. Little Annie
22. Montezuma Basin
23. Marble Mountain
24. Pioneer
25. White Pine
26. Marshall Pass

Interstate 70 Corridor
27. Adam's Rib
28. Meadow Mountain
29. Climax
30. Hoosier Pass
31. Peak One
32. Porcupine Gulch

Steamboat Zone
33. Steamboat Lake
34. Emerald Mountain
35. Baker Mountain

Western Slope
36. Mesa Creek

Legend

Large Cities
Medium Cities
Small Cities

 Lost Ski Area

25 Interstate Highway

285 U.S./State Highway

82 State Highway

State Capital

○ City

CONTENTS

Preface *ix* • Foreword *x*

Introduction 1

Lost Ski Resorts in the Northern Front Range 9

Lost Ski Resorts in the Southern Front Range 69

Lost Ski Resorts in the San Juan Mountains 105

Lost Ski Resorts in the Central Mountains 131

PREFACE

or years my love affair with skiing in Colorado held dual citizenship: in the backcountry, and at the resorts. It wasn't until the 2005/2006 winter season that the two came together in a unique marriage, and it all happened because of an unassuming email from my good friend Tom.

"We should go find and ski these places," was the full content of his message, plus a hyperlink to an Internet website, www.coloradoskihistory.com. It was the Rocky Mountain manifestation of a movement that had started in New England years earlier, known as the New England Lost Ski Areas Project. Ski history buffs were documenting the history of "lost" ski areas, ones that had long since closed their doors and shut their lifts. Some researchers hiked the ski areas during the summertime, walking up their grassy slopes and snapping photos of old buildings, lift foundations, whatever they saw. As far as Tom and I knew, though, no one was actually skiing these places in winter.

Tom was onto something, I thought. His idea gave birth to "Powder Stash," an article I wrote for *5280: Denver's Mile-High Magazine*, about four of Colorado's lost ski areas. It was during the research phase of that article that another friend, Andrew, made the suggestion that resulted in this book. We were backcountry skiing at Geneva Basin, the fourth and final area of my magazine article. Andrew and I were halfway down a run, grinning at each other—it was a powder day at a "resort," and we had the runs all to ourselves. "Have you thought about writing a guidebook to these areas?" he offered. "I would definitely be interested in skiing at more of these places." Andrew had a point.

Since that day in March 2007, I've skied at nearly 40 lost areas throughout Colorado and southern Wyoming. It's been a fantastic journey in so many ways—days spent in the backcountry with good friends; touching the history and heritage of Colorado's skiing past; powder days like I haven't had in years.

I initially worried that researching and writing this book would "burn me out" on skiing. That, by making skiing my job for a winter, it would cease to retain its casual pleasure, and would become drudgery as I obsessed about meeting my deadlines. But to my great joy, *Powder Ghost Towns* has been a rewarding, enlightening, and most of all, fun experience. And I hope the information contained within these pages offers the same to you.

Peter Bronski
September 2008

FOREWORD

hen one considers skiing in Colorado in the 21st century, names like Aspen, Vail, Telluride, and Breckenridge inevitably come to mind. The ski resort industry in Colorado has grown immensely from its humble, pre-World War II beginnings into one of the dominant winter sports regions in the world. But what few modern skiers and snowboarders realize is that the history of skiing and ski areas in Colorado is as rich as the gold and silver that were mined from these hills.

Scattered throughout the seven major mountain ranges in Colorado lay many forgotten ski hills, some small and others large, but all overgrown relics of a once vibrant skiing community, a community focused solely on the experience of skiing, and not the bottom line. From the earliest ski hills at Chalk Mountain, Pikes Peak, and Cement Creek, to more modern "lost ski areas" like Ski Rio, Berthoud Pass, and Conquistador, the shared history of vibrant Front Range ski clubs hosting jumping events and miners using immense wooden skis to race each other back to the bars runs deep.

Fortunately, modern backcountry skiers can relive much of the colorful history of these lost ski areas with a keen appetite for adventure and a desire to relive the old days. As a lifelong skier and college history major, I have spent many days ski touring over the deep and untracked snows of lost resorts like Marble, Montezuma, Geneva Basin, Berthoud Pass, and Dallas Divide, soaking up the sense of good times gone by and imagining myself as a skier in the 1930s or 1940s. While skinning up, one can contemplate the ghost skiers that once carved turns down these slopes, and take solace in the fact that our sport evolved to what it is today because of the experiences of those skiers and ski area operators. I love inspecting the old rope tows and broken-down lift shacks, imagining the joy that these slopes and tows brought to generations of skiers.

Inevitably, these ski hills will fade into the memories of the skiers that cared about them, and unfortunately, modern skiers and snowboarders may not know or care enough to keep their memories alive. Fortunately for backcountry skiers and ski history buffs, Peter Bronski has taken the time to accurately and with great detail guide us into the past so that we all might relive the glory days of skiing in Colorado. *Powder Ghost Towns* will inspire skiers to search out the ski history that may lie in their own backyard. With this book I'm confident that many of our lost ski areas will get a chance to relive their glory days as skiers once again seek out the joys of skiing and riding on their slopes.

Enjoy,
Chris Davenport
Old Snowmass, Colorado
September 2008

Chris Davenport is a professional big-mountain skier (www.steep skiing.com) who has appeared in more than a dozen feature ski films, including ones from Warren Miller Entertainment and Matchstick Productions. He is the second person to ski all of Colorado's Fourteeners (http://www.skithe14ers.com), and the first person to complete the feat in a single year.

Introduction

HISTORY

ecause the individual chapters of this book discuss Colorado's skiing history in great detail, here I'll paint the picture using only the broadest of brushes, so as to put the individual backcountry destinations and lost resorts into historical context.

The earliest documented skiing in Colorado dates back to the 1850s. Guides, doctors and nurses, priests, mailmen, and miners all skied simply to get about their work and daily lives through the heart of Rocky Mountain winters. Those earliest skis were made from wood, and averaged 8 to 12 feet long. Animal skins strapped to the base of the skis served as the "skins" that allowed for uphill travel.

It wasn't long before those pioneering skiers were racing one another downhill. By the 1880s, Crested Butte and Gunnison were already hosting ski races. In 1883, the Ski Club at Irwin became the first documented organization devoted to recreational skiing in the state. By 1887, skiers at Ouray had developed "après skiing," enjoying wine and food together after a day on the slopes.

Colorado hosted the first Winter Carnival west of the Mississippi in 1912 at Hot Sulphur Springs. Many other Winter Carnivals soon followed, as did an influx of Norwegians, Swedes, Swiss, and other talented skiers. Soon, native Coloradans started to leave their own mark on the state's ski culture. By 1936, Colorado had its first rope tow; by 1939, its first overhead chairlift. Both of these "firsts" belong to ski areas that are now lost, as do other significant milestones—first night skiing, lowest elevation ski area, first double chair.

The 10th Mountain Division, which trained at Camp Hale near Leadville, ushered in another era of skiing for Colorado. When the soldiers returned from World War II, they founded many of the state's megaresorts that operate today.

Today, only a relative handful of ski areas remain open—27, plus or minus a few in any given year. They include the big resorts—Breckenridge, Vail, Aspen, Telluride, and Steamboat—and also mom-and-pop

A skier approaches Ironclad Ridge, with the Rock Creek drainage and lower slopes of Saint Vrain Mountain behind.

Looking down the lift line of Bear Bumps at Cuchara Mountain Resort

locations such as Eldora, Monarch, Wolf Creek, and Sunlight. These resorts continue Colorado's legacy as "Ski Country USA." But it was the
lost ski areas—which total perhaps as many as 200—that started it all.

They closed for many reasons. Competition. Not enough skiers.
Inconsistent snowfall. Financial woes. Yet they all share one common
attribute—they've become Colorado's "other" ghost towns. They are
powder ghost towns, reclaimed by the mountains with the passage of
time and falling of snow each winter season. But they remain accessible to the backcountry skier who is willing to leave the beaten track
and the lifts behind in search of untouched powder and tangible pieces
of Colorado's skiing past.

USING THIS GUIDE

This section describes how to use the guidebook, including how lost ski areas were selected for inclusion, as well as the information you'll find within each chapter.

CRITERIA FOR INCLUSION

The selection process for deciding what lost ski areas would be included in the book was, in part, a subjective one. As the author of the book, I had the luxury of deciding which ones did and didn't make the cut. In general, every ski area had to have a blend of good history and good skiing. But I did try to bring a degree of objectivity to the table. Every ski area also had to satisfy three basic criteria:

- It had to be legally and publicly accessible (about half of Colorado's lost ski areas are on private property);

- It had to have enough vertical to make the skiing worthwhile (many lost ski areas were small rope tows with vertical measured at a few hundred feet or less);

- It had to have reliable snowfall (more than a few lost ski areas, especially those in the Front Range, closed for lack of consistent snowfall).

Those criteria were more guidelines, though, than hard and fast rules. In the end, I made choices intended to give you—the reader and backcountry skier—the best skiing. If it made sense to link up a smaller lost ski area with a larger area of backcountry terrain above it, I did so. In a select few cases, a historically significant ski area was fully or partly on private property, but the mountain above it or adjacent to it was perfectly public. In those cases I've sent you nearby. And in an equally small number of cases, I've included significant ski areas that were proposed but never built.

The remainder—the vast majority—are exactly what you'd expect; lost ski areas where you'll backcountry ski the same runs that were once served by lifts. In some instances, those areas are old enough to have become overgrown almost beyond the point of recognition. In other instances, the lost ski area remains so intact—with buildings and lifts and chairs hanging from those lifts—that the feeling is almost spooky. They genuinely feel like "powder ghost towns."

In the end, though, the areas selected for inclusion in this book all guide you to my original goal: good skiing blended with good history.

And in so doing, they offer a new world of backcountry possibilities to satisfy your powder dreams.

CHAPTER SECTIONS

Every chapter in this book includes the following information for each lost ski area:

The Essentials	Basic statistics that summarize the area.
The History	Just what it sounds like.
The Trailhead	Where to start.
The Approach	How to get there.
The Descents	How to get back down.
The "Buzz"	What other backcountry skiers have to say about it.
The Après Ski	Where to get food and drink when you're done on the slopes.

While most of those sections are largely self-explanatory, the first section—The Essentials—requires greater elaboration. Every chapter begins with a basic summary of statistics that summarize the ski area. Those statistics include:

Nearest Town

The closest town where you can expect to find basic services like gas and dining. This may not necessarily be the closest town as listed on a map, which might not provide those services.

Distance

The one-way distance from the trailhead to the highest point from which you'd start your ski descent.

Vertical

The amount of vertical gain you can expect from the trailhead en route to the high point. Typically, this is listed as the net vertical gain. However, if there is a significant difference between the net gain and the cumulative gain, the overall (cumulative) vertical gain will be listed parenthetically.

Season

The best time to ski the area.

Elevation Range

The highest and lowest elevations you'll encounter during your outing.

Difficulty Rating

An overall measure of the effort required to ski the area, listed as easy, moderate, or strenuous. Keep in mind that this is an overall estimate. Routes that have significantly shorter mileage but are off-trail through deep snow may be listed as more difficult than routes that have much longer mileage, but are on packed trails. This is not a measure of the difficulty of the skiing.

Skiing Rating

How good is the quality of the skiing? Indicated by one, two, or three ❄ symbols. One ❄ symbol indicates an area where the skiing experience is enhanced by the history of the place, even if the skiing isn't great. Two ❄ symbols indicates an area with good skiing, well worth returning to many times. Three ❄ symbols indicates great skiing—add it to your list of pilgrimage sites.

SNOTEL Station

SNOTEL is a program of the Natural Resources Conservation Service, and is an acronym for Snowpack Telemetry. The system is made up of a network of automated stations throughout the western United States that collect snowpack and climate data. The daily readings from those stations can be invaluable in deciding where to ski on a particular day. Each ski area lists the nearest SNOTEL station by both name and number. In order to view the data for a given station, select the SNOTEL site from the map or the drop-down menu on the following websites: www.wcc.nrcs.usda.gov/snotel/Colorado/colorado.html and www.wcc.nrcs.usda.gov/snotel/Wyoming/wyoming.html.

Forest Zone

Lists the jurisdiction in which the lost ski area is located. Full contact information, including street addresses and telephone numbers, are listed alphabetically for all forest zones in the Resources section on page 235. These are typically national forest ranger districts, although they may also be state parks, city or county open space programs, or other landowners.

CAIC Zone

Lists the zone in which the lost ski area is located. CAIC stands for the Colorado Avalanche Information Center. CAIC evaluates the stability of the snowpack regularly throughout the state, and posts daily updates on its website—http://avalanche.state.co.us—including an assessment of the avalanche hazard.

The author digs a snow pit to assess avalanche hazard in Montezuma Basin, near Aspen.

USGS Quad

The appropriate topographic map published by the U.S. Geological Survey.

Weather

Lists the code for the latest Zone Area Forecast, a mountain range-specific weather forecast provided by the National Weather Service. In order to review the forecast for your zone, visit the following website (in place of the "XXXXXX" at the end of the web address, type the six-digit letter and number code listed for the ski area): http://forecast.weather.gov/MapClick.php?zoneid=XXXXXX

Waypoints

Select GPS waypoints are given in the text for trailheads and topographic features of ski run approaches and descents. The Universal Transverse Mercator (UTM) system of map coordinates was used to establish the waypoints. The UTM system is based on lines of latitude and longitude, dividing the world into zones, and then subdividing those zones into a network of grids. UTM coordinates allow you to locate the correct grid, and then plot an "easting" and a "northing" to pinpoint a particular waypoint. For more information on the UTM grid, see the USGS website at http://erg.usgs.gov/isb/pubs/factsheets/fs07701.html.

SNOWPACK AND HAZARDS

Colorado's continental climate is notorious for creating an unstable snowpack. Please use safe travel techniques. Read a book about evaluating snowpack stability, avalanche hazard, and avalanche rescue (see the snow safety section in the Resources on page 237 for some suggested reading). Better yet (much better yet), take a class. Practice your skills to keep them fresh. Always wear a beacon, and carry a shovel and probe. Always travel with partners, and make sure that they do the same (and know how to use the equipment). Since entire books have been written about this topic, I won't say more here. But do take the hazard seriously. Your life depends on it.

PUBLIC AND PRIVATE LAND

Finally, I wanted to say a brief word about public and private lands. If you ski every run in this book and use every approach, you'll be on public land more than 90 percent of the time. But there will be times when you'll cross private land (on legal easements and rights-of-way), or will be skiing above or next to private property. Please respect private property. Although it may be tempting to poach runs—particularly in instances when the landowner is absentee and out of state—I don't recommend or condone such practices. If you make the decision to trespass on private property (and I hope you don't), you do so of your own free will and motivation.

Also, although it is unlikely, it is entirely possible that land will change hands from public to private, and vice versa, or that easements or rights-of-way will change. It is also possible, in a rare number of cases, that a lost ski area will be revived and reopen its doors, or that an application for a new special use permit may result in unexpected restrictions on areas that are otherwise public. All of these scenarios could affect the approaches and descents listed in this book. Always respect the current state of affairs, and please notify me, the author, of any such changes so that I may incorporate them into future editions of the guide. You may contact me through Wilderness Press at info@wildernesspress.com.

TOPOGRAPHIC MAPS AND AERIAL PHOTOS

Every ski area in this book is accompanied by a corresponding topographic map that shows trailhead locations, approach routes, and descents. For a subset of ski areas—those that still have a complex network of runs in the trees—I've also included an annotated aerial photograph, in order to make the runs and the terrain clearer than could be described in the text or on the topographic maps. All aerial photos are courtesy of the U.S. Geological Survey.

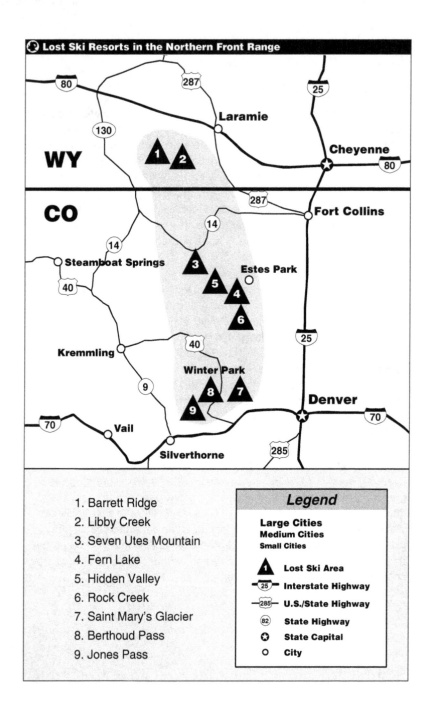

Lost Ski Resorts in the Northern Front Range

1. Barrett Ridge
2. Libby Creek
3. Seven Utes Mountain
4. Fern Lake
5. Hidden Valley
6. Rock Creek
7. Saint Mary's Glacier
8. Berthoud Pass
9. Jones Pass

Legend

Large Cities
Medium Cities
Small Cities

1 Lost Ski Area
25 Interstate Highway
285 U.S./State Highway
82 State Highway
State Capital
City

8

Lost Ski Resorts in the
Northern Front Range

The Northern Front Range describes the region stretching from the Medicine Bow Mountains and the Snowy Range in southern Wyoming south to Interstate 70, and extending west from Denver to Loveland Pass and the Eisenhower Tunnel. This section of the guide includes nine lost ski areas, though over the years many, many more have operated on the slopes of these mountains. Many of the lost ski areas closest to Denver and the Plains closed for a simple lack of snow—Magic Mountain in Golden, Genesee Mountain along I-70, Chautauqua Meadows in Boulder, and many more. Many others date back to the earliest days of lift-served skiing in Colorado—Fourth of July above Nederland, numerous sites around Granby, and Hot Sulphur Springs. Today, a scant few lift-served resorts remain: Winter Park, Sol Vista, Eldora, and Snowy Range. The lost areas are listed from north to south.

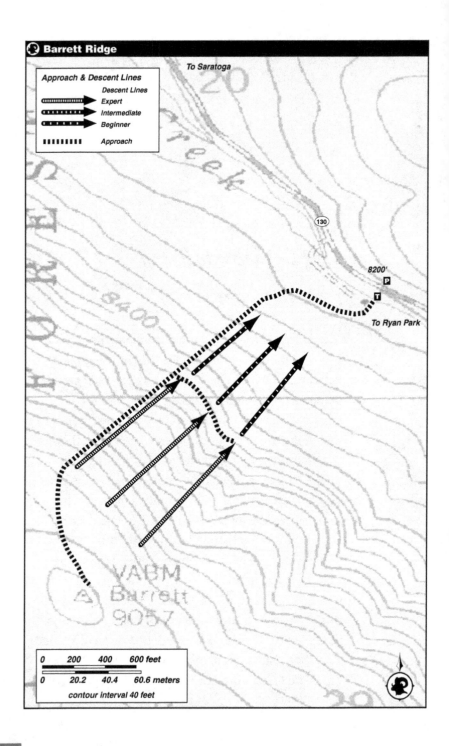

BARRETT RIDGE

THE ESSENTIALS

Nearest Town	Saratoga, WY	**SNOTEL Station**	South Brush Creek (772)
Distance	0.6 mile	**Forest Zone**	Medicine Bow National Forest, Brush Creek/ Hayden Ranger District
Vertical	800'		
Season	December to April		
Elevation Range	8200' to 9000'	**CAIC Zone**	None
Difficulty Rating	Easy	**USGS Quad**	Ryan Park, WY
Skiing Rating	⬥	**Weather**	WYZ063

THE HISTORY

Despite its relatively recent closure (sometime in the 1970s), painfully little is known about the old Barrett Ridge ski area. It had a lift, and at least two dominant ski runs. Beyond that, no one—not the area's museums, or national forest office, or local residents—seems to know or remember much at all. Barrett Ridge is an enigma and was one of the only lift-served ski areas on the west side of the Snowy Range.

Around the same time that Barrett Ridge operated, however, the U.S. Forest Service received a proposal for another ski area on the west side of the Snowy Range. To be called "Silver Creek," it would have been southwest of Snowy Pass and Medicine Bow Peak on a south-facing slope in the South French Creek drainage. Unique among ski areas in the Rockies, it would have been a "top base" ski area: You'd park your car at the top, and then ski down and ride the lifts back up to your car. The planned ski area had 1700 feet of vertical, but building it would have required plowing the Snowy Range Scenic Byway, which was closed in winter miles below the proposed ski area. It also would have required a new access road from the byway to the base area, a water source, electricity, and telephone lines. In spite of such challenges, the Forest Service thought it had potential. The agency's one recommendation: locate the base area at mid-height, so that if the lifts broke down, guests would only have to climb half the height of the ski area to get back to their cars.

Access to the area was planned via Saratoga and Ryan Park, and Silver Creek reportedly had the strong support of the Saratoga Inn (whose winter economy surely would have benefited from the skier traffic). Silver Creek almost got off the ground, but never did.

THE TRAILHEAD

Begin at the Ryan Park Ski Slope Trailhead on Highway 130. From Saratoga, Wyoming, drive south on combined Highway 130/230 for 8 miles. Turn left (east) onto Highway 130, and continue for another 13 miles. The road will make a sharp right turn, heading south. At this point, you'll cross into Medicine Bow National Forest. Three-tenths of a mile beyond the national forest boundary, you'll pass the Brush Creek Visitor Center (closed in winter) on your left, and 0.8 mile beyond the visitor center (and 1.1 miles beyond the national forest boundary), you'll arrive at the Ryan Park Ski Slope Trailhead, with a parking lot on the east (left) side of the highway (**UTM: 13 372947 4576890**). If you reach Ryan Park Road and the minuscule town of Ryan Park, you've gone too far.

Alternatively, from Riverside, Wyoming, drive north on Highway 230 for 10 miles, turn right (east) onto Highway 130 and continue as above.

The "Buzz"

If you like getting away from the crowds, this is the place to do it. There are no major towns for a long way in any direction. With the minimal approach, if this area were located anywhere else closer to a population center, it'd be swarmed with skiers and sledders.

—The author

THE APPROACH

The old Barrett Ridge ski area is literally roadside, and the approach is about as short as it can get. From the parking lot, cross to the west side of Highway 130, descend to Barrett Creek and cross to the base of an open, snowy meadow. You're at the base of the ski area. Three primary runs are visible from here. Looking up-slope, there is a main run on the left, a main run in the middle, and the lift line on the right. The simplest approach is to pick your line and skin up it. If you're intent on reaching the 9000-foot crest of Barrett Ridge (**UTM: 13 372228 4576360**) to squeeze out the most vertical, the easiest passage to the top is via the lift line. A trail traverses the slope at about mid-height, allowing easy movement between the various runs. About two-thirds of the way up the slope, the lift line appears to close out in a stand of trees. Continue up the fall line, and the lift line will become evident once again. Stay the course and finish in an open stand of evergreens atop the ridge.

THE DESCENTS

Barrett Ridge has three primary runs. Standing atop the ridge, there is **a large run on skier's right**, **a large run on skier's left**, and **the lift**

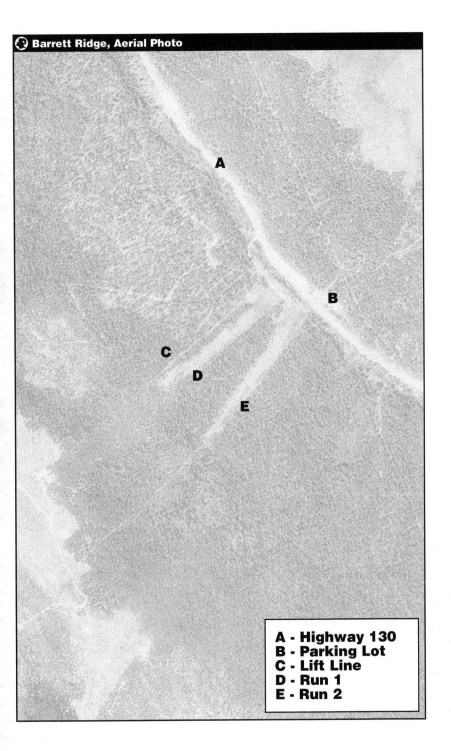

Barrett Ridge, Aerial Photo

A - Highway 130
B - Parking Lot
C - Lift Line
D - Run 1
E - Run 2

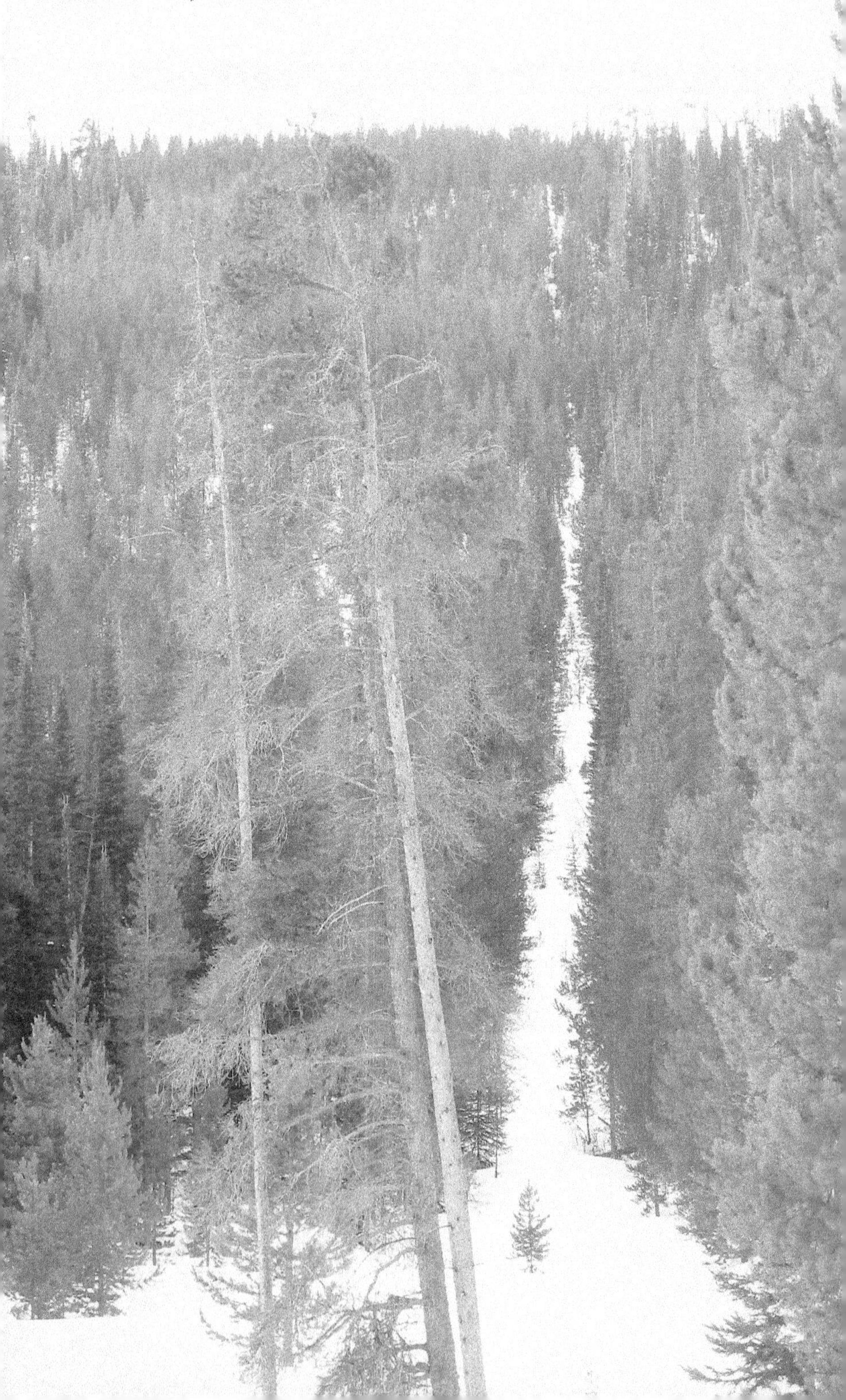

line farthest to the left. All three runs have similar slope angles (more gentle at the bottom, steeper high in the trees). If you want to do lots of short laps on wide-open runs, stick to the bottom half of your chosen run. If you want to get in more vertical per lap, and enjoy skiing steeper lines through tight trees, ascend the lift line to the top of Barrett Ridge.

THE APRÈS SKI

Don't expect much of an après ski scene in this quiet corner of Wyoming. But you can try these options in Saratoga:

Espresso Bellissima, 1st and Bridge streets, (307) 326-3477

Hotel Wolf Restaurant, 101 East Bridge Street, (307) 326-5525, www.wolfhotel.com

Silver Saddle Restaurant, Saratoga Inn, 601 East Pic Pike Road, (307) 326-5261, www.saratogainn.com

Warm Springs Cafe, 405 North 1st Street, (307) 326-5046

In Riverside (population: 59), try the **Mangy Moose Saloon** (no listed phone number or address, but you can't miss it on Highway 230).

Looking up the lift line at Barrett Ridge

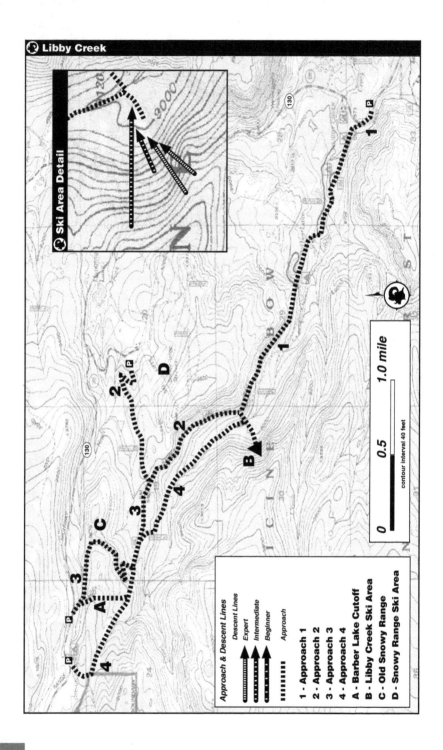

Libby Creek

Ski Area Detail

Approach & Descent Lines

Descent Lines
Expert
Intermediate
Beginner
Approach

1 - Approach 1
2 - Approach 2
3 - Approach 3
4 - Approach 4
A - Barber Lake Cutoff
B - Libby Creek Ski Area
C - Old Snowy Range
D - Snowy Range Ski Area

0   0.5   1.0 mile
contour interval 40 feet

LIBBY CREEK

THE ESSENTIALS

Nearest Town	Centennial, WY
Distance	3 miles max.
Vertical	600′ to 1400′
Season	December to April
Elevation Range	8573′ to 9800′
Difficulty Rating	Moderate
Skiing Rating	❷ ❷ ❷

SNOTEL Station	Brooklyn Lake (367)
Forest Zone	Medicine Bow National Forest, Laramie Ranger District
CAIC Zone	None
USGS Quad	Centennial, WY
Weather	WYZ063

THE HISTORY

The history of the old Libby Creek ski area is complicated by the fact that it was once known as the Snowy Range ski area, and that, over time, a total of four ski areas (three lost, and one still in operation) have had the name "Snowy Range ski area." For the sake of clarity, I will refer to them as:

- Barrett Ridge (the old ski area near Ryan Park on the west side of the Snowy Range; see the previous trip)

- Old Snowy Range (an old ski area north of Libby Creek and west of present-day Snowy Range ski area)

- Snowy Range (currently operating)

- Libby Creek (the subject of this trip)

The Snowy Range in southeastern Wyoming (southwest of Laramie) is an extension of the Medicine Bow Mountains that begins at Cameron Pass in Colorado. The earliest history of lift-served skiing in the Snowies, as they're known locally, seems to belong to the Old Snowy Range ski area. The details, though, have been lost to the sands of time. Very little is known about this area, including its years of operation. Its location, on the other hand, is known: it operated on the slopes of a small, rounded mountain in the area bounded by Nash Fork/Highway 130, the Barber Lake Road, and Forest Road 351-g.

Then, sometime in the 1930s, the Libby Creek ski area came onto the scene. It was one quarter mile south of present-day Snowy Range ski area, and one mile south of Old Snowy Range ski area. Though its exact opening year is uncertain, its "glory days" spanned the late 1930s and throughout the 1940s (in 1938 the U.S. Forest Service documented 6800 skiers at Libby). It was considered too steep for most skiers (most runs were "expert"), and had a small, avalanche-prone area (called

"Gully" in "The Descents"). It operated sporadically throughout World War II and into the 1950s.

Libby Creek had only limited parking along the side of old Highway 130 (Barber Lake Road). You couldn't actually drive to the base of the ski area. From the roadside parking along the highway, you'd walk down a set of wooden stairs that descended a scree and talus slope. From the bottom of the stairs, you'd clip into your skis and ski across a meadow to the base lodge. From there you could at last hop on one of two rope tows or a chairlift. At the end of the day you had to hike out back to your car.

By 1957 or 1958, Libby Creek closed. But soon, a new area was coming into its own. In March 1959, Forest Service rangers made a reconnaissance of the Nash Fork (near present-day Highway 130). They drove to the Libby Creek ski area, and then headed north on foot and on skis. The official opinion: the potential ski area was more desirable than both Libby Creek and Happy Jack (an area along Interstate 80 east of Laramie). Building the new ski area, however, would require an access road (present-day Forest Road 351-g—Approach 2 in the following sections).

The Forest Service, though, didn't think anyone would want to develop it. Nevertheless, the agency opened it up for bids on August 1, 1959. Six short months later, in January 1960, a Kansas City group signed a 30-year permit. The Nash Fork ski area opened as Medicine Bow for the 1960/1961 season with two T-bars serving 600 feet of vertical, a shelter house, restaurant, and parking lot. Later, in the 1980s, a chairlift was added, and the name changed again to Snowy Range Ski Area. Today, Snowy Range has four chairlifts and a "magic carpet" serving 1000 feet of vertical on 27 trails. As of April 2008, Snowy Range Ski Area was for sale, everything included, for the price of $6.5 million.

Libby Creek, meanwhile, has become a consummate backcountry destination.

THE TRAILHEAD

The old Libby Creek ski area is located in the Snowy Range along Barber Lake Road, which is closed in winter. Because of this, there are four possible trailheads, and four corresponding approaches, for the Libby Creek ski area. No one option is necessarily better than another. It's simply a matter of personal preference (mine is for Approach 3, but pick your poison). I describe them here in the order they're encountered as you drive west up into the Snowy Range from Centennial.

From Centennial, Wyoming, continue west on Highway 130 (Snowy Range Scenic Byway) for 1.75 miles to the Medicine Bow

National Forest/Centennial Information Center on the right-hand side of the road. Park here for **Approach 1**.

One quarter mile beyond the information center, pass the lower junction of Highway 130 and Barber Lake Road (remember it's closed in winter). Continue on Highway 130. Three miles beyond the information center, you'll arrive at the turnoff for the Snowy Range Ski Area. For **Approach 2**, turn left here, as if you're going to the ski area. The road descends toward the ski area. Shortly before arriving at the base of the ski area, the road forks. The left fork descends to the ski area parking lot and base lodge. The right fork ascends slightly to a maintenance area and parking lot for snow-grooming equipment. Although it may feel wrong, this is where you're supposed to go. Park here for the Medicine Bow Trailhead, the start of **Approach 2**.

The *"Buzz"*

The northeast aspect of the ski area holds powder really well, even when there hasn't been a fresh snowfall for a while. Though the trailhead was bitterly cold and windy, Libby Creek stayed well-protected and was a ton of fun.

—Josh W.

Otherwise, remain on Highway 130 heading west, and after another 2 miles, arrive at the upper junction of Highway 130 and Barber Lake Road. This junction is marked by a sign, an abundance of trucks and trailers for snowmobiles, and a sign indicating the winter closure of the Snowy Range Scenic Byway just beyond. Park here for **Approach 3**.

Finally, for **Approach 4**, continue another 0.75 mile beyond the upper junction of Highway 130 and Barber Lake Road, and park at the Green Rock Trailhead on the left-hand side of the road. This trailhead is for skiers only; snowmobiles aren't allowed in the parking lot or on the trails.

THE APPROACH

The four possible approaches are described here in the same order as their corresponding trailheads in the previous section:

Approach 1
Uphill on the way in, downhill on the way out

From the information center, shoulder your skis and walk west along the shoulder of Highway 130 for a quarter mile to the lower junction of Highway 130 and Barber Lake Road. Click in to your skis and skins and follow Barber Lake Road west. After 1 mile, pass Barber Lake, and after 2 miles, you should be directly across the valley from the old Libby

Creek ski area. The road is on the north side of the valley, beneath some small, south-facing cliffs. The valley drops down to the south, and the open runs and arrow-straight slot in the trees that was the lift line should be plainly visible to the southwest. As an additional landmark, the road here rounds a sharp bend, turning from west to north. From here (**UTM: 13 400416 4576042**), drop off the road, descending a talus slope and then a tree-covered slope to the base of the valley. Here you'll intersect the Barber Lake Trail, which follows Libby Creek. Turn left (southeast) on the trail, and follow it to a small opening in the trees where the trail meets the creek. Cross the creek, and then continue southwest through the trees to a large, open meadow at the base of the ski area (**UTM: 13 400166 4575906**).

Approach 2
Uphill and downhill on the way in, uphill and downhill on the way out
From the Medicine Bow Trailhead at the Snowy Range Ski Area, follow Forest Road 351-g west-southwest for 1 mile to its intersection with Barber Lake Road. At Barber Lake Road, turn left (southeast) and continue for another mile. From here, drop off the road and continue as for **Approach 1.**

Approach 3
Downhill on the way in, uphill on the way out
From the upper junction of Highway 130 and Barber Lake Road, start out heading east on Barber Lake Road. **Almost immediately, you'll have to make the first of two decisions.** After less than a quarter of a mile, the Barber Lake Trail Cutoff heads right (south) into the trees. You can either stay on the Barber Lake Road (which has good views of the valley but is exposed to wind and open to snowmobile travel), or take the Barber Lake Trail Cutoff, which ducks into the protection and quiet of the trees, and is slightly shorter.

If you stay on Barber Lake Road, continue for three-quarters of a mile to a pair of sharp switchbacks before the road heads dead east. If you take the Barber Lake Trail Cutoff, head south for a quarter mile to the junction with the Barber Lake Trail (marked with blue diamonds). Turn left (east) and continue for another quarter mile until the trail merges with Barber Lake Road at the base of the last switchback. For the next quarter mile, the road and trail routes are the same.

Then it's time for the second decision: remain on the Barber Lake Road again, or take the Barber Lake Trail. If you've never been to Libby Creek before, staying on the road can be useful for navigation, and identifying exactly when you should cross Libby Creek and head southwest to the base of the old ski area. If you've been to Libby Creek before, are confident in your navigation, or enjoy the quiet and protection of the trees, take the trail. If you choose to stay on the road, after a quarter mile you will reach the junction with Forest Road 351-g. Continue as for Approaches 1 and 2. If you choose to take the trail, follow blue diamonds mounted on trees on the valley floor along the north side of Libby Creek for roughly 1 mile. Shortly before you reach the creek crossing, a yellow metal sign on a tree reads: ROCKS ON TRAIL, CAUTION, 100 FEET AHEAD. Shortly past that sign, the Barber Lake Trail enters a small clearing where the trail meets up with the creek. Cross here and continue as for **Approach 1**.

Approach 4
Downhill on the way in, uphill on the way out

From the Green Rock Trailhead, start out going southwest on the combined Barber Lake/Libby Creek trail (marked with blue diamonds). The route swings through the east edge of a large, open meadow (often brutally cold and windswept) before turning to the east-southeast. After a half mile, the Libby Creek Trail turns sharply right (south). Do not take this trail. It will add significantly to your mileage! Continue straight on the Barber Lake Trail. This junction is well-marked. After another half mile, the Barber Lake Trail Cutoff comes in from the left. Continue as for **Approach 3** on the Barber Lake Trail.

THE DESCENTS

There are five primary descents at Libby Creek. Looking up at the ski area from the base, and describing them from right to left, they are: **Lift Line, Main Run, Glade, Pitch,** and **Gully.** For **Lift Line** and **Main Run,** you can either skin directly up your intended run, or, to preserve the powder, skin up in the trees to climber's right of the ski runs. The second option is also a more mellow angle, which is nicer for the skinning, though it does add distance. For the remaining three runs—**Glade, Pitch,** and **Gully**—from the meadow at the base, skin directly up to your intended descent route.

Lift Line: From the top of the lift line, ski straight down. End in the meadow. 30 degrees.

Main Run: From the top of the lift line, make a descending traverse to skier's right for 50–75 yards before beginning your descent. You'll soon intersect the open run. As each stretch of open run closes out in the trees, stair-step to skier's left to link up with more open runs. Eventually, this will funnel you into the largest ski run, which overlaps at the bottom with the lift line. End in the meadow. 25–30 degrees.

Glade: The Main Run and the **Pitch** are separated from one another by a stand of trees open enough to enjoyably link turns. 25-30 degrees.

Pitch: From the meadow, trend to climber's left until you intersect a narrow open slot that leads up through the trees. Follow this slot up—it gets steep for skinning. When it seems to peter out, continue up and right, emerging into a much more open area. Follow the run up to its topmost point. 35 degrees.

Gully: From the top of the **Pitch,** continue up to climber's left, intersecting an open, treeless gully. 40 degrees.

Looking down the lift line at Libby Creek

EXTRA CREDIT

Ski one of the *other* lost Snowy Range ski areas, which you pass on your way to Libby Creek if using approaches 2, 3, or 4. Refer to the topo map for their specific locations.

THE APRÈS SKI

The après ski scene isn't exactly thriving in Centennial (population: 100), but the town has an authentic Wild West feel and you can find a beer and steak when you need 'em. Try the **Old Corral Steakhouse** (2750 Highway 130, 307-745-5918, www.oldcorral.com).

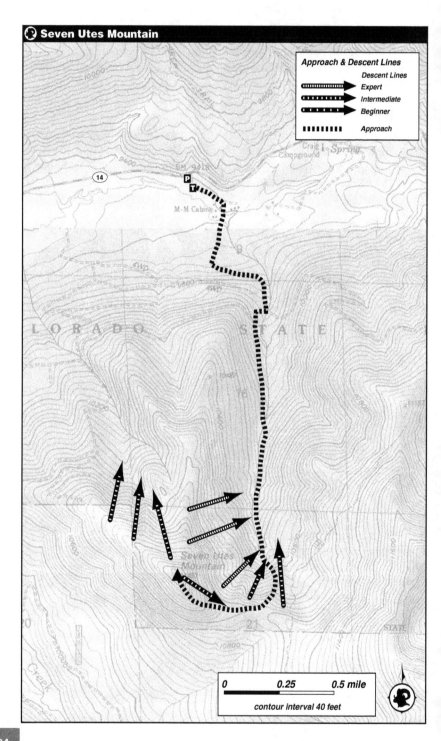

Approach & Descent Lines

Descent Lines
Expert
Intermediate
Beginner

Approach

0   0.25   0.5 mile

contour interval 40 feet

SEVEN UTES MOUNTAIN

THE ESSENTIALS

Nearest Town	Gould	**SNOTEL Station**	Joe Wright (551)
Distance	2.6 miles	**Forest Zone**	Colorado State Forest
Vertical	2000'	**CAIC Zone**	Front Range Mountains
Season	December to April	**USGS Quad**	Mount Richthofen
Elevation Range	9418' to 11,453'	**Weather**	COZ033
Difficulty Rating	Moderate		
Skiing Rating	❷ ❷ ❷		

THE HISTORY

Over the years, the Cameron Pass area has hosted a number of relatively small ski areas—rope tows and the like. The earliest documented lift-served skiing in the vicinity of Seven Utes dates to 1946, when the North Park Ski Hill operated on the north side of Highway 14 directly across from the old M-M Cabins and the trailhead for Seven Utes Mountain. A 1947 issue of the *Jackson County Star* reported that on March 21, 1946, 75 skiers showed up for a Sunday of skiing. The rope tow, which was operated by the North Park Ski Club, was 1100 feet long and gained about 600 feet of vertical. A warming hut was in the making. For members of the club, a season pass cost $5 for children, $10 for adults, or $15 for a family pass. Nonmembers could pay $1 per day for a lift ticket.

The North Park Ski Hill wasn't the only or earliest lift-served skiing in the area, however. On the east side of Cameron Pass, 5 miles below the pass and 2 miles above Chambers Lake, another ski area got its start in the winter of 1938/1939. It is generally known as the Chambers Lake ski area. In that first season, skiers and members of the Colorado Mountain Club cut test runs, checked snow depths, and obtained funding for a new ski area. The county agreed to keep the road open in winter. The U.S. Forest Service and Civilian Conservation Corps took over cutting more ski trails. Meanwhile, the Cameron Pass Ski Club converted an old cabin at the base of the area into a shelter house for skiers and ski patrol members. Hot lunches were served on weekends. The area had two primary runs, each with 300 feet of vertical drop: one a quarter mile long, the other three-eighths of a mile long. Some 125 people eventually joined the ski club, and the area probably remained open until 1951. At one point over those years it extended one of its lifts onto an adjacent ridge to access more terrain.

But the North Park Ski Hill, Chambers Lake ski area, and others like it, were nothing compared to what would have been built on Seven Utes Mountain. Rumors of a large, potential ski area on Seven Utes first publicly surfaced in 1968. Denver was anticipating making a bid to host the 1976 winter Olympics. It needed sites for the downhill and slalom ski races, and the state set its sights on a number of potential areas. Seven Utes was one of them.

A January 1969 report stressed the "recreational and scenic importance" of the Seven Utes-Cameron Pass area. Meanwhile, potential investors in the would-be Seven Utes ski area came to the table claiming $25 million in available funds to start the project. Updated reports estimated that only $3 million was needed to actually start work on the new ski area. But throughout the 1970s and 1980s, a series of additional studies—environmental, skier, wetlands impacts, socioeconomic—held up the process. Over that time, the earlier investors lost interest and walked away.

Even so, the state considered Seven Utes a great site. It had a north-facing aspect, good snow, favorable terrain, and more than 2000 feet of vertical. On the spectrum of potential locations for new ski areas statewide, the Forest Service rated Seven Utes "exceptionally good." The agency estimated that the ski season could run from November to April, with a natural 50-inch base in February, an average annual snowfall of 250 inches, and a maximum annual snowfall of 450 inches.

Then, in 1993, California developer Fred Sauer unveiled a new plan. Sauer's idea was to build a new ski resort, Seven Utes Resort, on the north face of Seven Utes Mountain. In addition to skiing, the development would have included a major hotel, ice-skating rink, golf course, spa, tennis facilities, and more. The base area would have been located near Ranger Lakes, close to the site of the present-day visitor center. The sum total of the development would have been an incredible 4500 acres, putting it almost on par with Vail for sheer size.

Almost from the beginning, though, the proposed ski resort was mired in challenges. The land on which Sauer desired to build was located within Colorado State Forest. In other words, if he wanted to build, he would need to buy some prime real estate outright. The sale of state trust land is prohibited, however, and the execution of Sauer's plan would have required a complicated land exchange of 1200 acres. In addition, the resort would have bordered both Routt National Forest and Rocky Mountain National Park, further complicating the legalities. The Poudre Canyon Group of the Sierra Club rose up against the project. Also, despite the likelihood that the development would have brought an economic boost to the region, nearby residents of tiny, rural

Skinning up to the saddle between Seven Utes Mountain and Mount Mahler

Gould fought Sauer. Led by Don Ewy, a self-employed logger, the group of community activists, environmentalists, ranchers, loggers, and residents successfully opposed the resort.

By mid-November 1993, the State Land Board had received more than 2200 comments, including 1600 letters. Of those 2200 comments, fewer than 900 were supportive of Seven Utes. Governor Roy Romer publicly opposed the project. By December 15, 1993, Seven Utes Resort was dead.

Today, the Seven Utes and Cameron Pass area remains one of the least populated and least developed corners of Colorado's High Country. The land is wild, the scenery is largely uninterrupted by human development, and the backcountry skiing draws a passionate and dedicated following of folks, including a large contingent from the Fort Collins area. The closest you'll come to lift-served skiing here is the Diamond Peaks Ski Patrol, an all-volunteer group of backcountry skiers trained in search and rescue and avalanche awareness. Otherwise, to ski Seven Utes Mountain and the would-be Seven Utes Resort is to experience the kind of great conditions that caused developers like Sauer to dream of building a ski area here in the first place.

THE TRAILHEAD

Begin at the Seven Utes Trailhead (**UTM: 13 420910 4484022**), which is located on the south side of Colorado Highway 14 between Gould and Cameron Pass, at the old road to the M-M Cabins. If you're coming from the east, from the summit of Cameron Pass, drive west on Colorado 14 for 4 miles. If coming from the west, measure from the junction of Colorado 14 and County Route 21 in the town of Gould. Drive east on Colorado 14, passing the Moose Visitor Center (State Forest Headquarters at Ranger Lakes) at mile 4.0, and arriving at the trailhead at mile 5.6.

THE APPROACH

From the trailhead, follow the well-defined road south-southeast, and then east-southeast for 0.2 mile. Here, the road passes through a small stand of evergreens with a state forest gate before the terrain opens up again into a wide meadow. Do not continue east across the meadow. Instead, turn south on an unnamed trail, descend slightly to cross the Michigan River, and continue south-southwest on a well-beaten trail.

The turnoff for this trail on the west end of the meadow can be difficult to find. Take your time.

Once on the well-established trail south of the Michigan River, follow it. At mile 0.5, the route makes a sharp left turn, heading east as it makes a gentle, rising traverse of the lower north slopes of Seven Utes Mountain. At mile 0.75, the route makes a right turn, again heading due south. Here, the forest opens up into a small clearing, and the slope falls away to your left (west) into an unnamed creek drainage. The trail climbs through the central and western portions of the clearing, before joining a Jeep road that sees snowmobile use in the winter. Follow the now-wider route out of the southwest corner of the clearing. The road here goes west before making a switchback to the southeast. At the next switchback—where the road again turns sharply northwest—leave the road and head due south into the trees on a narrow, and at times (especially if no one's broken trail before you) faint trail through the trees (**UTM: 13 421377 4483034**).

The route now continues due south, contouring—and very subtly gaining elevation—across the western side of the Seven Utes drainage. At mile 1.4, you'll reach the valley floor, and then cross to the eastern side of the drainage. Continue to subtly contour up the east side of the drainage until you intersect an unmistakable old Jeep road. Turn south-southwest on that road. As you continue, views will open up to the west of the north ridge of Seven Utes, and of the mountain's summit and avalanche chutes to the southwest. At mile 1.9, the road will deposit you into an open meadow (**UTM: 13 421393 4481483**) at the base of several prominent gullies, and beneath the headwall of the Mount Mahler-Seven Utes saddle. Hug the east edge of the meadow, and then switchback up the 30-degree headwall until you surmount the 11,000-foot saddle (**UTM: 13 421350 4481049**).

From here, turn east and follow the crest of Seven Utes' east ridge. Several skiable gullies will be below you to your right (north). As you crest treeline at 11,100 feet, stay away from the northeastern edge of Seven Utes' east ridge and summit area, where a large cornice builds and the starting zones for several large avalanche paths begin. Arrive at the 11,453-foot summit at mile 2.6 (**UTM: 13 420783 4481299**).

THE DESCENTS

Three routes lie in a north-facing bowl beneath Seven Utes' summit, bounded by the mountain's north and northwest ridges:

Far Northwest Ridge: From the summit, continue northwest for 0.4 mile down the northwest ridge. Before reaching treeline, drop off the ridge onto a northeast-facing 25-degree pitch.

The meadow and avalanche chute at the base of the Seven Utes headwall

Northwest Ridge: From the summit, continue northwest for 0.3 mile down the northwest ridge. Drop off the ridge onto a northeast-facing 27-degree pitch separated from the previous run by a stand of trees.

North Face: From the summit, descend due north into a large, open bowl with a maximum pitch of around 28 degrees.

All three runs on the north side of the mountain funnel into a single creek drainage. To return to the trailhead, you can ascend back to the summit and retrace your approach, or follow the creek drainage north-west to where it intersects an old 4WD road just below the 10,200-foot elevation contour. Follow that road, bearing right at all forks, to return to the switchback where you diverged into the trees of the Seven Utes drain-age on the approach.

Two runs descend the east face of Seven Utes' north ridge:

The *"Buzz"*

You can ski right from the summit, most of the mountain is sheltered from the wind—so it holds great powder on a primarily north-facing aspect—and the angle of the runs is comfortable.
—Sara A.

Far North Ridge: From the summit, head north down the mountain's north ridge for 0.3 mile. From there, drop east. The run starts out around 29 degrees before reclining to a fairly constant 26 degrees.

North Ridge: From the summit, head north down the mountain's north ridge for 0.15 mile. From there, drop northeast into a gully that runs to the valley floor. Beware of avalanche hazard.

Four runs descend Seven Utes' east ridge and the north face of the Mount Mahler-Seven Utes headwall:

East Ridge: From the summit, descend the east ridge you ascended on the approach. Use this run to access the remaining three.

West Gully: From the shoulder of the east ridge, drop into a northeast-facing gully that descends to the meadow at the base of the headwall. The angle is steepest at the rollover where you drop off the ridge into the gully. The lower portions of the gully are strewn with rock outcrops and small cliff bands that can be avoided with careful routefinding, or could serve as terrain traps in the event of an avalanche or fall.

Central Gully: Descend the east ridge. As you reenter treeline, hug the north edge of the headwall and contour through the trees until you reach an open gully perched at 30 degrees. Enjoy.

Nearing the summit of Seven Utes Mountain

Headwall: Return to the Mahler-Seven Utes saddle and descend the treed slopes of the headwall. The trees are open enough to provide enjoyable skiing with linked turns.

Runs 4 through 9 all return you to the drainage used on the approach. Regain your skin track and easily cruise back to the trailhead.

THE APRÈS SKI

Your only option for nearby pub and grub is in the town of Gould, west of Seven Utes on Highway 14. Try **Drifters Cookhouse,** 55278 Highway 14, (970) 723-8300, www.drifterscookhouse.com. It's the only game in town.

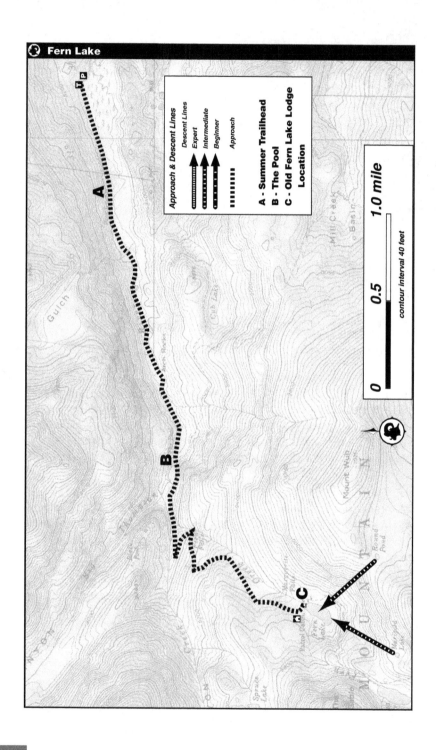

Approach & Descent Lines

Descent Lines

Expert

Intermediate

Beginner

Approach

A - Summer Trailhead
B - The Pool
C - Old Fern Lake Lodge
     Location

0   0.5   1.0 mile

contour interval 40 feet

FERN LAKE

THE ESSENTIALS

Nearest Town	Estes Park	**SNOTEL Station**	Bear Lake (322)
Distance	4.5 miles	**Forest Zone**	Rocky Mountain National Park
Vertical	2300'		
Season	December to April	**CAIC Zone**	Front Range Mountains
Elevation Range	8100' to 10,400'	**USGS Quad**	McHenrys Peak
Difficulty Rating	Moderate	**Weather**	COZ033
Skiing Rating	🔥 🔥		

THE HISTORY

Fern Lake is unique in this book, in the sense that it never had lift service of any type, but it is included for its historical significance. The beginnings of skiing at Fern Lake date back to 1909, when Dr. William J. Workman—from Ashland, Kansas—traveled to Colorado and built a lodge at his favorite fishing location, Fern Lake. The original lodge was constructed during 1910, and completed by 1911. Up to 500 guests visited the lodge each winter, and every guest was asked to sign a red leather-bound log book. Eventually, adjoining and nearby smaller cabins and tents were added.

Through the efforts of Enos Mills, F. O. Stanley (of the Stanley Hotel), and Joe Mills (for whom the mountain above Fern and Odessa lakes is named), six years later, on September 4, 1915, Rocky Mountain National Park was dedicated. By then, tourism oriented toward the scenery and outdoor activities surrounding Estes was quickly becoming the mainstay of the economy. Ski trips from Estes Park into Rocky Mountain were increasingly popular. By 1924 a trip had even been completed over the Continental Divide and down into Granby on the west side.

In February 1916, just months after the dedication of the park, the Estes Park Outdoor Club guided directors of the Colorado Mountain Club into Workman's lodge at Fern Lake for a "snow frolic." That initial trip started an annual tradition. Each winter, the lodge would open for two weeks and host members of the Colorado Mountain Club for their winter outing. Supplies were primarily brought in during the fall and stored until winter. However, Ranger Jack Moomaw also skied in with crates full of fresh eggs. The National Park Service helped to improve the ski runs, and skiers also used readily available open slopes. Lectures were hosted at the cabin during annual Winter Festivals that took place every February or March. The presentation in 1918 was titled, "The National Park and Winter Sports."

In May 1922, the Estes Park Chamber of Commerce hosted a banquet. National Parks Director Stephen Mather was the guest of honor. Leading up to the banquet, Mather had spent time inspecting the "ski courses" at Fern and Odessa lakes. He praised Rocky Mountain National Park for its "fine skiing," and proclaimed that skiing could continue easily into the month of May. Mather planned for a road to be built to the Pool on the Big Thompson River, which would reduce the approach to Fern Lake by 2 miles. (No such luck—the trailhead remained 2 miles back, and the current winter road closure even farther away.)

During March 1924—around the same time that a group made a ski traverse over the Divide—Fern Lake hosted what must have been one of the earliest action sports films. Some 20 to 40 skiers were filmed over a 10-day period. Snow drifted as high as the peak of the roof of the Fern Lake cabin, and skiers were filmed skiing directly off the roof of the cabin. In another scene, one of the lodge's two doors was completely drifted under. Skiers opened the door from the inside, and tunneled into the snow to within inches of the surface. Then, with the cameras rolling, they burst out of the seemingly pristine snowbank, jumped into the snow, got on their skis, and went off skiing.

One year later, in 1925, ranger Moomaw brought in a portable radio, which added a touch of comfort to the otherwise rustic lodge. The annual ski outings continued until around 1934, when the Colorado Mountain Club shifted its annual outing from Fern Lake to Grand Lake. Between 1934 and 1958, the lodge slowly faded out of use until its permit expired. Ownership changed hands several times. The once lavish dinners offered were scaled back to lunches, and then light snacks, and then simply refreshments. In 1938 the lodge closed for the winters, remaining open only during summer. Its National Park concession lease expired on December 31, 1958.

In 1959, the lodge was padlocked, and the other secondary buildings removed. Fern Lodge was kept for its historic value. Visitors could peer in through the windows and see a snapshot of life in yesteryear (some of the furniture from Fern Lodge is currently on display in the Moraine Park Museum). Sadly, the years 1969–1973 saw vandalism take a toll on the lodge. The National Park Service made one last attempt to save the building, but in 1976, burned it to the ground and "took back the land and restored it to its natural state."

The site of the lodge is still visible—it's a bare section of raised earth (a small, grassy meadow in summer) on the northeast side of Fern Lake, bounded by fencing and designated with an ENVIRONMENTAL RESTORATION sign. One can still see a cabin at the lake, however. In 1924, the park built a ranger cabin (closed to the public) in the trees on the northwest side of the lake. That cabin, renovated over the years, still stands.

THE TRAILHEAD

Begin at the Fern Lake winter trailhead, located within Rocky Mountain National Park. From downtown Estes Park, follow Route 36 to the Beaver Meadows Entrance. From the entrance gate, continue west for one quarter mile on Route 36 before making a left turn onto Bear Lake Road. After approximately 1.3 miles, turn right and follow signs for Moraine Park and Fern Lake. At mile 0.6, the road splits. Straight ahead, the road leads to Moraine Park. Turn left to continue to Fern Lake. Pass the Cub Lake Trailhead on your left, and arrive at the winter road closure for Fern Lake at mile 2.0 (as measured from when you turn off of Bear Lake Road). Park here (UTM: 13 447374 4467599).

The "Buzz"

Fern Lake is great for an outing to a spectacular location. It has more of a feel of exploration than of visiting an old ski area. Going there today must feel much like it did when the original CMC members made their outings decades ago.

—Kelli B.

THE APPROACH

From the trailhead, the first portion of the approach travels west on the road for 0.75 mile beyond the gate and the winter road closure, leading to the true Fern Lake Trailhead. Even in midwinter, this low-elevation road is likely to be melted out or blown clear to the gravel base by the wind. Strap your skis to your pack and hike it. At the true Fern Lake Trailhead, continue west on the well-signed and well-traveled Fern Lake Trail. Sections here can be icy or blown clear. Keep your skis on your back for now. After 1.7 miles (2.45 total), you'll arrive at the Pool, where a bridge crosses the Big Thompson River (UTM: 13 443955 4466728). Finally, click into your skis and skins. Immediately after the Pool the trail forks. The left fork goes to Cub Lake. Take the right fork, which ascends a short rise before continuing west en route to Fern Lake. After about a half mile, you'll reach a series of switchbacks that rapidly gain elevation

The National Park Service ranger patrol cabin on the north shore of Fern Lake

(especially compared to the flat valley you just hiked) as you climb past Fern Falls. Two miles beyond the Pool, pass a signed trail junction for the primitive Spruce Lake Trail. Continue for 0.1 mile farther on the Fern Lake Trail, arriving at the north shore of Fern Lake after a total of 4.55 miles (**UTM: 13 442597 4465496**). The National Park Service Patrol Cabin, closed in winter, sits just in the trees off the northwest corner of the lake. If conditions permit, skin out onto the lake and admire the views of Joe Mills Mountain, the Little Matterhorn, and Notchtop. Otherwise, travel east and south around the northeastern perimeter of the lake on the continuation of the Fern Lake Trail to reach the base of the runs.

THE DESCENTS

Though trails were rumored to have been cut here, most descents around Fern Lake are of the "wild" variety—true backcountry skiing. Opportunities are nearly limitless in the cirques to the west of the lake. But for nearby runs, try two options: Round Pond and Marigold Lake.

Round Pond: From the eastern shore of Fern Lake, climb steeply up to Round Pond, at the saddle between Joe Mills Mountain and Mt. Wuh. Descend your ascent route.

Marigold Lake: From the southern shore of Fern Lake, climb south-southwest up to Marigold Lake, which sits beneath the steep north face of Joe Mills Mountain. Descend a series of open runs back to the lake.

THE APRÈS SKI

The nearest town, Estes Park, is littered with restaurant options. Visit www.estesparkcvb.com/dining.cfm. When you're ready for dessert, the caramel apples at **Laura's** are divine (129 East Elkhorn Avenue, 866-586-4004, www.laurasfudgeofestes.com).

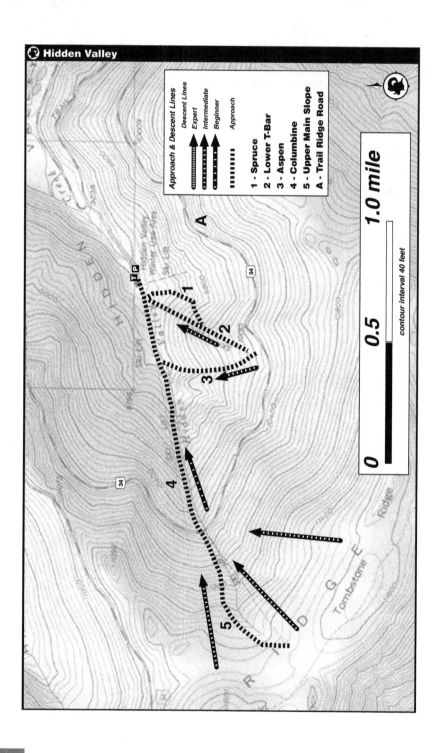

HIDDEN VALLEY

THE ESSENTIALS

Nearest Town Estes Park
Distance 1.8 miles max.
Vertical 2200'
Season December to April
Elevation Range 9400' to 11,600'
Difficulty Rating Moderate
Skiing Rating ❷❷❷

SNOTEL Station Bear Lake (322)
Forest Zone Rocky Mountain National Park
CAIC Zone Front Range Mountains
USGS Quad Trail Ridge
Weather COZ033

THE HISTORY

The Hidden Valley ski area, as with many others, got its start with hearty backcountry skiers who schussed its slopes before lifts ever came to town. An above-treeline area along Trail Ridge known as the Big Drift was their first target. Soon, there was a rope tow, and by the 1940s, three rope tows (each powered by old auto engines). Ranger Jack Moomaw (of Fern Lake fame), reportedly cut a trail discreetly, one tree at a time. His project—the Federation Internationale du Ski, also known as "Suicide"—supposedly dropped 1200 feet in less than a mile, and was just wider than a bridle path.

In 1949, a lift ticket cost just 50 cents. Then, in the 1950s, surplus military buses were used to shuttle skiers up Trail Ridge Road, and a basic lodge was installed at the base of the ski area. Ski Hidden Valley officially opened in 1955 with a combination of T-bars and Poma lifts. The Estes Park Recreation District operated the area, which flourished throughout the 1960s, despite having a reputation for the worst record in medical emergencies (mostly broken bones and knee injuries).

In December 1971, the ski area finally succeeded in convincing the national park to permit the installation of a double-chairlift. But Rocky Mountain National Park didn't like it. Sometime during the 1970s, the park took over ownership and operation of the ski area. By 1977, the double-chairlift had been removed. The tows and other lifts soon followed, and the buildings were demolished. Ski Hidden Valley closed down in 1991.

Since that time, the national park has built a new base lodge, which today serves as a ranger station, warming hut, and restroom facility for the winter sports sledding area nearby. It's also a launching point for backcountry skiers intent on schussing the old runs of Hidden Valley.

THE TRAILHEAD

Begin at the Hidden Valley winter use recreation area (**UTM: 13 444349 4471630**), located within Rocky Mountain National Park. From downtown Estes Park, follow Route 36 to the Beaver Meadows Entrance. From the gate, continue west on Route 36, which becomes Trail Ridge Road. Shortly after the Beaver Pond Trailhead, the road makes a switchback where it turns back sharply to the east. At the apex of the switchback, turn right, follow the signs for Hidden Valley, and park in the lot at the National Park Service ranger station. The station has public restrooms, a warming room, and historic photos of the old Hidden Valley ski area.

Alternatively, from downtown Estes Park, follow Route 34 to the Fall River Entrance. From the gate, continue west on Route 34 through Horseshoe Park. Route 34 ends at a T intersection with Trail Ridge Road. Turn right and continue past the Beaver Pond Trailhead, joining the directions above.

The "Buzz"

Hidden Valley is great when there's high avalanche danger elsewhere. It has a low enough angle that it doesn't present a lot of risk. The warming hut at the base, and its proximity to the Front Range are great. Navigation is easy—you can't make many wrong turns here. On the other side of the coin, it gets a lot of traffic, and on the way in you have to dodge tourists taking pictures of the elk. The top—where the best skiing is—can be exposed to the wind, but it's great for laps if conditions are good.

—Tom H.

THE APPROACH

Begin at the Hidden Valley winter use recreation area. From the lodge, start out west up the floor of the valley. Almost immediately you'll pass a small sledding hill on your left. At mile 0.1, you'll see the lift line for Lower T-Bar and the ski trail, Spruce, on your left (**UTM: 13 444213 4471566**). Turn left here if you intend to ski these runs. Otherwise, continue west up the main ski trail, Columbine, which by now is well-defined.

At mile 0.35, you'll come to a prominent fork in the trail (**UTM: 13 443810 4471422**). The left fork is the ski trail, Aspen. You can ascend it all the way to Trail Ridge Road, where it intersects the top of the Lower T-Bar lift line. Do so if you plan to ski it. Otherwise, continue on Columbine.

At mile 1.1, you'll reach Trail Ridge Road (**UTM: 13 442699 4471187**). This is the top of Columbine. If conditions look good, cross Trail Ridge Road and continue your ascent up the "Big Drift," also known as Upper Main Slope.

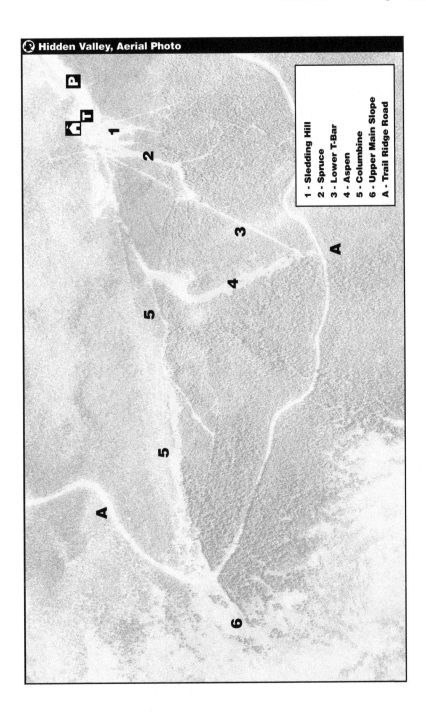

Hidden Valley, Aerial Photo

1 - Sledding Hill
2 - Spruce
3 - Lower T-Bar
4 - Aspen
5 - Columbine
6 - Upper Main Slope
A - Trail Ridge Road

THE DESCENTS

The descents are most easily seen on the topo map and aerial photo. However, the following major landmarks will serve to orient you to the possibilities:

Spruce and Lower T-Bar: the first runs encountered on climber's left as you ascend the ski area (beware of three large fallen trees across the bottom section of Lower T-Bar—either make sure there's enough snow coverage, or watch for them);

Aspen: the first major left-hand fork beyond Spruce and Lower T-Bar;

Columbine: the main run that leads all the way up to Trail Ridge Road at the head of the valley;

Upper Main Slope: the above-treeline terrain beyond Trail Ridge Road.

Keep in mind that there are other runs that create a network on the mountain. Most of the additional runs are tight, and some are partially overgrown. They are visible on the aerial photo, and I leave it to you to explore them at your leisure.

Looking up the Spruce and Lower T-Bar runs at Hidden Valley

THE APRÈS SKI

The nearest town, Estes Park, is littered with restaurant options. Visit www.estesparkcvb.com/dining.cfm.

When you're ready for dessert, the caramel apples at **Laura's** are divine (129 East Elkhorn Avenue, 866-586-4004, www.laurasfudgeofestes. com).

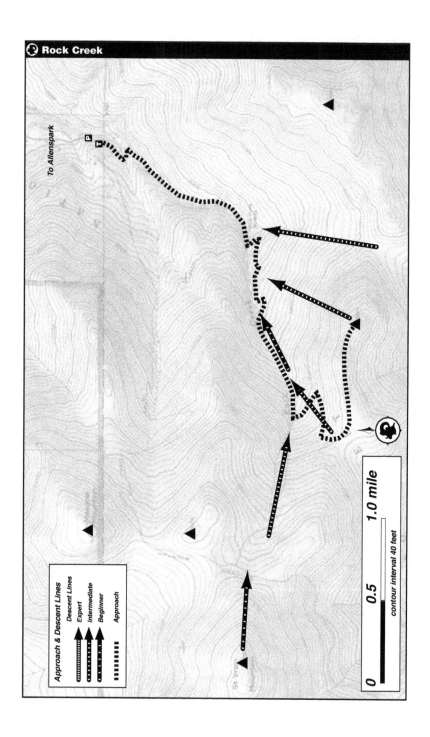

To Allenspark

P

Approach & Descent Lines

Descent Lines
Expert
Intermediate
Beginner
Approach

0   0.5   1.0 mile

contour interval 40 feet

ROCK CREEK

THE ESSENTIALS

Nearest Town Allenspark
Distance 4 miles
Vertical 2100'
Season January to March
Elevation Range 8700' to 10,810'
Difficulty Rating Moderate
Skiing Rating ❄ ❄

SNOTEL Station Wild Basin (1042)
Forest Zone Roosevelt National Forest, Boulder Ranger District
CAIC Zone Front Range Mountains
USGS Quad Allens Park
Weather COZ035

THE HISTORY

Allenspark and Rock Creek have a long history of skiing that dates back to 1896, when 10 men laid out the town site. One of them, "Big Jim" Scobee, was the first to have skis. He made them himself using wood flooring boards that were 4 inches wide. Other men in town teased him that his skis were "large enough for Paul Bunyan."

The first ski hill in town dates to 1918. Lars Haugen, who carried the mail from Allenspark to Ward, and Hans Hansen, who worked for Carl Howelsen in Steamboat Springs, built the run, which was called the Haugen Slide. Reportedly, the run was still visible in 1999, though I didn't find evidence of it in 2008.

Three years later, the Allenspark Ski Club came into existence, and one year after that—in 1922—a second ski hill did. Known as Willow Creek, it was used primarily for ski jumping and tournaments. A series of articles in the *Longmont Ledger* chronicled the rise of skiing in Allenspark that year. On February 3, 1922: the ski area was constructed, and the *Ledger* noted that it was "necessary to cut down considerable timber," and that the slope was reclined at a 33 percent grade. On February 10, a tournament was held, and the new ski area was heralded a success. On March 17, 150 cars carrying five people each arrived to watch the skiing. In those early days, prizes for winning one of the skiing tournaments were humble: a pocketknife, one pound of peanuts, a brush, a handkerchief, three bars of soap, an apron, a box of candy, a toothbrush, gloves, a clock.

One season later, on January 26, 1923, one boy dislocated his shoulder while skiing. Another hurt his knee. On the way home, one car slid off the road and into a snowbank. (Sounds a lot like a modern-day Sunday afternoon on Interstate 70!) Over time, a total of five ski areas were constructed in Allenspark. In addition to the Haugen Slide and Willow Creek, there was Thelma Course, Cooperrider/Butterbowl, and Point-O-Pines.

For the rest of the 1920s and into the 1930s, the ski areas of Allenspark hosted sanctioned tournaments as a member of the U.S. Western Ski Association. In 1939, lift service was finally added—a 1000-foot-long rope tow at Willow Creek, run off the rear wheels of a 1926 Dodge chassis. With the addition of lifts, the Allenspark ski areas were used by Colorado State University in the 1940s for the school's Winter Sports Festival, and the University of Colorado at Boulder supposedly used the hills as well.

Meanwhile, the Allenspark Ski Club, which had faded out of existence not long after its founding, was reinstated in 1938 as the Saint Vrain Ski Club by Clint Baker, the owner of nearby Fern Cliff Lodge. Then, in December 1946, the ski club opened the Rock Creek ski area. That Christmas, there were two rope tows—one 600 feet long with 200 feet of vertical, and another also 600 feet long, but with only 100 feet of vertical.

Rock Creek boasted three runs, a 30-meter jump, and numerous open snowfields. A warming hut was available thanks to an old, deserted log cabin from 30 years earlier that skiers put to the new use. The skiable acreage totaled 800. According to many sources, Rock Creek claimed a 3200-foot vertical drop, which would have qualified it for use in Olympic-level downhill skiing. However, lifts never served such terrain, and a 3200-foot vertical drop makes sense only if you extend the ski area from its base in the Rock Creek drainage to the summit of 12,162-foot Saint Vrain Mountain. (That's not entirely unreasonable—the east face of Saint Vrain Mountain is a common backcountry ski destination, and can easily be linked with the Rock Creek drainage immediately below it.)

In October 1947, Boulder County extended a road to the base of the ski area, and the ski club expanded Rock Creek's terrain, adding more lifts: a 2000-foot rope tow powered by the 1926 Dodge from Willow Creek, and a 4000-foot rope tow powered by a 1946 John Deere G engine. Lift tickets cost just $1 per person per day. A vehicle transported skiers from the parking lot in Allenspark to the base of the lifts, in what must rightly be called an early form of complimentary shuttle service.

By 1948, Rock Creek had grown in popularity, and nearby accommodations started offering combination "ski, eat, stay" packages. Baker's Fern Cliff Lodge, considered a luxury lodge, offered what it called the American Plan: $10 per person per night for a private room with double or twin bed and bathroom. If 20 or more people made a group

Typical glade terrain in the Rock Creek drainage

reservation for a week-
end, the price was $7.
If either of those options
proved too expensive, you
had the option to stay in a dorm
in the basement with a common
toilet and shower for $6 per person.
The Wild Rose Inn offered an altogether more
desirable option: three-room cottages for $5 per night
per cabin. Food was not provided, but the Wild Rose had cooking
facilities and gas. If you were good at negotiating, the owners were
willing to go the extra mile for you—a group of students from Fort Collins arranged for Saturday lunch, dinner, bunk bed at night, breakfast
Sunday morning, and lunch . . . all for $5 per person!

Alas, Rock Creek closed in March 1952, plagued by underfund-
ing, occasional high winds, the struggle of maintaining the 3-mile road
to the base, and temperamental rope tows that broke down regularly.
All was not entirely lost, however; Rock Creek was nearly revived six
years later in November 1958. The U.S. Forest Service made a reconnaissance of the area, hoping to entice new developers with a plan for
an expanded ski area. The Forest Service's vision would have involved
moving the base area a half mile farther up the valley and building
three new lifts that would have provided access to a variety of terrain
with 1600 to 1800 feet of vertical. Two lifts would have started from
the old base area and gone up to the summit of Point 10,810 and to
the saddle to its east. A third lift would have gone from the new base
area up to the 11,000-foot elevation on the southeast shoulder of Saint
Vrain Mountain. The Forest Service issued a prospectus, but no one
bid to develop the mountain, and Rock Creek has remained closed ever
since.

THE TRAILHEAD

Begin at the fork of Forest Roads 116-1 and 116-2 (**UTM: 13 455081
4447166**). Exit the Peak to Peak Highway (Route 7) in Allenspark. From
town, travel south on Ski Road (County Route 107). After 0.1 mile, the
road turns sharply left. After another 0.1 mile, the road turns sharply
right. At mile 1.3, cross into Roosevelt National Forest, at which point
Ski Road/County Route 107 becomes Forest Road 116. At mile 1.6 the
road forks. The right fork is Forest Road 116-1, and leads to the Saint
Vrain Mountain Trailhead. The left fork is Forest Road 116-2, and leads
to the old Rock Creek Ski Area. Park here at the fork! This is the standard
winter parking area for people venturing up the Rock Creek drainage.

Resist the urge to continue driving on Forest Road 116-2, even if it looks tempting and passable. From the fork, the road descends steeply before crossing a creek and then turning up the Rock Creek drainage. Many people have gotten their cars stuck trying to press their luck. Don't become one of them.

THE APPROACH

From the fork, follow Forest Road 116-2. The road descends southwest for 0.1 mile to a creek crossing, where it turns back briefly to the east. At 0.2 mile, the road turns sharply again, renewing its southwest course and genuinely entering the Rock Creek drainage. Continue to follow the road up the valley, arriving at the old base area of the Rock Creek Ski Area at mile 1.1 (**UTM: 13 454270 4445788**). The base area is evidenced by a large meadow where the buildings once stood, as well as some open runs and young evergreens in the forest immediately to the south. It's likely that the route up until this point has been well-traveled by snowmobiles.

The *"Buzz"*

Although it can be windy on Ironclad Ridge, the Rock Creek drainage is well-protected and holds powder. The old ski area is in a beautiful valley with a straightforward approach.

—Karla T.

Beyond the old base area, Forest Road 116-2 becomes a narrower track. At mile 1.25, the track goes through a pair of switchbacks before continuing west up the valley. From this point onward, the route is marked by a series of gold, yellow, or blue diamonds on trees, as well as brown Forest Service stakes. At mile 1.7, the route switchbacks twice again. From here the route climbs steadily west through the trees until mile 2.5. Here, Trail 116-2C (marked DEAD END) continues straight and right. Do not take this trail. Make a hard left to remain on course, which is marked simply "116" from this point onward. A series of trails—both official and unofficial—lace the mountain valley to climber's right. If you're in doubt of the proper route, take the left-hand option. As you continue to climb, you'll gain improving views of the upper Rock Creek drainage. After making the hard left (turning southeast) to remain on 116, the route makes a switchback at mile 2.7 (turning southwest). At mile 3.0, the route makes a switchback again (turning south), and at mile 3.1, yet again (turning northwest). Leave the trail at this switchback (**UTM: 13 452270 4444943**).

Climb directly south-southeast through the trees for less than a tenth of a mile. Here you are on the crest of Ironclad Ridge, which is really an extension of the southeast ridge of Saint Vrain Mountain.

From the crest of the ridge, turn directly east and continue for 0.8 mile, arriving at the 10,810-foot summit of Rock Creek Ski Area at mile 3.9 (**UTM: 13 453374 4444681**).

THE DESCENTS

The runs of the old ski area are still visible, but faint (they've grown in quickly over the years). Even so, four primary options are available for descents: the **Road, Glade, Summit,** and **Saddle.**

The Road: Simply reverse your ascent route and carve turns down the road you skinned up. It's like your own personal groomer.

The Glade: From Ironclad Ridge, avoid the road and its switchbacks. Instead, drop straight down the fall line, schussing through open trees at a steady pitch the whole way.

The Summit: From the summit of Point 10,810, drop north or northeast. Immediately below the summit, watch for rocks. Beyond that, the tree skiing is divine. The descent spits you out on the approach road. Turn right (east) to head home.

The Saddle: From the summit of Point 10,810, descend east to the saddle at 10,100 feet. From the saddle, descend directly north and follow the fall line. End at the old base area.

EXTRA CREDIT

From Ironclad Ridge, instead of turning east toward the summit of Point 10,810, turn west-northwest and head toward Saint Vrain Mountain. Ski the upper Rock Creek drainage, or continue all the way to the summit of Saint Vrain Mountain and ski the broad, low-angle snow slope that makes up its east face.

THE APRÈS SKI

Allenspark offers the closest meal. Try the **Meadow Mountain Cafe** (441 Business Highway 7, 303-747-2541). Otherwise, Estes Park to the north, and Lyons and Nederland to the south are your next closest options.

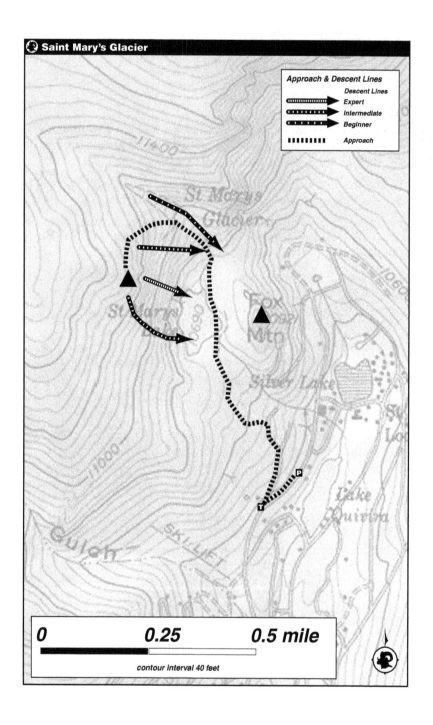

SAINT MARY'S GLACIER

THE ESSENTIALS

Nearest Town Idaho Springs
Distance 1 mile
Vertical 1000'
Season November to June
Elevation Range 10,380' to 11,400'
Difficulty Rating Easy
Skiing Rating 🎿 🎿

SNOTEL Station Lake Eldora (564)
Forest Zone Arapaho National
Forest, Clear Creek
Ranger District
CAIC Zone Front Range Mountains
USGS Quad Empire
Weather COZ034

THE HISTORY

The history of skiing at St. Mary's is really the history of two side-by-side ski areas: the historical skiing that took place at St. Mary's Glacier, and the lift-served skiing that evolved on the forested slopes adjacent to the glacier. St. Mary's Glacier is home to some of the earliest recreational skiing in Colorado. The permanent, year-round snowfield provided a ready-made venue for the fast-growing sport. By the early 1920s, St. Mary's was a regular destination for Denver-based ski outings. Then, in 1923, the Denver Rocky Mountain Ski Club organized the first annual Fourth of July Ski Tournament at St. Mary's Glacier.

Lift-served skiing probably arrived at St. Mary's in the 1950s, when development began in Anchor Gulch, directly south of the lake and glacier. At least as early as 1961, the University of Colorado ski team began using the area for informal training. By the 1970s, the ski area was firmly established as Ski Saint Mary's.

During the late 1970s, a series of changes in ownership also resulted in a series of name changes for the ski area. It first became Silver Lake, and then—for the 1979/1980 season—Silver Mountain. But people didn't recognize the new name, and couldn't figure out where it was located. The following year—the 1980/1981 season—the name changed again, to the more recognizable Saint Mary's Glacier Resort.

The lifts ran from Wednesday through Sunday, and lift tickets cost $5 midweek, and $7 on weekends. A combination of rope tows, T-bars and other lifts served terrain that gradually expanded from 550 feet of vertical to 1260 feet of vertical over time. Despite such improvements, St. Mary's never became an overwhelming success, and eventually shut down in 1986. It has remained closed since, but in recent years, serious talks have surfaced about reopening the portion of the ski area that sits on private property as a snowboard-oriented terrain park. The

new facility will be called Eclipse Snow Park, and is currently negotiating the final phases of approval from Clear Creek County. Residents of Alice and St. Mary's have fiercely opposed the new area. If successful, Eclipse is hoping to do for St. Mary's what Echo Mountain did for Squaw Pass, another lost ski area successfully reopened as a terrain park in Clear Creek County.

Thankfully, though, St. Mary's Glacier and the historic ski terrain north of Anchor Gulch are permanently public, offering year-round backcountry skiing on one of the West's oldest ski areas.

THE TRAILHEAD

Begin at the St. Mary's Glacier trailhead in St. Mary's. From Interstate 70, take the Fall River Road exit, west of Idaho Springs. Continue on Fall River Road, passing through the tiny town of Alice. Beyond Alice, you'll pass the old St. Mary's ski area, enter the community of St. Mary's, pass a trailhead sign for the "glacier hike," and at last arrive at a parking area on the left side of the road. The parking area (the only legal parking for St. Mary's) is located on private property. While the landowner once offered this parking for free, a fee of $5 per vehicle now applies.

THE APPROACH

From the parking lot on the northwest side of the road, walk back (southwest) along the road for 50 yards to the trailhead (**UTM: 13 444934 4408791**). It is well signed: GLACIER HIKE: ¾ MILE TO BASE OF GLACIER. A cluster of historical log cabins also sit alongside the trailhead behind a length of chain-link fence. This is an extremely popular trailhead. Expect to see backcountry skiers, snowshoers, dogs, even tourists in jeans and sneakers. Follow the north-trending and well-trodden path for 0.5 mile to St. Mary's Lake at 10,690 feet. From here, the permanent snowfield known as St. Mary's Glacier is to your north, while a sub-summit of Point 11,716 rises steeply out of the lake directly to the west. Either continue north across the frozen lake, or do the same on the trail as it squeezes between the lakeshore and the small peak known as Fox Mountain. Once at the base of the glacier, turn west and begin your

The "Buzz"

St. Mary's has great skiing conditions and a long season. The approach is super quick and easy—there's good snow within a mile of the road. The only downsides are that it can be busy, and I wish there was more vertical per run.

—Kelli B.

Remains of an old lift and the lift line at Ski St. Mary's

ascent. Continue about halfway up the glacier to the 11,100-foot elevation. Then turn toward climber's left (south) and ascend the shoulder of the unnamed sub-summit.

THE DESCENTS

St. Mary's Glacier is home to four primary descents: the **Glacier, Right Shoulder, Gullies,** and **Left Shoulder.**

The Glacier: Ski the main tongue of the low-angle glacier to far looker's right.

The Right Shoulder: Between the summit of the peak rising above the western shore of St. Mary's Lake and the glacier is a broad shoulder to looker's right of an island of rocks. Pick your line. The higher you go, the more vertical you gain per run, and the steeper the slope angle becomes. It can hold great powder, but can also be wind-loaded and avalanche prone.

The Gullies: The sheer east face of the summit of St. Mary's Lake is streaked with a series of gullies that provide passage through cliff bands. They can provide great skiing, but beware of the consequences of an avalanche or fall that would leave you with no runout, ending on the frozen, flat icy surface of the lake.

Remains of log cabins near the base of St. Mary's Glacier ski area

A skier carves turns
on the right shoulder
of St. Mary's Glacier.

Northern Front Range   55

The Left Shoulder: To looker's left of the summit is a long,
snowy shoulder that provides great
skiing back to the south shore of the lake.
There are several opportunities to drop off the shoulder and down the lower sections of the east face.

THE APRÈS SKI

Nearby Idaho Springs is your best bet. Visit www.clearcreekcounty.
org/idaho-springs-colorado-dining.htm.

Try out these favorite locales:

Beau Jo's, 1517 Miner Street, (303) 567-4376, www.beaujos.com

Buffalo Restaurant and Bar, 1617 Miner Street, (303) 567-2729,
www.buffalorestaurant.com

Tommyknocker Brewery, 1401 Miner Street, (303) 567-2688,
www.tommyknocker.com

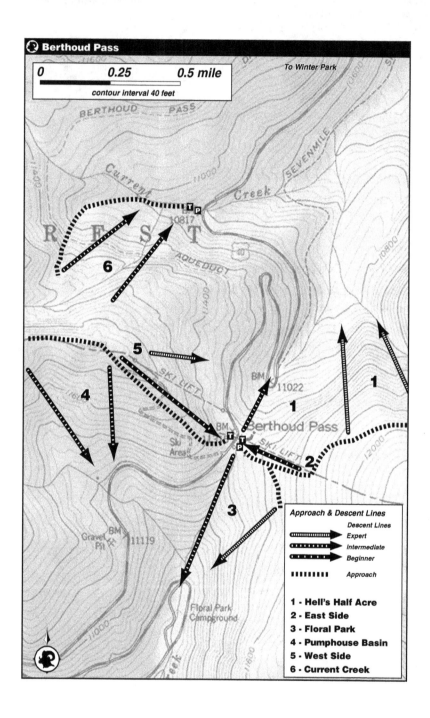

BERTHOUD PASS

THE ESSENTIALS

Nearest Town Winter Park
Distance 1.5 miles max.
Vertical 1400' max.
Season December to May
Elevation Range 10,800' to 12,400'
Difficulty Rating Easy to moderate
Skiing Rating ⚫⚫⚫

SNOTEL Station Berthoud Summit (335)
Forest Zone Arapaho National Forest, Sulphur Ranger District
CAIC Zone Front Range Mountains
USGS Quad Berthoud Pass
Weather COZ034

THE HISTORY

Skiing at Berthoud Pass has genuinely come full circle over the years. The earliest organized skiing dates to the 1930s, when a small ski area existed near the West Portal of the Moffat Tunnel, close to present-day Winter Park. In 1939, 26 racers participated in a May Day Slalom down the Current Creek Headwall. But it was Berthoud Pass that really attracted the skiers. In the earliest days, they would ski from the 11,314-foot summit of the pass down both sides. At the bottom of their chosen run, they'd load into cars and drive back to the top.

Then, in the 1936/1937 winter season, Berthoud opened the state's first rope tow (excepting a competing claim by Glen Cove). Financing for the effort was provided by the May Company department store, and by a Denver Ford dealer who donated an engine to power the tow. The 848-foot-long rope tow was completed for the sum of $2500. Bud Barwise, manager of Denver's Merrill Lynch office, was the first to ride it. J. C. Blickensderfer, of the Ski Club Zipfelbergers, was the second. The day was February 7, 1937—the first day of lift-assisted skiing in the state. Also on that day, two men—Joseph Oppenheimer and John Oberdorfer—were killed in an avalanche skiing elsewhere at Berthoud Pass. They were the first recreational skiing fatalities in the state, and their bodies weren't found until spring.

An inn that sat atop the pass since 1920 burned down in 1939. A new lodge was built, and opened in December 1949. Two years earlier, Berthoud claimed another skiing "first"—the first double-chairlift. The ski area needed the expanded capacity—in 1946, the U.S. Forest Service estimated that of the state's 100,000 skiers, 30,000 skied at Berthoud.

The decades that followed saw a fairly cyclic pattern: financial woes, closures, new owners, reopenings, permit and lawsuit fiascos, and upgrades (and promised upgrades that were never built). In 1987, new owner Peter Crowley introduced a new idea: off-piste skiing. In addition to the lift-served groomed runs, Crowley offered shuttle buses that would pick up skiers below the pass and bring them back to the top. Berthoud, in a way, was connecting with its earliest roots.

Before shutting down, Berthoud had one more trick up its sleeve: Berthoud Powder Guides, a cat-skiing operation that operated on the slopes above both sides of the ski area. Alas, Berthoud was on its way out. Lift-served skiing shut down after the 2000/2001 season. Cat-skiing folded on March 10, 2003. A nonprofit group, Friends of Berthoud Pass, lobbied to keep the lodge atop the pass standing as both a testament to history and as a home base for backcountry skiers. It was not to be. The Forest Service tore down the lodge in spring 2005.

The *"Buzz"*

Berthoud is super popular among backcountry skiers, and for good reason. It's accessible, and has tons of terrain. You probably won't be alone here, but that's part of the vibe—it's a social skiing experience.

—The author

Today, Berthoud has come full circle. One of Colorado's most popular backcountry skiing destinations and most well-known lost ski areas, skiers once again schuss both sides of the pass, using cars to shuttle themselves back to the top. Take your turn at this legendary lost resort.

THE TRAILHEAD

Before I describe the trailheads, I should first describe the skiing. The old Berthoud Pass ski area is best divided into six sections, which co-incide with the old trail maps. On the east side of the pass are Hell's Half Acre, East Side, and Floral Park. On the west side of the pass are Pumphouse Basin, West Side, and Current Creek. Use the Berthoud Pass Summit Trailhead for all but Current Creek, which has its own eponymous trailhead.

If you're using the Berthoud Pass Summit Trailhead, from downtown Winter Park and points north, drive south on Highway 40 for 14 miles to the summit of Berthoud Pass. Park here on the east side of the pass in a large lot where the old lodge once stood. From Empire and points south, drive north on Highway 40 for 13 miles to the summit of the pass.

If you're using the Current Creek Trailhead, from the Berthoud Pass summit drive north on Highway 40 (descending off the pass) for 2 miles to the trailhead.

One of the main ski runs on the west side of Berthoud Pass

THE APPROACH

When planning your approach and descents, it's useful to keep in mind that Berthoud Pass is an extremely popular backcountry skiing area, one that in many ways has a culture and an ethic all its own. Many runs end at a road, and often, at a hairpin turn. You could use your skins and set a skin track to climb back up to the pass and your car, but in practice, most skiers either use a shuttle car, or simply hitch a ride. Of course, this won't apply if your chosen run either descends back *to* the pass, or if it doesn't end at a road. Plan accordingly.

The approaches are described for each of the six divisions of the old ski area:

East Side: From the trailhead, climb east directly up the old ski run and lift line for 0.25 mile. Finish at treeline.

Hell's Half Acre: From the trailhead, ski directly off the north side of the pass. Or, approach as for East Side, but contour north until above your chosen line. Note: beyond Hell's Half Acre lies the once-operating area for Berthoud Powder Guides, including lines known as Vortex, Mines 1, and Mines 2. Beware of avalanche danger. People have died here.

Floral Park: From the trailhead, ski directly off the south side of the pass. Or, approach as for East Side, but contour south until above your chosen line.

West Side: From the trailhead, carefully cross the road to the west side of Berthoud Pass. Climb west directly up the old ski run adjacent to the lift line for 0.9 mile. Finish atop Point 11,963. Note: beyond West Side lies more of the once-operating area for Berthoud Powder Guides. Continue west up the ridge to Point 12,391, arriving in another 0.7 mile. Beware of avalanche danger.

Pumphouse Basin: Approach as for East Side. Instead of skiing east and northeast to return to the pass, drop south off of Point 11,963 and into Pumphouse Basin.

Current Creek: From the Current Creek Trailhead, head west up Current Creek, arriving at your destination 0.5 to 1.0 mile from the trailhead.

THE DESCENTS

Berthoud has a simply overwhelming amount of backcountry skiing terrain. It would be too cumbersome to list all the individual descents

Looking down on Berthoud Pass from the slopes of Colorado Mines Peak, with the parking area below and the west-side ski runs visible across the road

here. Instead, I'll describe them in aggregate by area of the mountain. Consult the corresponding topo map for additional detail on locations.

East Side: Intermediate and beginner terrain. End at the parking lot.

Hell's Half Acre: Primarily serious expert terrain in trees and gullies. End at the hairpin turn at 11,022 feet, or farther down the Fraser River Valley.

Floral Park: Primarily expert and intermediate terrain in the trees. End at the hairpin turn at 10,700 feet.

West Side: Primarily intermediate, with some beginner and some expert terrain. End at the summit of the pass across the road from the parking lot.

Pumphouse Basin: Primarily expert and intermediate terrain. End at the road at 11,200 feet.

Current Creek: Primarily expert terrain. End at the Current Creek Trailhead.

THE APRÈS SKI

Nearby Winter Park is your best bet. Visit www.winterparkguide.com/dining/index.php.

Try out this favorite locale:

Hernando's Pizza & Pasta Pub, Highway 40, (970) 726-5409, www.hernandospizzapub.com

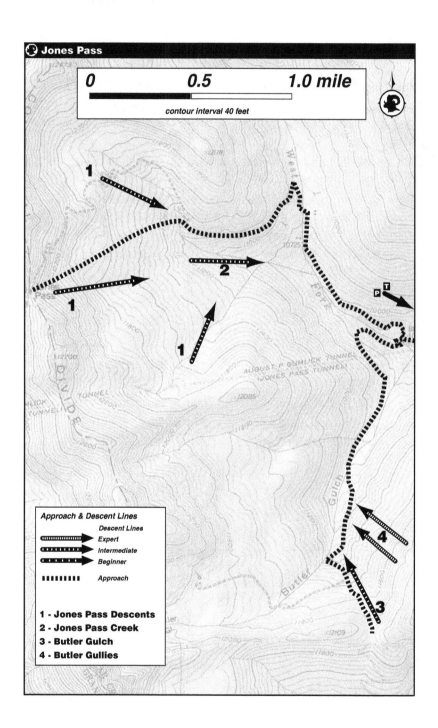

0   0.5   1.0 mile

contour interval 40 feet

Approach & Descent Lines

Descent Lines
━━━━━▶ Expert
━ ━ ━ ▶ Intermediate
• • • ▶ Beginner

▪▪▪▪▪▪▪▪ Approach

1 - Jones Pass Descents
2 - Jones Pass Creek
3 - Butler Gulch
4 - Butler Gullies

JONES PASS

THE ESSENTIALS

Nearest Town Empire
Distance 2.8 miles
Vertical 2000'
Season March to May
Elevation Range 10,400' to 12,400'
Difficulty Rating Moderate
Skiing Rating 🎿🎿🎿

SNOTEL Station Jones Pass (970)
Forest Zone Arapaho National Forest, Clear Creek Ranger District
CAIC Zone Front Range Mountains
USGS Quad Berthoud Pass
Weather COZ034

THE HISTORY

As the population of Denver and the Front Range grew during the early 20th century, so too did the demand for water. Bringing water to thirsty cities and towns was the unlikely beginning of skiing at Jones Pass.

In 1921, Denver filed for water rights on the Williams Fork River, which sits west of the Continental Divide directly below Jones Pass. By the early 1930s, two things happened: the City of Denver was ready to start on a tunnel that would carry water from the Williams Fork to the east side of the divide, and backcountry skiers had discovered the slopes of Jones Pass.

During the winter of 1935/1936, an article in the *Rocky Mountain News*, "Skiing in Colorado," proclaimed Jones Pass the next best known skiing destination after St. Mary's Glacier. The article praised the "good open slopes, the best of which are above timberline," and noted that the width of the snowfield was several miles, with steeper slopes nearby and a "schuss of two or three miles" easily made. Later that fall, on November 12, the *Rocky Mountain News* published an article noting that the City of Denver was building log cabins near the base of Jones Pass for the engineers who were working on the water tunnel project (today called the Jones Pass Tunnel, and before that, the Williams Fork Tunnel, or unimaginatively, Denver Water Tunnel Diversion Project). When the tunnel project was completed, the city planned to turn the cabins over to skiers. Frank Ashley, interviewed in the article, said that overnight "shelter houses" were sorely needed, as were more ski trails. "Get the facilities and you will get the skiers," he noted. Ashley also thought that Jones Pass needed lifts.

One year later, on February 28, 1937, the Colorado Mountain Club held a down-mountain Kandahar ski race. The club hoped to make it a yearly tradition.

The next year, 1938, proved pivotal. First, on May 5, the *Glenwood Post* published U.S. Forest Service winter use statistics, which showed that Jones Pass had seen 1200 skiers during the course of the previous winter. Nearby Berthoud Pass, by comparison, had opened its first rope tow in 1936/1937, and by 1938 claimed 26,000 skiers per season. Secondly, also in 1938, Red Mountain Lodge was built by J. C. Blickensderfer and other members of the Denver ski contingent. It was built in the style of a Swiss chalet at the foot of Red Mountain, 1 mile above the Jones Pass turnoff of the Berthoud Pass road. Red Mountain Lodge would become a valuable base of operations for skiers. Thirdly, the City of Denver hired Blickensderfer, along with Bob Balch and Dick Mitchell (a ski instructor from Sun Valley), to survey the Jones Pass area for skiing development. The trio spent two weeks skiing the slopes of Jones Pass, exploring the upper Vasquez Basin. Despite great conditions, they didn't think the area was accessible enough for large numbers of skiers. Regardless, on December 18, 1938, the *Rocky Mountain News* published a glowing article about Jones Pass. "Skiers will find conditions as good as Berthoud," it declared. There is a "tremendous natural basin with excellent open ski slopes, reached by driving to the camp of the Denver Water Diversion Tunnel Project, and then proceeding on foot." Jones Pass was particularly recommended for spring skiing.

Less than five years after that glowing recommendation from *Rocky Mountain News,* the Forest Service received its first lift-served skiing proposal for Jones Pass, submitted by E. G. Constam, well-known as a builder of T-bar lift systems for ski areas. The proposal moved slowly, and Constam's vision was never built.

Seven years later, in 1950, the Forest Service conducted a skiing study of the east side of Jones Pass, focusing on the area between the 10,400-foot and 12,000-foot elevations. The agency proposed a 6500-foot-long lift serving 1500 feet of vertical. The entire proposition was stimulated by the Red Mountain Lodge, and by Denver's desire for closer areas with great skiing. Again, no lifts were built. Jones Pass received one final opportunity for lift-served ski development in 1958, when the Forest Service again did a reconnaissance of the area, this time to Butler Gulch. It was accessible, with good skiing, but by then, plans were underway for the Interstate 70 tunnel that would go under present-day Loveland Ski Area, and the potential Butler Gulch development was squashed in favor of other ski areas that were better positioned along the improving I-70.

THE TRAILHEAD

Begin at the Jones Pass Trailhead (**UTM: 13 427073 4402615**). From the town of Empire, drive west on Highway 40 for 7 miles to the first hairpin turn below Berthoud Pass. At the hairpin curve, turn off onto a snow-covered gravel road, which is well-signed for Jones Pass and the Henderson Mine. Drive west on this road for 1.7 miles to the entrance to the Henderson Mine. Here, the road makes a jog to the right and bypasses the mine, arriving at the Jones Pass Trailhead at mile 2.2. Park here.

THE APPROACH

From the trailhead, start out heading west on the Jones Pass Trail. After 0.2 mile, the trail forks (**UTM: 13 426759 4402650**). The left fork leads to Butler Gulch. Follow the right fork to continue to Jones Pass.

To Jones Pass

The well-defined, snow-covered road continues in the trees, slowly turning north as it contours around the bottom of Vasquez Peak following the West Fork of Clear Creek. At mile 1.1, you'll break out of the trees into a very large, high-alpine meadow and valley.

Continue north on the road, although here it can be difficult to follow. Watch for an ENVIRONMENTAL RESTORATION AREA sign, and a split-rail fence that may be buried up to its topmost posts in the snow. Shortly after passing these landmarks, keep an eye on the left (west) slope of the valley. There, a PTARMIGAN CONSERVATION sign marks the continuation of the road. Follow the road north to mile 1.25, at which point the route cuts back sharply to the southwest. You'll soon cross a series of open slopes (great skiing; some backcountry skiers even build kickers here for jumps), and then reenter the trees briefly. You're now heading west up into the Jones Pass basin proper.

At mile 2.0 and 11,300 feet, you'll crest treeline. From here, nothing but open snow slopes and 1000 feet of vertical separate you from the Jones Pass summit. Leave the road and head directly west-southwest en route to the 12,461-foot summit of Jones Pass, which is reached at mile 2.8 (**UTM: 13 423835 4403031**).

The "Buzz"

There's tons of terrain within a relatively short distance of the trailhead. The Jones Pass side can be noisy with snowmobiles, but the snow slopes above treeline are worth it. Butler Gulch is a backcountry skier's quiet paradise. The trees and lower slopes above treeline are excellent midwinter, while the massive snow slopes higher on the mountains are begging to be skied in spring.

—Kelli B.

To Butler Gulch

Follow the left fork, crossing the West Fork of Clear Creek, and then climbing the hillside on a trail through the trees. The trail makes one large switchback before turning into Butler Gulch and trending south-southwest. When you reach treeline at approximately 11,400 feet, do not continue on the main trail west into upper Butler Gulch. Instead, head south and climb to the saddle (**UTM: 13 426494 4400456**) between Point 12,109 and Point 12,317.

THE DESCENTS

Jones Pass Basin: The eastern slopes of Jones Pass are essentially one big playground. Pick your line and ski it.

Jones Pass Creek: Below Jones Pass and the road is an unnamed creek. Following that creek drainage can yield additional good descents.

Jones Pass Road: Retrace your steps and ski the road you came up.

Butler Gulch: Ski the north-facing slope from the saddle between Points 12,109 and 12,317.

Butler Gullies: From near the saddle, traverse north above treeline onto the northwest-facing slopes of Point 12,317. Several enticing gullies descend this face and lead into the trees. Follow the fall line or path of least resistance back to the trail below.

THE APRÈS SKI

Empire, along Highway 40, offers the closest option:

Jenny's Restaurant, 4 West Park Avenue, (303) 569-2570, www.jennysofempire.com

Hard Rock Cafe, 18 East Park Avenue, (303) 569-3450 (This is not part of the national chain. It predates the international franchise, and is named for the "hard rock" miners that worked the surrounding mountains.)

A skiable gully below treeline en route to Jones Pass

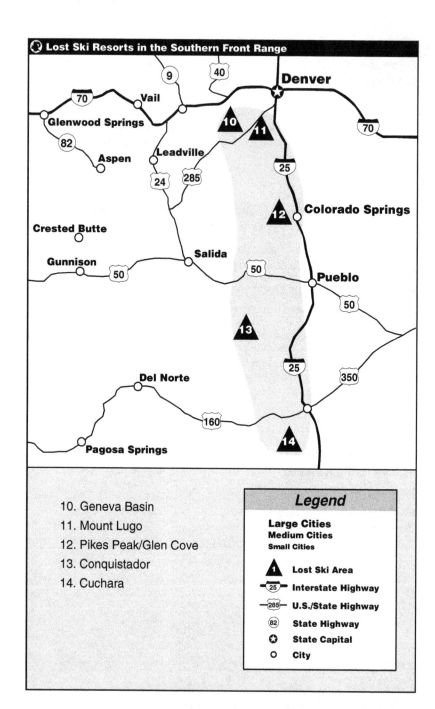

Lost Ski Resorts in the Southern Front Range

10. Geneva Basin
11. Mount Lugo
12. Pikes Peak/Glen Cove
13. Conquistador
14. Cuchara

Legend

Large Cities
Medium Cities
Small Cities

🔺 Lost Ski Area
🛣 25 Interstate Highway
285 U.S./State Highway
⑧ State Highway
✪ State Capital
○ City

Lost Ski Resorts in the
Southern Front Range

The Southern Front Range describes the region stretching from Interstate 70 south to the New Mexico border, and from Colorado Springs west up to and including the Sangre de Cristo Mountains. This section of the guide includes five lost ski areas. There are many more lost ski areas, but the ones not included here are all on private property. One of those worth mentioning is Raton Ski Basin, southeast of Trinidad and a stone's throw from the New Mexico border. During the winter, the only way to access this ski area is from New Mexico, where you drive north through Sugarite Canyon and back into Colorado to the base of the ski area. That nuance earned Raton the slogan, "New Mexico's only Colorado ski area." With the exception of the recent reopening of Echo Mountain Park, no major lift-served ski areas remain here. The lost areas are listed from north to south.

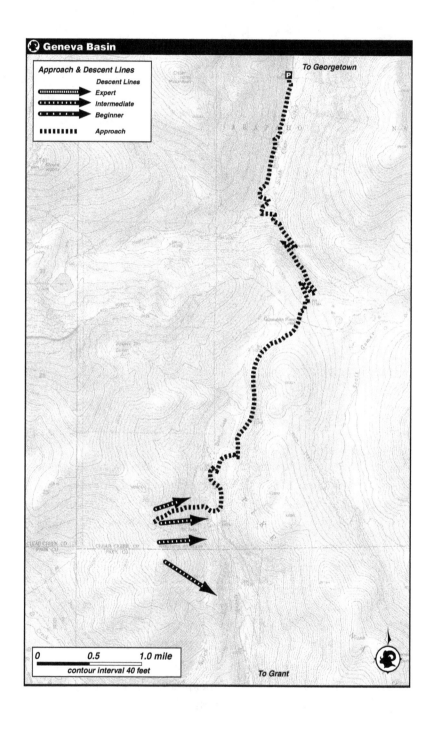

GENEVA BASIN

THE ESSENTIALS

Nearest Town Georgetown	**SNOTEL Station** Jackwhacker Gulch (935)
Distance 7 miles	
Vertical 1600' net (2400' gross)	**Forest Zone** Pike National Forest, South Platte Ranger District
Season December to April	
Elevation Range 10,400' to 12,000'	
Difficulty Rating Strenuous	**CAIC Zone** Front Range Mountains
Skiing Rating ❷ ❷ ❷	**USGS Quad** Mount Evans
	Weather COZ034

THE HISTORY

ike St. Mary's, Geneva Basin has had a tumultuous history of openings, closings, and reopenings under different owners and different names. The story begins in mid-December of 1961 when the area first opened as Indianhead. More than two years of preparation led up to opening day, which was delayed when the initial developers went broke. By October 1961, Indianhead had a two- or three-story chalet, and two rope tows bought from the defunct Magic Mountain ski area in Golden. The road up from Grant was being improved in the hopes of easing access for skiers.

But Indianhead didn't succeed, eventually defaulting on its loans because the ski area just didn't get enough skiers—it only achieved 25 percent of its lift capacity.

During the summer of 1964, Walter Burke, president of the Geneva Ski Corporation, purchased Indianhead at auction from the Small Business Administration. That following 1964/1965 season was great—the new Geneva Basin ski area achieved 80 percent lift capacity. Geneva Basin added a new double chair and T-bar, both of which were slated for completion prior to the 1965/1966 season. A Saint Bernard named Heidi was the ski area's new mascot.

In 1970, Roy Romer—who would become Colorado's governor in 1986—bought Geneva Basin along with several business partners. He and his partners had 15 children among them, and joked that it was cheaper to buy the whole ski area than it was to buy them all individual lift tickets. The kids worked in the parking lots, sold lift tickets, and ran the lifts. Romer and company were reportedly the only owners to ever make money at Geneva Basin.

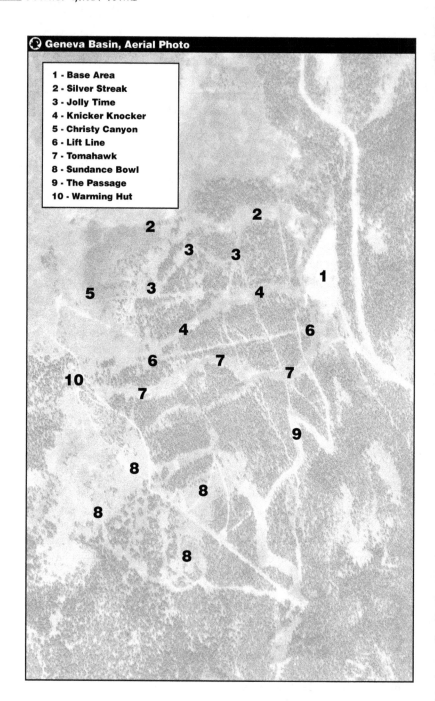

Geneva Basin, Aerial Photo

1 - Base Area
2 - Silver Streak
3 - Jolly Time
4 - Knicker Knocker
5 - Christy Canyon
6 - Lift Line
7 - Tomahawk
8 - Sundance Bowl
9 - The Passage
10 - Warming Hut

In 1975, the ski area was sold again and new investors upgraded the facilities, but by January 1983, Geneva Basin had earned the nickname "Generic Basin," owing to its no-frills environment that contrasted sharply with the megaresorts. A lift ticket cost $13, and the mountain saw some 50 to 70 skiers on weekdays, and up to 400 on a weekend day. But it was a challenging area, with 35 percent expert terrain, and 45 percent intermediate terrain.

The "*Buzz*"

I had my best skiing of the season here in June 2007. The long approach is brutal, but the skiing is totally worth it.

—Andrew J.

In November of 1984, the ski area sold again. The new owners changed the name to Alpenbach, and charged $16 for a full-day weekend lift ticket, and $12 on weekdays. But Alpenbach didn't open for the 1984/1985 season; an empty chair fell off one of the lifts, and the Colorado Tramway Board condemned the lift and shut the ski area.

By February 1986, Alpenbach was hopeful of completing a massive revitalization project. But investors couldn't pay for the completion of the improvements, and the area went into bankruptcy, never opening for the 1985/1986 season.

Old log cabins and ski chalets near Duck Lake at the base of Geneva Basin

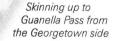

Skinning up to Guanella Pass from the Georgetown side

Later in 1986, the U.S. Forest Service terminated the area's special use permit, citing nonperformance, and in 1991 announced its intention to dismantle the ski area and allow it to return to a natural state. That announcement prompted a flood of support from locals who wanted to reopen the ski area. Several proposals went nowhere. In one final death rattle, during November 1993 voters turned down, by a wide two-to-one margin, a Park County ballot initiative suggesting a recreation tax to fund the ski area's reopening. Two days later, the Forest Service burned the lodge to the ground. The ski area was no more.

In the final days of lift-served skiing at Geneva Basin, a five-person family pass cost $175, there was a 1200-foot vertical drop, and a "courtesy patrol" of three young mothers cruised the novice and intermediate trails, handing out Kleenex tissues, glove liners, and needle and thread for mending tears.

Although the lodge is gone, and the lift towers have been taken away, several things remain at Geneva Basin. The ski runs and lift lines are remarkably intact, offering a superb skiing experience. Chalet-style cabins on private property near Duck Lake avoided the fate of the base lodge, and are a sight to behold, tucked into the trees and easily viewable from Guanella Pass Road and the public land surrounding Duck Lake. A ski patrol and warming hut still stands on the apex of the ridge at the top of the primary lift line. Robber's treasure is supposedly buried on the mountain . . . somewhere.

And lastly, Geneva Basin is reportedly home to a resident spook (fitting for a powder ghost town, no?). The ghost is named Eddie the Head. Eddie was Ed Guanella, the son of Paul Guanella for whom the pass was named. Ed was involved in the construction of the ski area. He was tragically decapitated during an accident stringing the cable on the bull wheel for one of the lifts, and in the years following, ski area employees reportedly have seen him walking around at night at the top of the Duck Creek lift. So when you're skiing Geneva Basin, keep a watchful eye for one more "person" on the slopes.

THE TRAILHEAD

Begin at the winter road closure on Guanella Pass Road on the north side of Guanella Pass south of Georgetown (**UTM: 13 438988 4387261**).

THE APPROACH

The base of Geneva Basin ski area was once accessible by car in winter. But beginning with the 2006/2007 winter season, Clear Creek County stopped plowing the road over the pass in winter. That budget-saving decision greatly increased both the distance and the difficulty of the approach to Geneva Basin. Now, you must climb to the summit of the pass, descend to the Geneva Basin ski area, and then ascend the ski area. Keep in mind that when you're done skiing, you must still reclimb to the summit of the pass before descending to your car.

From the winter road closure, continue south on the Guanella Pass Road. At mile 1.5, pass the Beaver Ponds on your left. At mile 2.2, reach the turnoff for Naylor Lake (**UTM: 13 438371 4384684**). In recent seasons, the winter road closure has been located just above the Naylor Lake turnoff. This reduces the one-way approach mileage to Geneva Basin by about 1.5–2.0 miles. Bypass the turnoff and stay left on the Guanella Pass Road. From here, the road trends southeast, going through two separate pairs of switchbacks as you ascend above treeline and reach the 11,669-foot summit of Guanella Pass (**UTM: 13 438955 4383085**) at mile 4.0.

From the summit of the pass, continue south on the road, trending south-southwest. Square Top Mountain is visible directly across the valley to your west. As you round the northwest slopes of Point

Looking up the Silver Streak run

Looking up at more runs and lift lines at Geneva Basin

11,990, Duck Lake will become visible below you to the south. Remain on the road, passing above Duck Lake on the east. The road here turns west and descends to Duck Creek a short distance south of the outflow from the lake. From here, several chalets and other cabins are visible—remnants of the old ski area. However, the cabins and the land in the immediate vicinity of the lake are private property. Stay on the road and continue farther south still. Finally, at mile 6.4, you will be directly across from the base of the Geneva Basin ski area.

Leave the road and head west, crossing Duck Creek and reaching the bottom of the ski runs (**UTM: 13 437640 4380220**). Choose a run and skin uphill, reaching the crest of the ridge at mile 7.0 and an elevation of about 11,800 feet.

Alternatively, Geneva Basin can be approached from the south by taking the Guanella Pass Road from Route 285 in Grant and following it to the winter road closure. Then continue along the road until you reach the base of the ski area. This road closure is much more variable, and thus, so is the potential approach mileage. However, it does avoid the inconvenience of having to surmount Guanella Pass on both the approach and the return to the car if coming from the north (Georgetown) side.

Sandwiched on a tiny parcel of private land between the old Geneva Basin ski area and Duck Lake is Alpendorf on the Lake, (303) 569-2681. Accessible only by ski or snowmobile in winter and run by a delightful proprietor, Alpendorf offers rustic cabins for rent if you want to spend the night. Another even more basic option is the old ski patrol hut, which still stands atop the ridge in a small stand of trees near treeline. Maintained by volunteer backcountry users, it features a wood-burning stove, bunks, a small kitchenette, and a common room with table and chairs. Even if you're just out for the day, it's a great place to get inside and out of the elements, warm up, and have a bite to eat before beginning your descent. Please remember to leave it in as good or better condition than you found it.

THE DESCENTS

See the topo map and aerial photos for detailed location information.

Silver Streak: From the ridgetop, descend far skier's left down an open snow bowl and rollover to treeline. Follow the leftmost run to the base.

Jolly Time: From the ridgetop, descend the fall line down the open snow bowl and duck into the trees onto a partially overgrown run.

Christy Canyon: From the ridgetop, descend to skier's right, intersecting the main lift line.

Knicker Knocker: Descend the run immediately to skier's left of the lift line.

Lift Line: Ski it.

Tomahawk: Descend the run immediately to skier's right of the lift line.

Sundance Bowl: Descend the southeast facing terrain to far skier's right on the mountain.

THE APRÈS SKI

Georgetown, along Interstate 70, is your best bet. Visit www.george town colorado.com/dining.htm.

Try out this favorite locale:

Red Ram Restaurant and Saloon, 604 6th Street, (303) 569-2300

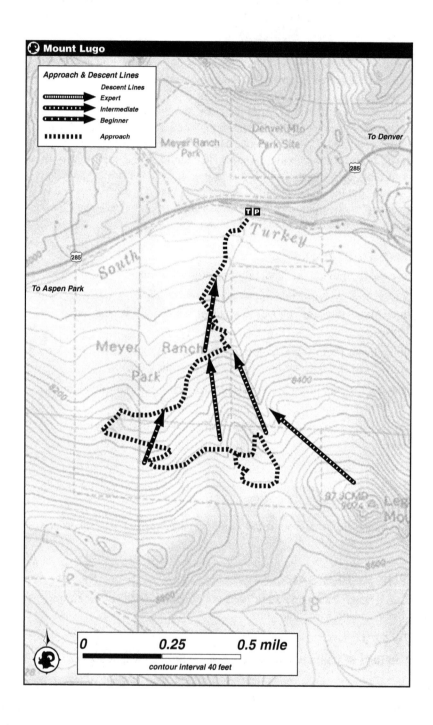

MOUNT LUGO

THE ESSENTIALS

Nearest Town Aspen Park	**SNOTEL Station** Echo Lake (936)
Distance 2.7 miles	**Forest Zone** Jefferson County Open Space
Vertical 900'	
Season February to March	**CAIC Zone** Front Range Mountains
Elevation Range 7900' to 8800'	**USGS Quad** Conifer
Difficulty Rating Easy	**Weather** COZ036
Skiing Rating 🌀	

THE HISTORY

The old Mount Lugo ski area is located within the present-day boundary of Meyer Ranch Park, part of the Jefferson County Open Space system. The park is named for Norman F. and Ethel E. Meyer, who purchased the 397-acre ranch in 1950 and used it for grazing and haying.

The earliest known history of the ranch dates to 1870, when Duncan McIntyre and his family homesteaded on the property. In 1883, Louis Ramboz bought the property from the McIntyres and built the ranch house in 1889. Ramboz worked the land for hay, timber, and cattle. An unsubstantiated legend holds that the ranch served as the winter quarters for the animals of the P. T. Barnum Circus during the late 1880s, the time during which Ramboz owned the land. Interestingly, when Norman Meyer remodeled the ranch house in 1995, he found a wooden board with the inscription, "Circus Town, 1889."

Fast forward to the winter of 1940/1941, when the Mount Lugo ski area opened. A horse-drawn sleigh carried guests from the road up to the ski area high on the north face of Mount Legault. There, 173 acres of skiing were accessible via a 1200-foot rope tow that provided just 150 feet of vertical drop. It was developed by a man named Covert Hopkins, though little else is known about him save for his name.

The ski area operated again for the 1941/1942 season, but closed later in 1942 as a result of gas rationing (and the ski area's subsequent inability to run the tow motor). Remnants of the tow and the old motor are supposedly still on the mountain, though I didn't find evidence of them during my visit. Perhaps they were buried under snow. The old runs are evidenced by stands of young aspen. The name "Mount Lugo" was perhaps a permutation of Mount Legault, the peak's true name, although this is little more than my own speculation.

The Old Ski Run Trail at Mount Lugo leads to the aspen stand where the lift line and ski runs once hosted skiers.

THE TRAILHEAD

Begin at the Meyer Ranch Trailhead **(UTM: 13 476570 4377427)** on the south side of South Turkey Creek Road. From the Town of Aspen Park, drive east on Highway 285 for one half mile. Exit for South Turkey Creek Road, and almost immediately pull into the parking lot for Meyer Ranch on the right (south) side of the road.

THE APPROACH

From the Meyer Ranch Trailhead, start out heading south on the well-packed and well-traveled Owl's Perch Trail through an open meadow. A hill just to the west of the trail is popular with families for sledding. After 0.4 mile, you'll pass a restroom facility, and at 0.5 mile, the Owl's Perch Trail splits. The right fork skirts the top of the sledding slope. The left fork continues more directly up the mountain. Take the left fork for 0.2 mile to its junction with the Lodgepole Loop Trail. Stay straight (do not turn right) on the Lodgepole Loop Trail as it climbs through a small meadow and then enters the trees. The trail switchbacks two or three times before the Lodgepole Loop is intersected by the Sunny Aspen Trail after another 0.2 mile (0.9 total). Turn onto the well-marked Sunny Aspen Trail, and continue for 0.5 mile to a large stone picnic shelter (1.4 miles total). Here, turn once again, this time onto the Old Ski Run

Trail. The trail begins heading southwest, but then makes a sharp turn to the east-southeast as it traverses a slope. Halfway across this traverse, you'll intersect open stands of young aspen. These are some of the old ski runs. Continue on the trail past two switchbacks for a total of 0.7 mile to a final trail junction. This final trail junction is a loop addition of the Old Ski Run Trail, like the end of a lollipop on a stick. You can go either way around this 0.6-mile-long loop.

EXTRA CREDIT

At the height of this loop, leave the trail and continue south to the crest of a saddle in the ridge. Do not continue across to the south side of the saddle. Doing so puts you on private property. However, turning east and following the ridge offers the opportunity to gain additional vertical en route to the true summit of Mount Lugo, while remaining on Jefferson County Open Space property.

The "Buzz"

You won't have an epic day here, but it provides a nice, casual outing in the mountains close to Denver. Good skiing here, more than at other places, is very conditions-dependent because of its lower elevation and extreme Front Range location. Wait for the Front Range to get a few good snowfalls, so that the snowpack can build up and cover obstacles such as tree stumps. Then head up the mountain after a fresh snowfall.

—The author

THE DESCENTS

Trails: Simply reverse your route and follow the trail system back down.

Aspen: When you reach the old runs of the ski area, leave the trail and ski the open stands of aspen.

Mount Legault North Slopes: From the height of the trails, or from the saddle or higher on Legault, descend the north slopes, staying to skier's left of the prominent creek drainage to stay off private land and on Meyer Ranch Park property.

THE APRÈS SKI

Nearby Aspen Park has a number of fast food chains and local restaurants. You can also try the town of Conifer for more restaurant options: http://denver.chowbaby.com/restaurants/Conifer.

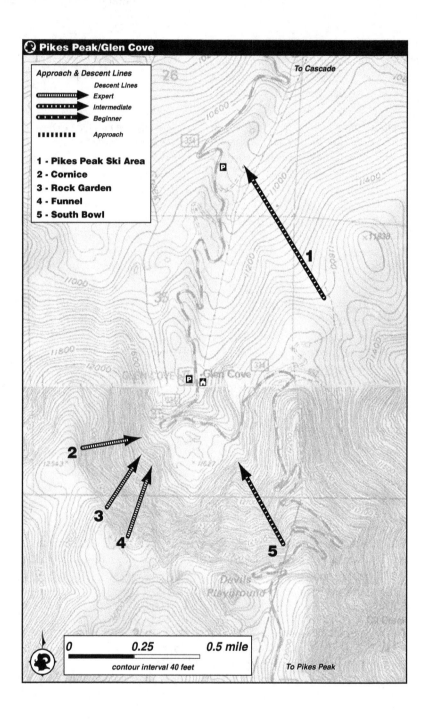

PIKES PEAK/GLEN COVE

THE ESSENTIALS

Nearest Town Manitou Springs
Distance 1 mile
Vertical 1000'
Season January to May
Elevation Range 10,800' to 12,700'
Difficulty Rating Easy
Skiing Rating 🏂 🏂

SNOTEL Station Glen Cove (1057)
Forest Zone Pike National Forest, Pikes Peak Ranger District
CAIC Zone Front Range Mountains
USGS Quad Woodland Park
Weather COZ082

THE HISTORY

In many ways, the history of skiing on Pikes Peak is intertwined with the history of the mountain itself. The Pikes Peak region was first obtained by the United States in 1803 as part of the Louisiana Purchase. Seventeen years later, in 1820, the mountain saw its first recorded ascent compliments of Dr. Edwin James, who was part of a larger expedition to the area. By 1873, the U.S. Army Signal Corps had built a weather station on the summit. Then things really started to accelerate.

Between 1886 and 1888, a carriage road to the summit was built. Following immediately on its heels, the Manitou and Pikes Peak Cog Railroad was built between 1889 and 1890. Then, beginning in 1914 (and completed December 1918), Fred Barr and his father worked on the improvement of a trail up the east face of the mountain, today the famous Barr Trail. One year later, in 1915, Spencer Penrose conceived of an automobile highway to the summit, using the route of the older carriage road. The project began in early 1915 and cost $500,000.

Then the era of skiing on the mountain began. Between the years 1916 and 1936, the highway was operated as a toll road with a $2 fee per person. As a result, throughout the 1920s and into the 1930s, skiers accessed the mountain by train on "ski outings." As early as June 1924, a ski-jumping competition was held on the mountain. That first competition was won by Louis Dalpez, an eighteen-year-old from Denver who was later inducted into the Colorado Ski Museum Hall of Fame in 1979.

Then, in 1936, the toll on the auto road was repealed. The cost of snow removal and road maintenance was too much, and the U.S. Forest Service assumed responsibility for the highway. Skiers flocked to the mountain, and the place known as Glen Cove in particular. Glen Cove claimed to have the state's first rope tow in 1936—a claim also

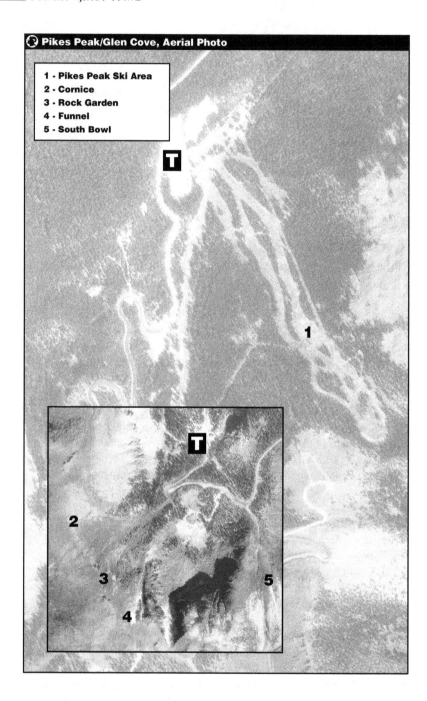

Pikes Peak/Glen Cove, Aerial Photo

1 - Pikes Peak Ski Area
2 - Cornice
3 - Rock Garden
4 - Funnel
5 - South Bowl

made by the Berthoud Pass ski area. Regardless, by 1940, Glen Cove had two rope tows to carry skiers up the snow slopes in the cirque. Meanwhile, during the 1938/1939 winter season, the Broadmoor Hotel in Colorado Springs advertised a series of ski descents on Pikes Peak, utilizing the railway, auto road, and Glen Cove rope tows.

By the end of the 1940s, the ski action was shifting away from Glen Cove and toward the new Pikes Peak Ski Area just 1 mile down the road. The area operated on the slopes immediately below Elk Park. There was a temporary lodge at the base, a series of runs, and a variety of lifts and bus service that accessed the trails. A lift ticket for the day cost just $3. A season pass was $25, and a family pass was $75.

In the late 1970s, the skiable vertical drop actually decreased from nearly 1000 feet to just 270 feet when the buses stopped running and guests could only use the small lifts. Ski area owners planned major expansion during the 1980/1981 season that they hoped would open the following year. The plans included greatly expanded terrain, new lifts that would restore the area's full vertical drop, and a permanent base lodge.

The *"Buzz"*

There's basically no approach. Access is easy, and the views are great. But conditions can be variable—you can find everything from fresh powder to bare ground to bulletproof wind slab, all on the same day. If it's windy, or the snow is in bad shape, it can be a drag. If you wait for spring, though, the skiing on the slopes and in the gullies above Glen Cove is phenomenal.

—Josh W.

Inconsistent snowfall, snowmaking problems, and high winds plagued the upgrade, and the Pikes Peak Ski Area never realized its expansion. The new Poma lift was installed but was then removed when the ski area couldn't pay for the $700,000 investment. The lodge was never built, and the new terrain never added. The ski area that hoped to draw 2000 people a day and operate seven days a week instead closed its doors for good in 1984, having seen just 300 skiers a day on a limited opening schedule.

Today, Pikes Peak remains the domain of hearty backcountry skiers, returning the mountain to its earliest form of skiing. Winter descents of the old Pikes Peak ski area, and spring descents of the cirque walls above Glen Cove—South Bowl, Funnel, Rock Garden, and Cornice—pay homage to the lift-served skiing of early pioneers and more recent downhillers alike.

THE TRAILHEAD

Since Pikes Peak and Glen Cove are two separate ski areas stacked one on top of the other, you have two options for trailheads, depending on which area you intend to ski. Access for both trailheads is provided on the Pikes Peak Highway, a toll road that in winter is open from 9 AM until 3 PM. Rates as of the 2007/2008 winter were $10 per adult, or $35 per car. To reach the toll road, from Manitou Springs, drive west on Highway 24 for 4.5 miles to the town of Cascade. Turn left onto Fountain Avenue, following signs for the Pikes Peak Highway. After 0.4 mile, bear left at a fork onto Pikes Peak Highway, passing the North Pole Santa's Workshop tourist attraction, and arriving at the toll gate.

For the Pikes Peak Ski Area Trailhead, from the guard's station/toll gate at the base of the mountain, reset your odometer. Do not go by the mile-markers on the road—they do not begin measuring at the same point, and subsequently don't coincide with your odometer reset at the toll gate. At the 10-mile mark, the runs of the old Pikes Peak Ski Area will be clearly visible to your southeast. A wide pullout on the east side of the road offers plentiful parking (**UTM: 13 493804 4304138**).

For the Glen Cove ski area trailhead, continue past the Pikes Peak Ski Area Trailhead to the Glen Cove picnic area and visitor center. If conditions on the upper mountain are unfavorable, the road will be

The Pikes Peak Ski Area from the roadside parking area along the Pikes Peak Memorial Highway

closed here. Whether it's open or not, park here. This is your trailhead (UTM: **13 493619 4302901**).

THE APPROACH

For the Pikes Peak ski area, descend the road bank to the east, crossing a small drainage and arriving almost immediately at the base of the ski runs. Choose your run and skin up it to evaluate snow conditions until you arrive near Elk Park at roughly 11,800 feet. It's well worth it to evaluate the snowpack—conditions, even in midwinter, can be highly variable, ranging from nearly bare ground to deep snow.

For the Glen Cove ski area, follow the road for about 0.3 mile to a sharp hairpin turn below a steep-walled cirque lined with snow-filled gullies. This is the Devil's Playground (technically, just below it). Again, choose your run and skin up it to evaluate snow conditions, which can range from bulletproof wind slab to beautiful spring corn.

THE DESCENTS

In the Glen Cove bowl, try the following runs: **South Bowl, Funnel, Rock Garden,** and **Cornice**. Check the topo map and aerial photo for detailed location information.

At the Pikes Peak Ski Area, runs were unimaginatively named **Main Run, Beginner Run**, etc. Pick your line and ski it. They're all comparable.

THE APRÈS SKI

At the end of the day head down the mountain and into Manitou Springs: www.manitousprings.org/dining.htm.

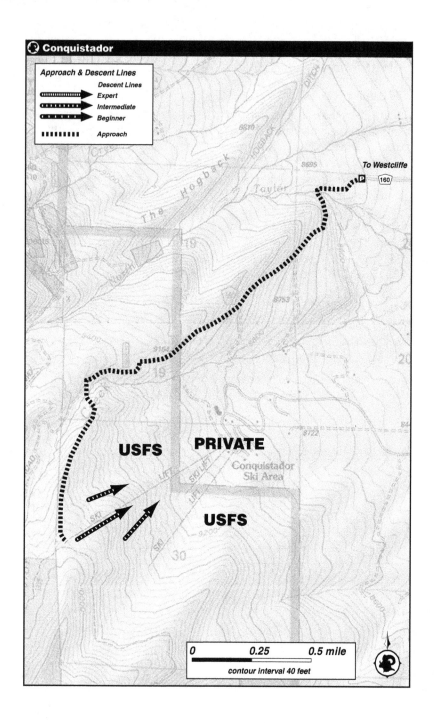

CONQUISTADOR

THE ESSENTIALS

Nearest Town	Westcliffe	**SNOTEL Station**	South Colony (773)
Distance	2.3 miles	**Forest Zone**	San Isabel National Forest, San Carlos Ranger District
Vertical	1300′		
Season	January to March		
Elevation Range	8700′ to 10,000′	**CAIC Zone**	Sangre de Cristo Mountains
Difficulty Rating	Moderate		
Skiing Rating	🎿 🎿	**USGS Quad**	Horn Peak
		Weather	COZ072

THE HISTORY

As a general rule of thumb, the Sangre de Cristo Mountains, and the Wet Mountain Valley to their east have not been home to significant ski areas. Most over the years have been small rope tows, operated either by local communities or by ranchers on private property. The vertical drop, the amenities, and just about everything else was on a very small scale. Ski San Isabel was a perfect case in point.

Located in the Wet Mountains, Ski San Isabel operated from 1956 until 1972. There was a 1300-foot-long rope tow—actually two rope tows attached to the same set of poles. Electric motors provided enough juice to carry 13 people up the slope at a time. There were two runs: right and left, and very little elevation gain. Most weekends the ski area would average 100 people a day, and each person paid just 99 cents for their lift ticket. It typically operated from mid-December until mid-March. The Pennington family, who owned the property, ran cows there in the summertime.

Conquistador, roughly 5 miles west of Westcliffe on the eastern slope of the Sangre de Cristos, was a shining exception. It became a major ski area, at least by the valley's standards, but crashed and burned spectacularly.

Conquistador began in 1964, when a local rancher sold 1120 acres to the developers. The ski area opened for the 1976/1977 season with two surface lifts, just 250 feet of vertical, and limited terrain—three runs mostly targeted at beginners. Even so, it attracted some 8000 skiers in that first season (which supposedly equaled Telluride's popularity that same year).

August of 1982 proved a seminal month. Conquistador underwent a $3.5 million expansion. The ski area added a triple chair, double chair,

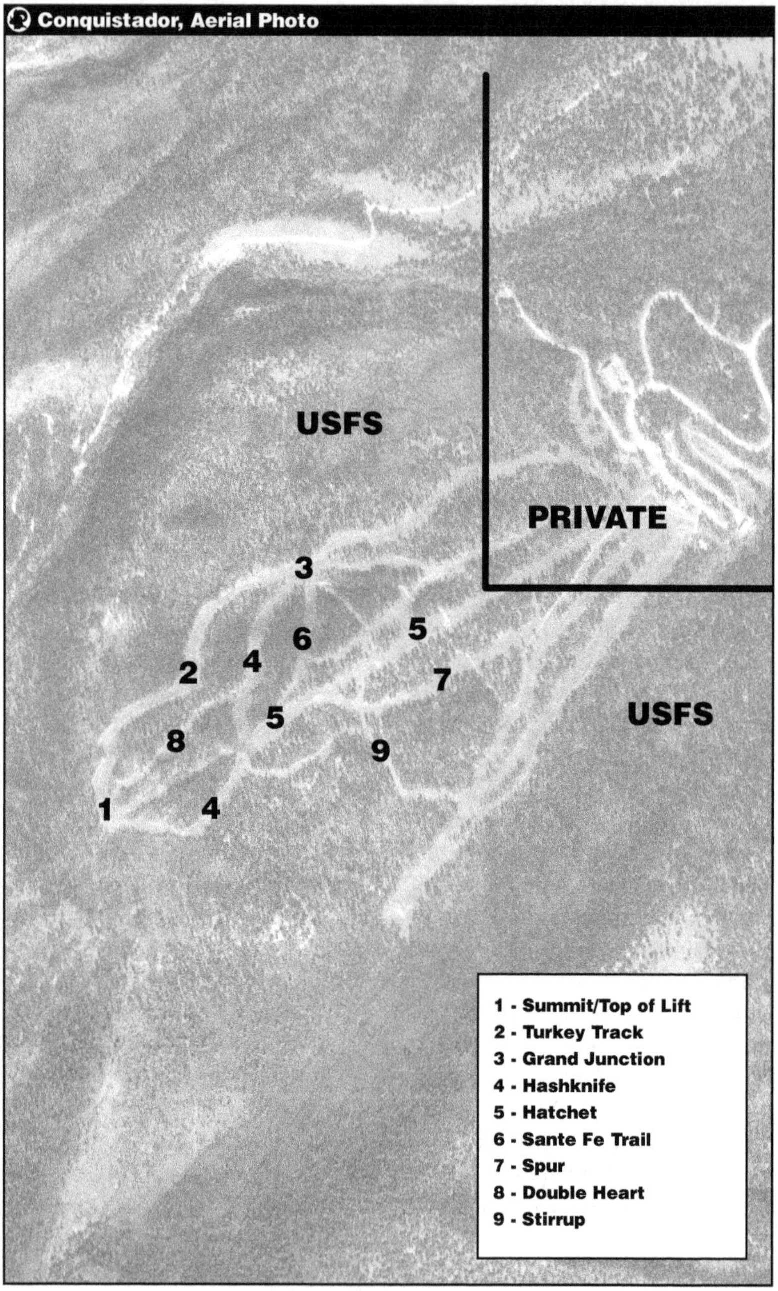

Conquistador, Aerial Photo

USFS

PRIVATE

USFS

3
6
5
2   4   7
5
8   9
1   4

1 - Summit/Top of Lift
2 - Turkey Track
3 - Grand Junction
4 - Hashknife
5 - Hatchet
6 - Sante Fe Trail
7 - Spur
8 - Double Heart
9 - Stirrup

and snowmaking capabilities that covered 90 percent of 15 new runs with 1200 feet of vertical drop.

One year later, Conquistador's owner—a New York-based business—foreclosed on the property. It had defaulted on $23 million in loans. The Small Business Administration assumed ownership of the resort, and operated it through the 1987/1988 season. In December 1988, the SBA tried to auction off Conquistador at a bargain-basement price. No qualified bidders showed up.

By October 1989, the collapse of Conquistador wiped out what little winter economy Westcliffe had. Although the ski area had been contentious within the community from the outset, it was also Custer County's biggest employer, supplying 130 jobs, maintaining an $850,000 payroll, and paying $50,000 in property taxes each year.

In July 1992, there was hope that the ski area would reopen for the 1992/1993 season. But that winter would prove the last time the resort opened to guests. Sometimes bad snow years, and sometimes too-warm weather earned the ski area the nickname "Mudcliffe."

In June 1995, 150 acres of the ski area sold once again, for $1.2 million. The remainder of the 3000 total acres that had made up the resort by then either belonged to the U.S. Forest Service or had been sold off as parcels for residential development. The new name for the ski area was the Hermit Basin Lodge and Ski Area, and it had no plans to operate for the 1995/1996 season.

Shortly thereafter, Hermit Basin switched gears. It removed the lifts, and the base lodge became a conference center. It renamed itself the Hermit Basin Christian Conference Center. Owing to these changes, in April 1996, the Forest Service issued a permit for the removal of all remaining lifts and on-mountain improvements. The mountain would be returned to wildlife habitat, and the San Carlos Ranger District of San Isabel National Forest regained authority over its lands. (Curiously, the next closest lost ski area—Horn Creek Ranch—also became a Christian conference center.)

The Hermit Basin Christian Conference Center continues to operate. The base lodge of the old ski area still stands and is used as the main conference center. And while the base area and the lower portions of the ski runs remain on Hermit Basin's private property, the vast majority of the mountain—including all its upper portions—are on national forest lands for the enjoyment of backcountry skiers with the drive to explore a unique lost ski area with a storied past.

THE TRAILHEAD

Begin at the winter road closure of Hermit Road, which is located at the junction of Hermit Road and Sampson Ridge Road **(UTM: 13 449610 4220783)**. From the town of Westcliffe, drive south on Highway 69. After a quarter mile, turn right (west) onto Road 160 (also known as Hermit Road, Hermit Basin Road, Hermit Creek Road, and Hermit Pass Road—they are all the same thing). Continue on Road 160 for 6 miles to the junction with Sampson Ridge Road.

In the likely event that Road 160 is drifted over in parts, follow signs to the Hermit Basin Christian Conference Center and Resort. After turning right (west) onto Hermit Road (Road 160), continue for 2 miles and then turn left (south) onto Road 137 (Kettle Lane). Take the first right (turning west again) onto Road 150 (Muddy Lane). Continue for 3 miles, and then turn right (north) onto Road 159. Drive north for 2 miles, and turn left (west again) at the stop sign onto Road 160 (Hermit Road). Continue for one quarter mile to the junction of Hermit Road and Sampson Ridge Road. This junction is marked by a brown Forest Service sign with information about the Hermit Pass Road, North Taylor Road, and Gibson Trailhead. In winter, the Hermit Pass Road can be difficult to see leaving this junction. Trust the Forest Service sign's location. If you continue past the sign, Sampson Ridge Road will make

The runs of Conquistador, with the Sangre de Cristo Mountains beyond, seen during the approach

a hard right turn, and you'll know you've gone too far. Park off the main road at the beginning of the Hermit Pass Road.

THE APPROACH

The approach to Conquistador is complicated by private property. The old base area, the bottommost portion of the ski runs, and the land east of the old ski area are all private. The only legal approach, while not difficult, takes the long way around these obstacles.

From the trailhead, follow the Hermit Pass Road. Over its first hundred yards, it can feel nondescript. However, after passing through a small stand of pine trees, the road becomes blatantly obvious. Follow it. The route descends slightly for 0.2 mile, where the road crosses North Taylor Creek. The road continues south for 0.1 mile, and then turns to the southwest for a long, rising traverse across an open, southeast-facing slope with great views of the broad valley far below, the base of the ski directly south, and the ski runs themselves to the southwest.

At 0.5 mile, the main road passes the first of two private roads that are gated and marked. At 0.8 mile, pass the second private road. Cross onto national forest land at mile 1.1. At mile 1.3 the road makes a brief switchback before continuing dead west. The road cut on your right tends to shed small rocks, while to the left, the road drops away steeply to Middle Taylor Creek below. Around mile 1.5, the road turns sharply southwest again, and you will be directly across from the terminus of the forested ridge that comes down to the north off of Conquistador (**UTM: 13 447792 4219444**). Here it is reasonable to descend to and cross Middle Taylor Creek.

From the bottom of the valley, take the path of least resistance up the northwest slope of the ridge to its forested crest. Once on the crest, turn south and continue your ascent. At mile 2.25, you'll pop out of the trees and onto the uppermost reaches of the ski runs. Traverse to the

The "Buzz"

Conquistador is great fun to ski, even though private property at the base complicates the approach and necessitates a skin up and over the mountain to get out at the end of the day. Even so, with good snow, the wide-open runs and distant views up into the Sangre de Cristos and down into the Westcliffe valley make it well worth the extra effort. Skiing here is almost eerie—the runs are so clear and the snow is so smooth, I kept stopping at trail junctions and looking uphill expecting to see other skiers, but I was the only one.

—The author

highest point, where the top of the lift line once terminated just below the 10,000-foot elevation **(UTM: 13 447650 4218425)**.

THE DESCENTS

The interconnecting network of trails on Conquistador can be difficult to describe. See the topo map and aerial photo for detailed location information. Most importantly, **do not** descend any run all the way to the base of the mountain. Doing so will put you on private property, and the owners don't like that. At about mid-height on the mountain, all runs are intersected by a cat track that cuts across the slope (it used to be called Upper Stirrup and Santa Fe Trail). Stop your descent here. It is a useful landmark. Public land extends a short way below it, but don't risk trespassing. Most of the runs all funnel to a large trail intersection called Grand Junction to the far skier's left of the cat track. Put your skins back on and head up to the top for another lap.

THE APRÈS SKI

Tiny Westcliffe (population: 463) is your best bet for food and drink at the end of the day: www.centralcolorado.com/westcliffe/dining/dining. htm.

The author's solitary turns on a ski run at Conquistador

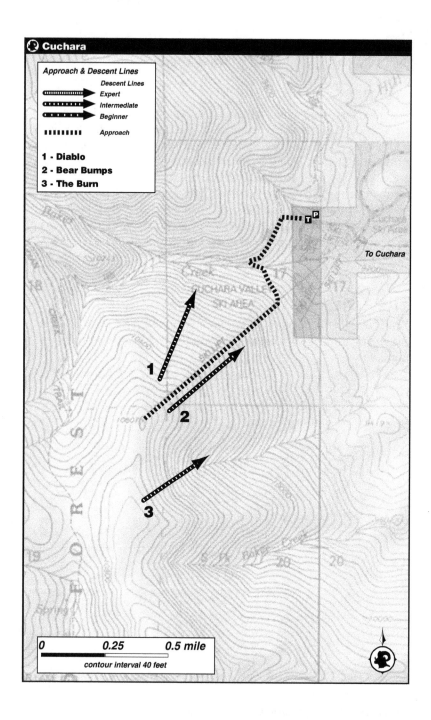

CUCHARA

THE ESSENTIALS

Nearest Towns Cuchara, La Veta
Distance 1.2 miles
Vertical 1400'
Season January to March
Elevation Range 9400' to 10,800'
Difficulty Rating Easy
Skiing Rating 🔩 🔩 🔩

SNOTEL Station Apishapa (303)
Forest Zone San Isabel National Forest, San Carlos Ranger District
CAIC Zone Sangre de Cristo Mountains
USGS Quad Trinchera Peak
Weather COZ074

THE HISTORY

At the far southern end of the Sangre de Cristo Mountains, near the Spanish Peaks, lies a beautiful and remarkably unpopulated stretch of country known as the Cucharas Creek valley. The nearest "big" town, Trinidad, is more than one hour away, and has a population of just 9000. Even so, the few people that live in this corner of Colorado wanted a place to ski.

Consequently, in the late 1950s the City of Trinidad contracted a study to examine the possibility of building a ski area for its citizens. That study focused on the Whiskey Pass area, and while there was some potential, nothing ever came of the study. Shortly thereafter, during the decade from 1960 to 1970, a small ski area named Cuchara Basin operated on private property near the town of Cuchara. It had a warming hut and snack bar, but just five trails that each had no more than 350 feet of vertical. Lift tickets were cheap—$2.50 per person—but people needed a "real" place to ski.

They got their wish a decade later, during the 1981/1982 season, when Panadero opened south of Cuchara. It had more than 1500 feet of vertical, a rope tow, plus two double chairs and 11 runs. In the more than 25 years since then, the mountain has had more than eight different owners over the course of its tumultuous history. These are the highlights:

Panadero operated again for the 1982/1983 season, and then set about on an ambitious expansion project that included a wealth of additional terrain and two more lifts—a double chair and triple chair. It reopened in 1983/1984 as Cuchara Valley, but the expansion left it saddled with debt and financial instability. By the 1985/1986 season, the bank refused to provide additional financial assistance, and the ski area closed early, in February, leaving season pass holders more than a little ornery.

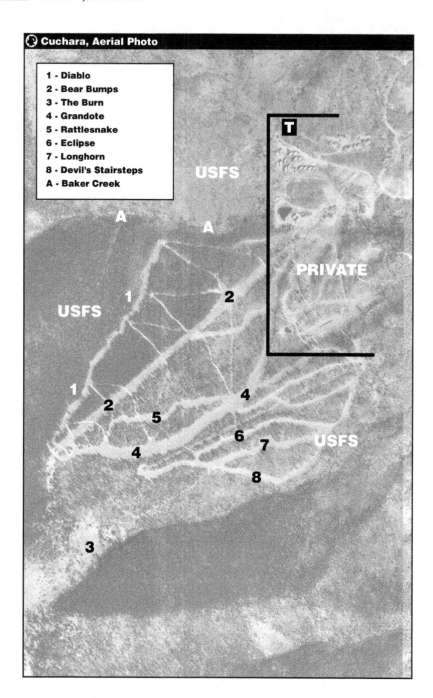

Cuchara, Aerial Photo

1 - Diablo
2 - Bear Bumps
3 - The Burn
4 - Grandote
5 - Rattlesnake
6 - Eclipse
7 - Longhorn
8 - Devil's Stairsteps
A - Baker Creek

Trail signs still mark the descents at Cuchara.

Cuchara opened again in 1987/1988, but a bad snow year and poor management resulted in low skier attendance. The ski area closed its doors from 1989 through 1992 while new owners were sought. Texas businessman Dick Davis came to the rescue, purchasing Cuchara for $1.1 million and opening the resort for the 1992/1993 season. He kept the mountain open for two seasons before he ran out of cash and sold the area in turn. Again, Texans coughed up the cash—this time Phillip and Donald Huffines paid $1.8 million for the resort. They operated Cuchara for the 1995/1996 season, but when the Colorado Tramway Board caught them operating in 1996/1997 without the appropriate permits, Cuchara shut down once again.

In 1997, John Lau (yet another Texan) purchased the base facilities and was issued a five-year ski area special use permit from the U.S. Forest Service. Cuchara reopened its doors as Cuchara Mountain Resort. By then it had a base lodge, hotels, restaurants, retail shops, ski patrol, rental shop, condominium developments, the works. Lau hit it lucky. When he opened Cuchara Mountain Resort for the 1997/1998 season, Colorado's Front Range was hit by a blizzard, resulting in great snow conditions and good attendance. Cuchara operated through the 1999/2000 season on a four-day schedule (Thursday through Sunday).

Then, on July 4, 2000, Cuchara Mountain Resort closed its doors and ceased all operations, including base property land sales. While the base facility is on private property, the 340 acres that make up the ski mountain itself (including the runs and lifts) are all located on national forest lands. The San Carlos Ranger District was responsible for the management of those lands, and for the administration of the resort's special use permit that allowed it to operate on federal property.

The early 2000s saw a series of owners go back and forth with the Forest Service, to no effect. Cuchara was finished. Local residents, though, have not been content to watch the area sit idle. In 2004 they formed a parks and recreation district with the hope of operating Cuchara as a nonprofit. That course of action resulted in a dead end. Most recently, in early 2008, citizens have just begun coming together in a series of informal meetings to talk about the idea of operating Cuchara Mountain Resort as a cooperative, similar to Mad River Glen in Vermont.

In the final analysis, the prospect of Cuchara reopening in the future remains grim at best. Getting the ski area off the ground requires surmounting a series of enormous obstacles: acquiring a new special

Fresh powder and solitude elicit wide smiles from a skier.

use permit, raising the funds to open the resort, and attracting enough skiers from an area that simply doesn't have enough people to supply. The Forest Service, for its part, doesn't anticipate having a ski area there in the future, at least not a lift-serviced resort as Cuchara once was. Now a backcountry skiing destination . . . that's another story.

THE TRAILHEAD

Begin at the Baker Trailhead (also known as the Baker Creek Trail, #1301) adjacent to the condos at the base of the old Cuchara Mountain Resort **(UTM: 13 488727 4133866)**. From the town of La Veta, follow Highway 12 south. At mile marker 11, you'll pass the Dikes of the Spanish Peaks (fins of rock outcrops) on your left. At mile marker 13, cross the Cucharas River. Just past mile marker 16 is the town of Cuchara. Continue through town, still heading south on Highway 12. Turn right (west) 0.3 mile beyond mile marker 18 onto Panadero Avenue. As of the winter of 2007/2008, a sign for Cuchara Mountain Resort marked this turn. Continue on Panadero Avenue. As you approach the old base lodge, the road forks. The right fork is Panadero Loop. The left fork is the continuation of Panadero Avenue. Take the left fork. Drive past the main parking lot of the old ski area, past the Aspen Leaf Village condos, and arrive at the end of the road. The Baker Creek Trail begins here. Do not use the parking for the condos. Instead, park at the base of the prominent blue water tower. This is the Forest Service–designated parking area for the public.

THE APPROACH

As with Conquistador, the base lodge and surrounding buildings are on private property. But unlike Conquistador, here you quickly pass onto Forest Service land, and the ski runs themselves are well onto public land.

From the blue water tower, follow the Baker Creek Trail west into the forest uphill for 100 yards. Make a hard left at a large sign that doesn't say anything meaningful, and contour south through the aspen trees as you emerge onto a southeast-facing slope with shrubs and views down to the base buildings. The trail gradually rounds the hillside, turning west into the Baker Creek drainage. At 0.3 mile, the trail descends to the creek (**UTM: 13 488417 4133579**). Here you have two options: continue west on the primary Baker Creek Trail until you intersect the base of a north-facing ski run (once called "Diablo"). Or turn left and backtrack along the creek, following flagging of red plaid fabric tied to

> ## The "Buzz"
>
> *Cuchara is a great mountain. There are endless opportunities for runs that are wide open. It supposedly closed in part due to inconsistent snowfall, but in late March we found a deep, consolidated snow-pack with a foot of fresh powder on top. The very short approach meant that we were able to do two laps and be back to the car within 15 minutes of reaching the bottom of our second lap . . . and the engine was still warm.*
>
> —Kelli B.

tree branches. This flagging leads you to a convenient crossing of Baker Creek. From the southern shore of the creek, head south-southeast in a gently rising traverse until you intersect what seems to be an old cat track or forest road. In earlier days, this was **Galina Gulch,** a novice ski run and the easiest way down the mountain. From Galina Gulch, turn left (south) and continue for 200 yards until you are beneath the main chairlift line. This run is **Bear Bumps**, and it's your ticket to the top. As a side note: private property is below you. During your descents, use your skin track from Galina Gulch as the lowest point you venture on the mountain. This will keep you safely on public land. Once on Bear Bumps, start setting your skin track up to the 10,800-foot summit of the mountain (**UTM: 13 487750 4132637**), arriving on top 1.2 miles from the trailhead.

THE DESCENTS

As with Conquistador, the interconnecting network of trails on the mountain make it hard to describe individual runs. See the topo map and aerial photo for detailed location information. The following major runs serve as useful landmarks:

Bear Bumps: The main run and lift line down the face of the mountain, facing the base area.

Diablo: The main run down the north face of the mountain into the Baker Creek drainage.

The Burn: A bowl and glades near the top of the mountain, south of the summit.

THE APRÈS SKI

The nearest town, Cuchara, essentially shuts down in winter. For dining, head north to La Veta. Visit www.lavetacucharachamber.com/member. php?i=c8.

Try out this locale:

Blue Rooster Saloon Bar and Grill, 923 South Oak Street, (719) 742-3093

A phantom lift line disappears up into the clouds on a snowy day at Cuchara.

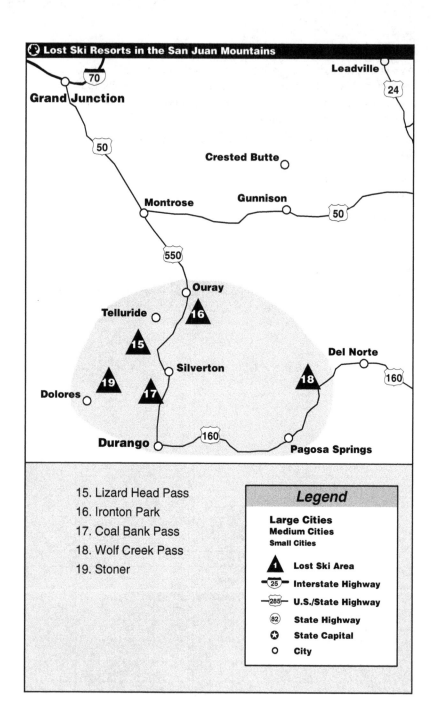

Lost Ski Resorts in the San Juan Mountains

Leadville
70
Grand Junction
24

50

Crested Butte

Montrose
Gunnison
50

550

Ouray
16

Telluride

15

Silverton
Del Norte

19
18
160

Dolores
17

Durango
160
Pagosa Springs

15. Lizard Head Pass
16. Ironton Park
17. Coal Bank Pass
18. Wolf Creek Pass
19. Stoner

Legend

Large Cities
Medium Cities
Small Cities

1 Lost Ski Area
25 Interstate Highway
285 U.S./State Highway
82 State Highway
✪ State Capital
○ City

Lost Ski Resorts in the
San Juan Mountains

The San Juan Mountains describes the region stretching from Montrose south to Durango, and from the San Luis Valley west to Cortez. This section of the guide includes five lost ski areas. The San Juans are known for their high avalanche danger, but also for their spectacular scenery and epic skiing. They also happen to routinely boast one of the deepest snowpacks in the state. For example, it's not uncommon for Wolf Creek Ski Area to receive more than 500 inches of snow in a season. During the 2007/2008 winter, the base at Wolf Creek Pass already exceeded 120 inches by early February. Because the San Juans are far from major population centers, they have relatively few lift-served ski areas, especially considering the great conditions. Wolf Creek Ski Area, Durango Mountain Resort, Telluride, and Silverton Mountain are the only major ones, while there are also a scattering of small, community rope tows, like the ones in Lake City, Silverton, and Ouray. The lost areas are listed from north to south, though they're spread throughout the region, and their order of listing is relatively insignificant.

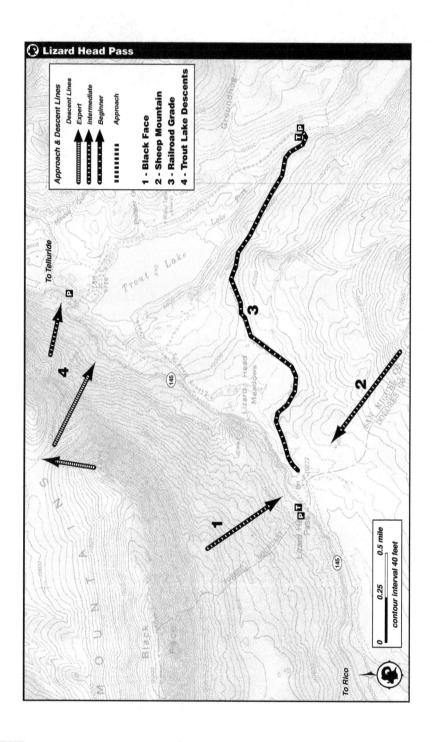

LIZARD HEAD PASS

THE ESSENTIALS

Nearest Town	Telluride
Distance	1.25 miles
Vertical	1800' max.
Season	December to April
Elevation Range	9700' to 11,700'
Difficulty Rating	Easy
Skiing Rating	❷ ❷

SNOTEL Station	Lizard Head Pass (586)
Forest Zone	Uncompahgre National Forest, Ouray Ranger District
CAIC Zone	Northern San Juan Mountains
USGS Quad	Mount Wilson
Weather	COZ018

THE HISTORY

It may be hard to believe that with Telluride's present-day reputation as a ski town, skiing in any major form is a relatively recent evolution here, but it's true. The town began in 1875, and for decades its existence was defined by mining. At its height in 1890, Telluride's population surpassed 5000. The town grew rich from the wealth of ore in the San Juan Mountains that surround it, so much so that Butch Cassidy and his Wild Bunch began their string of bank robberies at the San Miguel National Bank in 1889.

But with the silver crash of 1893, and World War I in 1917, Telluride's economy folded. There was a slow exodus of people and money. Even so, the hearty residents that remained sought to entertain themselves in the snows that came with winter. Their chosen playground was Lizard Head Pass. The pass was first seriously breached in 1890 and 1891 when Otto Mears spent $9 million to build the narrow-gauge Rio Grande Southern Railroad over the mountains, spanning 165 miles from Durango to Ridgway.

After the collapse of the mining boom in 1893, the trains shifted from carrying ore to carrying mail, lumber, coal, livestock, passengers, and skiers. There was just one problem: with declining revenues thanks to Telluride's economic collapse, the railway needed to cut costs. The solution was the Galloping Goose, a train system that required only a one-man crew. (The public transportation buses in Telluride today are called the Galloping Goose in homage to the first Goose, and an authentic Galloping Goose is on display downtown.)

When the winter snows came, the Galloping Goose was fitted with a plow. If that wasn't enough, larger locomotives with rotary snow plows did the work. And if *that* wasn't enough, crews of workers rode up on the trains and cleared the tracks by hand. By the 1920s, regular

Some of the ski descents above Trout Lake near Lizard Head Pass

ski trains brought skiers up from Telluride to the top of Lizard Head Pass, and to Trout Lake just below the pass on the north side. Rope tows were added in the 1950s. The exact location of the ski runs isn't clear, but based on the location of the old railroad grade, it can be reasonably surmised where those old-timers skied (see the **Trailhead, Approach,** and **Descents** sections).

During the 1960s, Telluride's population dropped to just 600. It was nearly a ghost town. But in the 1970s, the present-day Telluride ski area opened, and the town embarked on a rapid recovery thanks to its "white gold." The current population is somewhere around 2000. Nowadays, skiers have the luxury of riding the Gondola, which opened in 1996. The free public transportation system linking downtown Telluride with Mountain Village and the ski resort was the first of its kind in North America, making it unbelievably easy for skiers to get from town to the mountain. But try to imagine the sheer tenacity of early skiers in Telluride, who rode the Galloping Goose to the heights of Lizard Head Pass and skied the same San Juan snows enjoyed by backcountry skiers today.

THE TRAILHEAD

There are three possible trailheads, depending on where you plan to ski:

Lizard Head Pass

From the junction of Highway 145 and the Telluride spur, drive south for 12 miles on Highway 145 to the summit of the pass. Park in a lot on the north side of the road.

Trout Lake

Approximately 2 miles below the summit of the pass on the north side, park in a plowed pullout near the junction of Highway 145 and 626 Road.

Railroad Trestle

From Highway 145, turn east onto 626 Road and follow it for 1.75 miles to where it dead-ends at a public parking lot and a private driveway. The old railroad trestle is next to the parking lot.

The "Buzz"

The scenery is outstanding, the snow is deep, and the descents are fun.

—Kelli B.

THE APPROACH

There are three approaches, corresponding to your chosen ski destination and trailhead:

Lizard Head Pass Approach

If you plan to ski the south-facing slopes of Black Face or the northwest-facing slopes of Sheep Mountain, use this approach. From Lizard Head Pass, simply skin directly up your chosen route. For Black Face, head north up the forested slope. For Sheep Mountain, cross the road to the meadow on the south side of the pass and head for your chosen line on Sheep Mountain. 0.6 to 1.0 mile.

Trout Lake Approach

If you plan to ski the slopes of Point 11,302 or Point 11,747, use this approach. From the Trout Lake Trailhead, cross to the north side of Highway 145. Skin up the open slopes below Point 11,302, and then aim west for the open gully that climbs to the saddle between Points 11,302 and 11,747. From the saddle, turn southwest and continue to the summit of Point 11,747. 1.1 miles.

Railroad Trestle Approach

If you plan a more mellow day of skiing on the Nordic trails of the old railroad grade, begin at the Railroad Trestle Trailhead. The route trends generally west above the south shore of Trout Lake, through Lizard Head Meadows, and arrives atop Lizard Head Pass after 3.0 miles.

THE DESCENTS

Here I describe five possible descents, but you could easily conceive many others in the area of Lizard Head Pass and Trout Lake. These descents are meant to be those most likely used by the early skiers who frequented this ski area.

Black Face: Descend the lower south-facing slopes of Black Face. Beware of avalanche danger higher on the mountain above treeline and below the steep summit cliffs.

Sheep Mountain: Descend the lower northwest-facing slopes of Sheep Mountain.

Point 11,747: Descend the north-facing summit cone of Point 11,747, and then the gully that drops from the saddle between this peak and neighboring Point 11,302.

The old railroad trestle between Trout Lake and Lizard Head Pass, which once carried skiers on the Galloping Goose

Point 11,302: Descend the southeast-facing open snow slopes of the lower mountain below the saddle.

Railroad Grade: Descend the railroad grade, which today is a groomed Nordic track. Very mellow.

THE APRÈS SKI

The town of Telluride offers the best bet. Visit http://visittelluride.com/telluride/content/view/159/33/.

Try this favorite locale:

Las Montañas, 100 West Colorado Avenue, (970) 728-5114, www.lasmontanastelluride.com

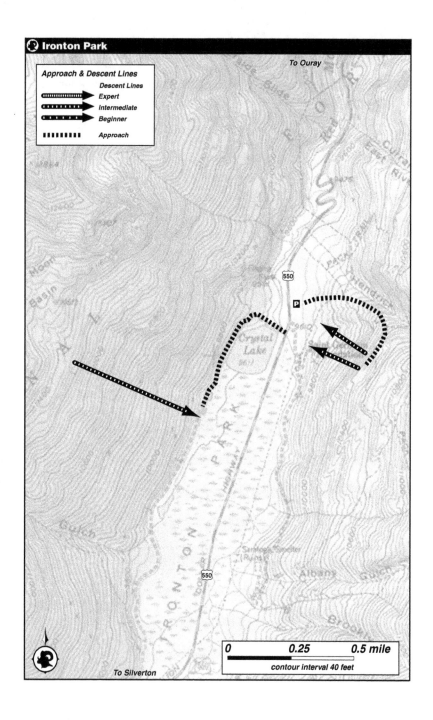

IRONTON PARK

THE ESSENTIALS

Nearest Town Ouray
Distance 0.6 mile
Vertical 850'
Season December to April
Elevation Range 9600' to 10,450'
Difficulty Rating Easy
Skiing Rating 🚩 🚩

SNOTEL Station Idarado (538)
Forest Zone Uncompahgre National Forest, Ouray Ranger District
CAIC Zone Northern San Juan Mountains
USGS Quad Ironton
Weather COZ018

THE HISTORY

The roots of skiing in Ironton Park and Ouray date back to 1887 and the Mount Sneffels Snowshoe Club, which was based in Ouray. "Snowshoe" was used as an early word for skis, and the Mount Sneffels club is often credited as giving birth to North America's après ski culture. Members of the club would ski for the day, then retire to a restaurant or someone's home for wine and food.

By the 1930s, Ouray at last had lift-served skiing. The place was called Ironton Park, a broad meadow in a high valley several miles above the town. The skiing took place on a northwest-facing mountain slope near the north end of the park. There were three downhill runs, and at least one lift. Even so, Ouray was never considered a "ski town." Robert Balch wrote in 1938: "Ouray is not a first-class skiing area, but its attractions as a resort may lead to winter sports facilities being provided in spite of difficulties . . . " Balch was right. Skiing in any major way never materialized in Ouray or Ironton Park. In fact, Ouray remains one of Colorado's few mountain towns with a thriving winter economy *not* based on skiing. But Balch could have hardly predicted what would drive the winter economy in skiing's place: ice climbing at the Ouray Ice Park in the Uncompahgre Gorge.

The Ironton Park ski area slowly faded away, and the stone lodge at its base became the property of the Saint Germain Foundation. In 1956, however, a U.S. Forest Service survey considering a new ski resort almost breathed new life into the area. The agency looked at Ironton Park, and the slopes of Hayden Mountain directly above, as a potential locale. Snow depths were more than adequate—Ironton Park had a 45-inch base in February, a 49-inch base in March, and a 39-inch base in April. The Saint Germain Foundation owned the park at the bottom of the slopes (that land eventually became public), where the

The old, partially overgrown ski runs of Ironton Park above Ouray

base facilities would be built. There was avalanche hazard, but it wasn't too severe, and could be easily controlled. There were two significant problems, though: no nearby population to support a major resort, and the narrow, winding road up to the area from Ouray that crossed more than a few significant avalanche runouts.

In that same year—1956—a second potential resort was also being studied, not above Ironton Park, but above Ouray itself. It was the brainchild of Warren Gibbs, who wanted to build a four-season, summer/winter resort with a series of lifts on Whitehouse Mountain and Twin Peaks. Some lifts would carry skiers from Ouray up onto the mountains, from which a second set of lifts would distribute them to the terrain and ski trails. Snow depths on the mountains were great—2.5 to 4 feet. But there were some significant hurdles. For one, the lower third of the mountain was riddled with several cliff bands that ruled out skiing, except by the most extreme skiers. Second, although there was great skiing on the upper two-thirds of the mountains, creating the ski trails would require very expensive cutting, clearing, and grooming of slopes blanketed in fir and spruce trees. The Forest Service came out against the proposal, and Gibbs' resort never came to be.

Instead, Ouray's most significant contribution to Colorado's lift-served skiing culture remains the après ski scene at the end of the day. Beyond that, skiing at Ironton Park and Ouray in general has reverted to backcountry, where intrepid skiers can enjoy untracked powder in the self-proclaimed "Switzerland of America."

THE TRAILHEAD

Begin at a pullout along Highway 550 at the north end of Ironton Park just north of the old stone building of the Saint Germain Foundation (**UTM: 13 266202 4204830**). From Ouray, drive south on Highway 550 for 6 miles. The parking area is on the left. From the summit of Red Mountain Pass, drive north on Highway 550 for 6.75 miles.

THE APPROACH

From the parking area, the old ski area and the ski runs are visible on a forested hillside directly to your east (just south of Hendrick Gulch). Begin heading east toward the trees across an open meadow. Arrive at the trees after less than 0.1 mile. Ascend a subtle ridge just north of the ski runs—this ridge has a more mellow angle and is a better option for uphill skinning. At approximately the 10,400-foot elevation, the ridge reaches a bench that cuts across the northwest face of the mountain. The slope is steeper both above and below this bench. Traverse this bench to the southwest until you're above your chosen run, arriving after 0.6 mile (**UTM: 13 266636 4204443**).

The "Buzz"

The old Ironton ski area is great because it's so close to the road and so easy to do laps on. Beyond the ski area itself, the Ironton Park area is surrounded by a tremendous amount of potential ski terrain—in springtime you're bound to see ski tracks on most slopes.

—The author

THE DESCENTS

There are two dominant runs at the ski area, and many other possibilities in the trees and on other runs that have overgrown over time. Both main descents end in the meadow behind the stone building.

EXTRA CREDIT

Cross to the west side of Highway 550 and follow a groomed cross-country trail west past the north end of Crystal Lake. The trail turns south and follows the bottom of Hayden Mountain and the west edge of Ironton Park. When you reach the base of a prominent avalanche path, climb it (assuming the snow is stable) to the bottom of Half Moon Basin at 11,400 feet. Start your descent from here. This was part of the Ironton/Hayden ski area proposed in the 1950s.

THE APRÈS SKI

Nearby Ouray is your best bet. Visit www.ouraycolorado.com/Dining.

Try this favorite locale:

The Outlaw Restaurant, 610 Main Street, (970) 325-4366, www.outlawrestaurant.com

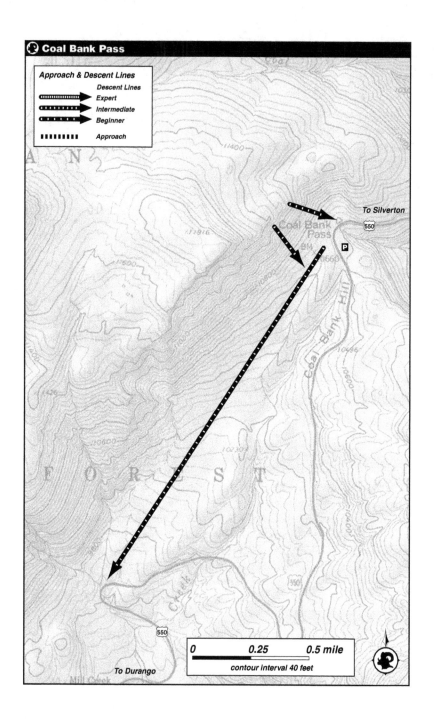

Coal Bank Pass

Approach & Descent Lines

Descent Lines
→ Expert
→ Intermediate
→ Beginner

Approach

To Silverton
550

Coal Bank Pass
P

Coal Bank Hill

FOREST

550

To Durango

0   0.25   0.5 mile

contour interval 40 feet

COAL BANK PASS

THE ESSENTIALS

Nearest Towns Durango, Silverton
Distance 1.75 miles
Vertical 1300' max.
Season December to April
Elevation Range 9700' to 11,000'
Difficulty Rating Easy
Skiing Rating 😊 😊

SNOTEL Station Molas Lake (632)
Forest Zone San Juan National Forest, Durango Ranger District
CAIC Zone Northern San Juan Mountains
USGS Quad Engineer Mountain
Weather COZ018

THE HISTORY

Over the years, the stretch of U.S. Highway 550—the Million Dollar Highway—between Silverton and Durango has been littered with small ski areas. No one was more instrumental in the development of those areas than Barney Yeager, who year to year moved a portable 400-foot rope tow from one locale to another: Columbine Lake in 1948/1949, Highway Camp (near Purgatory) from 1950 to 1953, Wildcat Ranch in 1955/1956.

Yeager wasn't the only one. The San Juan Basin Ski Club set up a rope tow at Haviland Lake in 1940/1941. A lift ticket cost 25 cents per day for adults. And there was Electra Lake and Chipmunk Hill, where a 1000-foot rope tow and, later, night skiing, existed from the 1930s through at least 1945. Durango had its own ski area, too: Calico Hill, at the south end of 3rd Avenue, operated by the city's recreation department from 1945 until at least 1968.

And then there was Coal Bank Pass, deep in the heart of the San Juans, midway between Silverton and Durango. When engineers were originally planning a travel route from Silverton to Durango, they chose the Animas River canyon. But the canyon wasn't wide enough for both a road and a rail line. The rail line won out, and the Durango-Silverton Narrow Gauge Railroad was built. Years later, the route over Coal Bank Pass was constructed (and later upgraded). It became known as the Million Dollar Highway. Several theories account for the origin of the name. Some suggest it was for the cost of construction. Others suggest it's a nod to the wealth that flowed out of the mines in Silverton.

One thing is clear: beginning in the early 1930s, the highest point on the Million Dollar Highway—Coal Bank Pass—was home to a lift-served ski area. It started out as a "drive up and ski down" area, but eventually installed a car-powered rope tow. From the summit of the pass, skiers would schuss down an open power line cut along Mill

A skier on the main run at Coal Bank Pass

Creek, beneath the cliffs of Engineer Mountain. Exactly how long the ski area lasted, no one knows for sure.

In 1960, however, there were plans to create a much larger ski resort superimposed on the Coal Bank Pass ski area. Known as Engineer Mountain (for the peak on which it would have been built), the project was spearheaded by a group of five developers (two of whom were loosely associated as investors at Sunlight Mountain Resort, near Glenwood Springs). The main area of the ski resort would have been the northeast and northwest faces of Engineer Mountain above Highway 550. They also planned for lifts below the highway, extending down to near Coal and Lime creeks.

During the month of January, U.S. Forest Service officials skied the mountain, surveying the proposal. They recommended that a special use permit not be issued. Engineer Mountain stalled in its tracks, and Coal Bank Pass remained the only lift-serviced ski area to operate on the pass.

Those initial surveys on Engineer did spawn additional surveys that ultimately resulted in the Purgatory ski area (today known as Durango Mountain Resort). The Forest Service also entertained the idea of building a ski resort on Sultan Mountain above Silverton. The plan had a favorable review, and the residents of Silverton were supportive, but Sultan ultimately failed because the residents of Durango wanted something closer to home.

Today, Coal Bank Pass and Engineer Mountain have returned to their original form of drive-up-and-ski-down skiing. Just remember your skins, be prepared to hitch a ride, or walk the road back up to your car parked atop the pass.

THE TRAILHEAD

Begin at the Coal Bank Pass summit parking lot (**UTM: 13 255137 4176076**). From downtown Durango, drive 35 miles north on Highway 550 to the summit of Coal Bank Pass. Park in a lot at the top of the pass below Engineer Mountain. From Silverton, drive south on Highway 550 for 12 miles to the pass.

THE APPROACH

Unlike most areas in this book, you'll actually use the approach *after* you've done the descent, since the skiing starts from the parking lot. To return to the trailhead, skin back up your descent route, use a shuttle car, or hitch a ride.

THE DESCENTS

The primary descent on Coal Bank Pass follows a power line cut down the south side of the pass. The run begins at the summit of the pass at approximately 10,660 feet. Descend following the power line, or the open slopes to either side, ending at the road at 9700 feet.

EXTRA CREDIT

You can also ski the lower slopes of Engineer Mountain right above the pass. Instead of descending off the pass to the south, climb up southeast-facing slopes directly west of the pass and ski back down.

The "Buzz"

The main run at Coal Bank Pass isn't steep enough for fresh powder, but it's good for spring skiing on firm snow. Its low angle and wide-open slopes make it a great place for entry-level backcountry skiers looking to get their feet wet.
—Kelli B.

THE APRÈS SKI

North of Coal Bank, the town of Silverton is your best bet. Visit www.silvertoncolorado.com/index.asp?DocumentID=213. South of Coal Bank, the town of Durango is well supplied with places to eat and drink. Visit www.durango.org/Restaurants/index.asp.

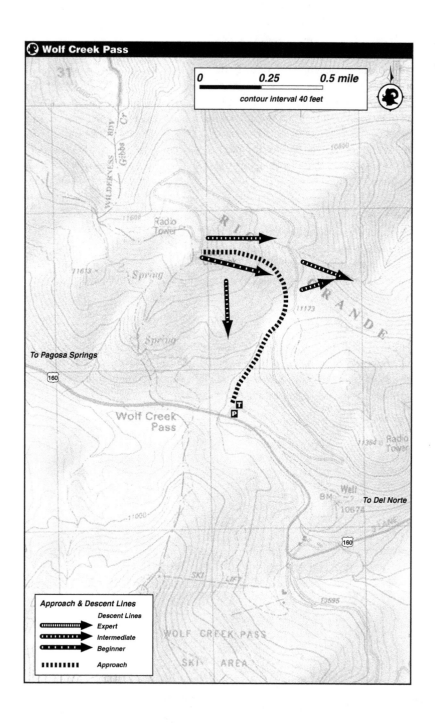

Wolf Creek Pass

0   0.25   0.5 mile

contour interval 40 feet

To Pagosa Springs

Wolf Creek
Pass

To Del Norte

Approach & Descent Lines

Descent Lines
Expert
Intermediate
Beginner

Approach

WOLF CREEK PASS

THE ESSENTIALS

Nearest Town	Pagosa Springs	**SNOTEL Station**	Wolf Creek Summit (874)
Distance	1.1 miles	**Forest Zone**	Rio Grande National Forest, Divide Ranger District
Vertical	950'		
Season	November to May		
Elevation Range	10,800' to 11,750'	**CAIC Zone**	Southern San Juan
Difficulty Rating	Easy	**USGS Quad**	Wolf Creek Pass
Skiing Rating	🌲 🌲	**Weather**	COZ068

THE HISTORY

Up to the early 1930s, Cumbres Pass, far to the southeast near the New Mexico border, was the only direct winter route through the mountains from the San Luis Valley to Pagosa Springs. But the snow atop Wolf Creek Pass had already earned a reputation as some of the deepest, lightest, and most stable in the state, a fact not lost on the region's earliest skiers. A March 1937 article in the *Valley Courier* summed up their sentiments:

> *San Luis Valley ski enthusiasts have placed their stamp of approval upon Wolf Creek Pass as the finest spot for winter sports in this section of the state . . . Therefore, no time should be lost in developing the Wolf Creek country for snow parties.*
>
> *Cumbres Pass is as good a place for sports as Wolf Creek, but it has the disadvantage of being accessible only by train, and ski trains are not always practical . . . On Wolf Creek a modern highway, open the year round, runs to the very summit of nearly eleven thousand feet where the snow is ideal for months at a time.*
>
> *Last year it was suggested that the Forest Service and the Civilian Conservation Corps do some work to develop the ground selected by ski organizations. The officials of the Rio Grande National Forest agreed to sponsor such a project, and it was indicated that the courses could be cleared of rocks and an attractive shelter house could be erected. The house would be so designed as not to clash with the scenery.*
>
> *Now that the skiing groups apparently have decided that Wolf Creek is the best place, there should be nothing in the way of carrying out such a program. If the valley is to have a real winter playground, let's make it a good one—the finest in the west, if possible.*

The Wolf Creek Pass Road was first dedicated in August 1916. During those first years, the pass closed in winter, and most years didn't reopen until at least June 1 because of deep snow. By 1938, the year after the above article appeared, the road over the pass was finally kept open in winter. It was suddenly open season for skiers.

A rope tow was installed on the north side of the pass. It was powered by an old Chevy truck engine, and lift tickets cost $1 per day. That summer, the Civilian Conservation Corps—under contract with the U.S. Forest Service—built the warming shelter skiers so desired. At the same time, the Colorado Department of Highways graded a dirt road that ran from the highway to the ski tow and warming hut. By the mid-1940s, the old Wolf Creek Pass ski area had a total of three lifts, the warming hut, lunches, and lodging in nearby towns on either side of the pass (Del Norte and Pagosa Springs).

The "Buzz"

Wolf Creek Pass has a short approach making for easy laps. The snow is so soft, light, and deep, this is the best skiing I've had in the last four years. The only negative is that it's far from anything else, but that helps keep the crowds away, which leaves more powder per person.

—The author

The year 1955, however, spelled the end of the Wolf Creek Pass ski area. In that year, the Wolf Creek Development Corporation began construction on a new ski area just below the pass on the east side—the beginnings of present-day Wolf Creek ski area that sits below Treasure Pass and Alberta Peak. The ski activity shifted from the pass to the new ski area, and the rest, as they say, is history. The Wolf Creek Pass ski area became a "lost" ski area, and today remains home to the same great backcountry snow that first got skiers excited about it back in the 1930s.

THE TRAILHEAD

Begin at the Wolf Creek Pass Trailhead (UTM: **13 341089 4149951**) on the north side of the 10,800-foot summit of the pass. From the east side (South Fork), drive west on Highway 160 to the summit of the pass. From the west side (Pagosa Springs), drive east on Highway 160. The summit of the pass is 0.8 mile above present-day Wolf Creek Ski Area.

THE APPROACH

With the exception of a forest road that leads to the radio towers atop Lobo Overlook, the north side of Wolf Creek Pass is off-limits to snow-mobiles, and is a designated nonmotorized winter recreation area. From the trailhead, head northeast on a trail up a creek drainage. The trail stays in the forest to the right (southeast) of the creek. At mile 0.4, the trail emerges onto the broad, open saddle (UTM: **13 341492 4150589**)

Gorgeous views of the southern San Juan Mountains from Lobo Overlook and the old Wolf Creek Pass ski area

between Lobo Overlook and Point 11,384. Here the trail and forest road merge briefly, heading north. The east ridge of Lobo Overlook is visible to your left.

Before the road enters the trees, and before you begin to descend off the backside of the saddle, turn left (west) and follow skin tracks (or make your own, if necessary) up the east ridge of Lobo Overlook. Arrive at the 11,700-foot summit of Lobo Overlook after 1.1 miles and 900 feet of elevation gain (**UTM: 13 340901 4150920**).

THE DESCENTS

The primary descents at Wolf Creek Pass are on the east slopes of Lobo Overlook. Immediately below the summit is a great 30-degree bowl. At the bottom of the bowl, you'll hit intermittent trees and open snow slopes at a lower angle that lead you back to the saddle. From the summit of Lobo Overlook, you can also drop northeast (just to the north of the power line that runs to Lobo's summit). Follow this drainage all the way to the road on the backside of the saddle. Also, from the saddle, you can drop northeast and east into a drainage and ski the open slopes until the forest definitively closes down on you several hundred feet below. Refer to the topo map for more details.

THE APRÈS SKI

Pagosa Springs, on the west side of the pass, offers the closest dining opportunities. Visit www.planetpagosa.com/pagosa_springs_restaurants.html.

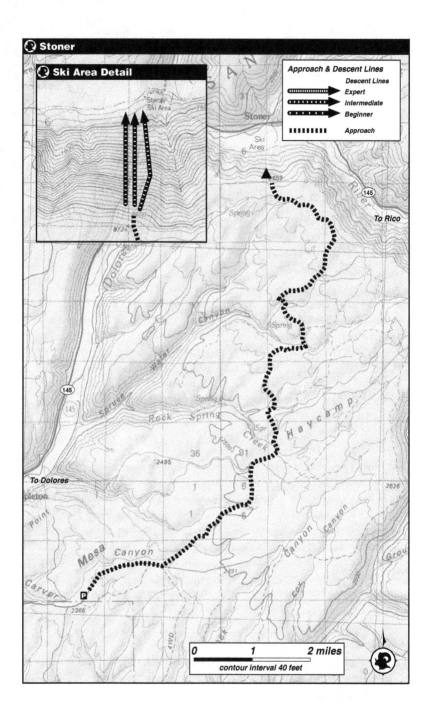

STONER

THE ESSENTIALS

Nearest Town	Dolores	**SNOTEL Station**	Scotch Creek (739)
Distance	11.5 miles	**Forest Zone**	San Juan National Forest, Dolores Ranger District
Vertical	1100'		
Season	January to March		
Elevation Range	7600' to 8700'	**CAIC Zone**	Northern San Juan
Difficulty Rating	Strenuous	**USGS Quad**	Stoner
Skiing Rating 🎿🎿		**Weather**	COZO19

THE HISTORY

The old Stoner ski area, located within San Juan National Forest, sits above the Dolores River in an unpopulated corner of southwestern Colorado. Stoner originally opened in 1948 with a T-bar and two rope tows. The Ski-Hi Ski Club in Cortez, 28 miles away, ran the area (they've also been called the Sky-Hi Ski Club and Cortez Ski Club, though Ski-Hi was their official and correct name). The ski runs were 3500 feet long and dropped 1050 feet of vertical. During that first 1948/1949 season, Stoner sold 300 lift tickets. By the 1951/1952 season, it was averaging 150–200 ticket sales per weekend, and the season ended with 1537 lift tickets sold.

In 1956, the ski area added a new slalom run. By then, lift tickets cost $2.75. If you wanted to ride the rope tows only, you'd pay $1.75. A single ride cost 50 cents. Stoner had also added some amenities—a large warming hut, a new lodge with a restaurant that sat 65 people, cabins, and a volunteer ski patrol. They opened on weekends and holidays, and ran their ski season from December through April 1.

Stoner significantly upgraded for the 1966/1967 season, thanks in large part to a Farmer's Home Administration loan. The old T-bar was extended in length to 4000 feet, and a second T-bar was added, as were additional runs. The upgrades helped to bring more skiers to the area. While Stoner had 1572 skiers in 1960/1961 and 3875 in 1964/1965, after the upgrade it drew in 10,000 skiers by 1969/1970.

But the ski area had to pay for its loan and upgrades, and lift tickets slowly rose in price to $4, then $5, and eventually $7. Unfortunately, after the 1969/1970 season, the popularity of the area began to wane. In 1974/1975 only 7200 skiers showed up over the course of the season. Finally, at the end of the 1982/1983 season, Stoner shut down. Its special use permit expired, the state Tramway Board wouldn't renew

Stoner, Aerial Photo

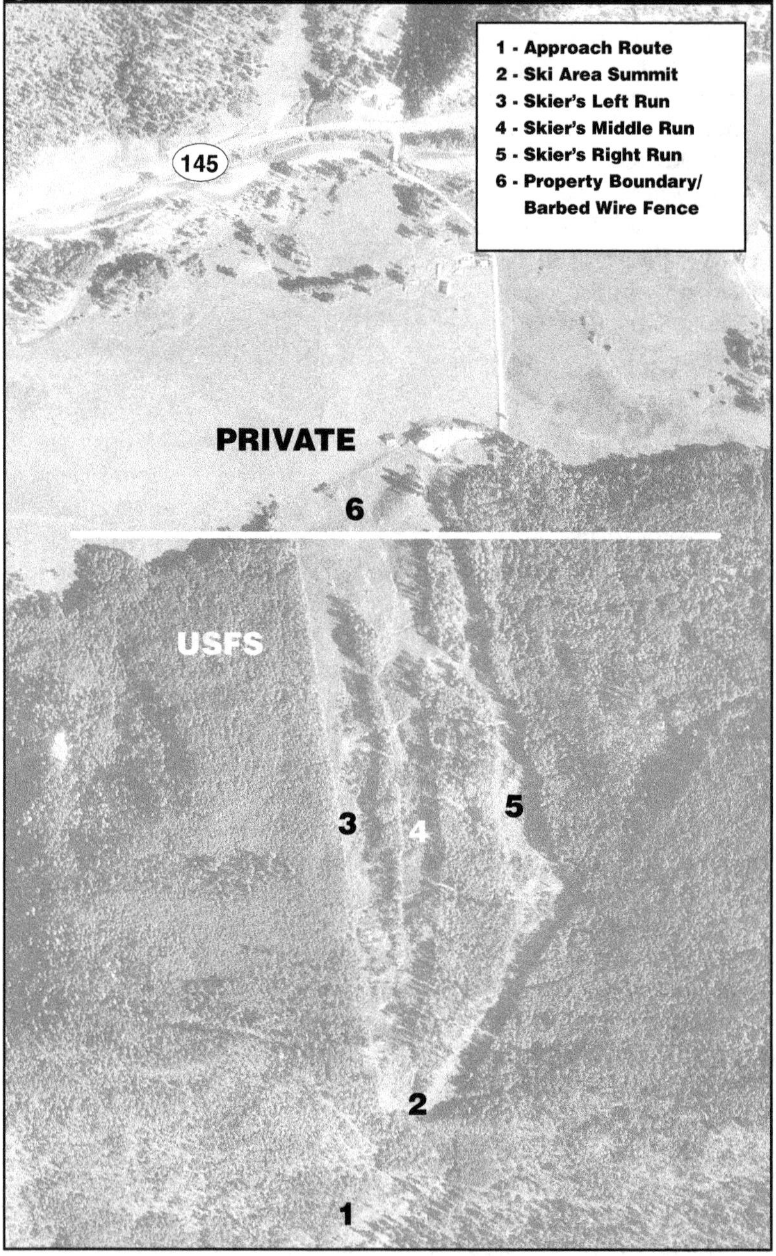

145

1 - Approach Route
2 - Ski Area Summit
3 - Skier's Left Run
4 - Skier's Middle Run
5 - Skier's Right Run
6 - Property Boundary/
    Barbed Wire Fence

PRIVATE

6

USFS

3   4   5

2

1

the licenses on the lifts unless they were renovated, and the ski area was over $100,000 in debt. In 1991, the base lodge and other facilities, as well as the on-mountain lifts, were removed, and the U.S. Forest Service rehabilitated the slopes.

Today, Stoner sits idle, nearly forgotten. But its runs are plainly visible. They're still wide open and begging to be skied. However, because of private property in the river valley at the ski area's base, you must today approach the ski area from the top and backside, even though you can drive to within 200 yards of the bottom of the runs.

THE TRAILHEAD

Because you're approaching the ski area from the backside, take the time to first drive to Stoner on Highway 145 and preview conditions on the ski runs before you commit to the long approach. Having said that: begin on Haycamp Mesa at the winter road closure of Forest Road 556 (**UTM: 12 731714 4150617**). This road closure is gated just beyond the national forest boundary line.

The *"Buzz"*

It's demoralizing that you can drive tantalizingly close to the base of the ski area, but are separated from it by private land. This major inconvenience greatly lengthens the approach. However, if you come with a sense of adventure, great skiing awaits those who are willing to put in the effort to get there.

—The author

From Dolores, drive west on Highway 145 to its junction with Highway 184. Turn south on 184. Pass the Dolores Public Lands Information Center. After 3.2 miles on Highway 184, turn left onto MC Road S. This turn is signed for HAYCAMP MESA. Continue on MC Road S for 6.4 miles. The road quickly turns from paved to dirt and gravel. The last 2 miles of the road pass through Lost Canyon Ranch. Just beyond the ranch, you'll cross onto Forest Service land, where the road changes names to Forest Road 556. Park here at the gated winter road closure.

THE APPROACH

This is of the most surreal approaches in this book. You'll pass through a Utah-esque mesa top with vultures and very little snow. Only views of the San Juan Mountains to the east remind you that there are mountains and snow nearby. With a one-way distance of 11.2 miles, technically, this is the longest approach in the book. However, I've listed Marshall Pass as the longest approach for one very important reason—Stoner is the only approach you'll probably do without snow, and the only one

I recommend you do with a mountain bike. Wait until it hasn't snowed for a bit, giving the road a chance to melt out, and then use a mountain bike with your skis on your back to quickly dispense with the approach. If the road is snow-covered, you might be able to use a snowmobile, but negotiating it around the gate and boulders at the winter road closure could prove problematic. No matter how you choose to tackle the approach, proceed as follows:

Continue on Forest Road 556 for 1.6 miles. At that point you will come to a three-way junction with Forest Roads 556, 557, and 393. Bear left to remain on 556. Continue for another 1.7 miles to another junction (with 556 and 398). Stay left again to remain on 556. Continue on 556 for another 1.6 miles. You'll pass several small side roads, and after 1.4 miles you'll cross Rock Spring Creek. At mile 1.6 you'll arrive at another juncture (with 556 and 558). Turn left onto Forest Road 558. Continue on 558 for 6.4 miles. (At mile 0.6 you'll cross a tributary of Rock Spring Creek; at 1.7 pass Forest Road 494; at 2.3 and 3.3 pass creeks that feed into Spruce Water Canyon; at 6.4 arrive at a spur road). At this spur road, turn right (north) and continue to the top of the Stoner ski area **(UTM: 12 736526 4162050)**.

The three ski runs of Stoner, viewed from Highway 145 and the Dolores River Valley

THE DESCENTS

Stoner has three main descents: **skier's left, middle,** and **skier's right**. All three runs have equal amount of vertical drop (about 1100 feet). Skier's left and middle are comparable in length, and basically follow the fall line. Skier's right makes a dog-leg turn, resulting in a longer run than the previous two. Important note: all three runs terminate at private land at the valley floor. The boundary between Forest Service and private land is demarcated with a barbed wire fence—a strong incentive not to descend too far.

THE APRÈS SKI

The town of Dolores, east of Stoner on Highway 145, offers the best bet. Visit www.doloreschamber.com/pages/dining.html.

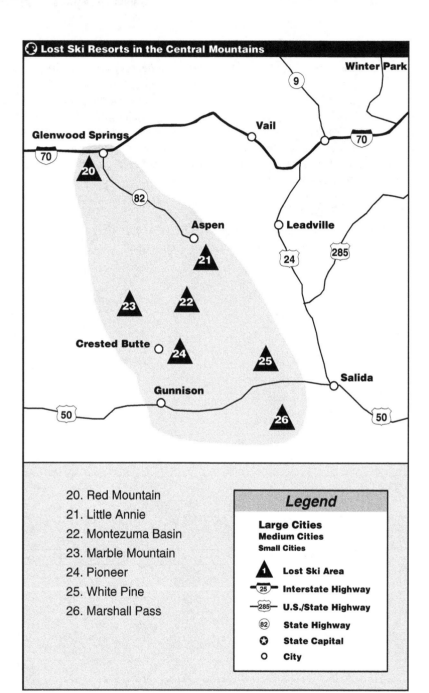

Lost Ski Resorts in the Central Mountains

Winter Park

9

Vail

Glenwood Springs

70

70

20

82

Aspen

Leadville

21

24

285

23

22

Crested Butte

24

25

Salida

Gunnison

50

26

50

20. Red Mountain
21. Little Annie
22. Montezuma Basin
23. Marble Mountain
24. Pioneer
25. White Pine
26. Marshall Pass

Legend

Large Cities
Medium Cities
Small Cities

1   Lost Ski Area
25   Interstate Highway
285   U.S./State Highway
82   State Highway
✪   State Capital
○   City

Lost Ski Resorts in the
Central Mountains

The Central Mountains describes the region surrounding Aspen and Gunnison. Generally, it spans the area stretching from Glenwood Springs south to Montrose, and from the Arkansas River Valley west to Paonia. This section of the guide includes seven lost ski areas. The Central Mountains are also home to some of Colorado's most popular lift-served ski areas today: Aspen, Aspen Highlands, Buttermilk, Snowmass, Crested Butte, Monarch, and Sunlight. The lost areas are listed from north to south.

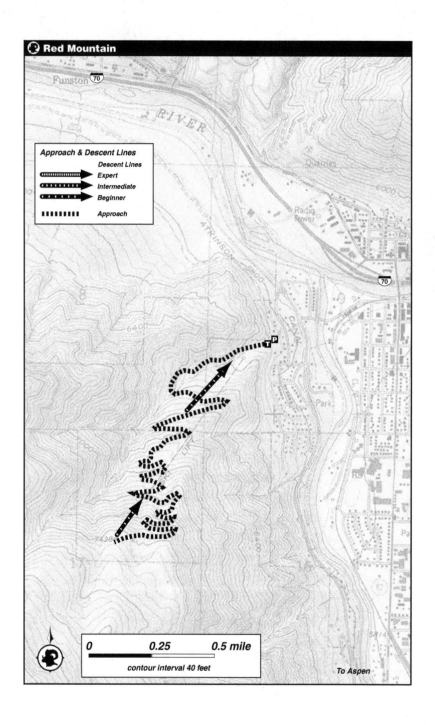

Approach & Descent Lines

Descent Lines

Expert

Intermediate

Beginner

Approach

| 0 | 0.25 | 0.5 mile |

contour interval 40 feet

To Aspen

RED MOUNTAIN

THE ESSENTIALS

Nearest Town	Glenwood Springs	**SNOTEL Station**	None
Distance	2 miles	**Forest Zone**	City of Glenwood Springs
Vertical	1500'		
Season	January to March	**CAIC Zone**	Aspen Area
Elevation Range	5900' to 7400'	**USGS Quad**	Glenwood Springs
Difficulty Rating	Easy	**Weather**	COZ008
Skiing Rating	❷		

THE HISTORY

Although skiers today may think of Glenwood Springs as a gateway to Aspen, the town was once home to a ski area that was virtually downtown: Red Mountain. Named for the unmistakable peak that stands directly above town, the ski area first opened in 1941. The Civilian Conservation Corps cut the mile-long run that gained nearly 1200 feet of vertical, and used parts salvaged from a steel mine near Ouray to build the single-chairlift. Later during that same 1941/1942 season, a skier was injured when the chair he was riding got caught in a lift tower. The lift was modified to fix the problem, resulting in the towers made from orange steel tubing that are still visible on the mountain today.

In 1942/1943 Red Mountain opened again, but by the 1943/1944 season, World War II severely limited the area's use. It shifted to a weekend-only operating schedule, and by 1952, had completely shut down.

A decade later, however, another ski area opened near the top of Red Mountain, virtually piggybacked onto the top of then-defunct Red Mountain ski area. Called Glenwood Park, it had a warming hut and a double chair that served just 200 feet of vertical. The area was open for just one season—1965/1966—before it closed down and sold its lift to Sunlight Mountain Resort, 15 miles away.

The Sunlight Ranch Company opened for business on December 16, 1966, operating on 420 acres of private land and 2081 acres of U.S. Forest Land (under a special use permit). That first year Sunlight saw 15,000 skier days. Since then, Sunlight has grown and expanded, changing its name to Ski Sunlight, and then Sunlight Mountain Resort. Its trails, lifts, and terrain have all changed, too. It remains an affordable locals' option, in contrast to the nearby megaresorts of the Aspen quartet: Aspen Mountain, Aspen Highlands, Buttermilk, and Snowmass.

THE TRAILHEAD

Begin at the Red Mountain Jeanne Golay Trailhead in Glenwood Springs (**UTM: 13 299410 4379918**). From Grand Avenue, turn west onto West 7th Street. Cross over the Roaring Fork River, and when the road ends at a T intersection, turn right onto Midland Avenue. Make your next left onto Red Mountain Drive, and then a right onto West 9th Street. The winter road closure ends at the Red Mountain Jeanne Golay Trailhead.

THE APPROACH

From the trailhead, you're essentially standing at the base of the old ski area, which went up Red Mountain above you. The main run is still evidenced by the open snow slope at the bottom, while the old lift towers—bright orange steel pipe—still stand in the thick brush alongside. You have two options: follow the Jeanne Golay Trail, which heads straight up the middle of the steep for 1400 vertical feet, or follow the snow-covered gravel road, which switchbacks up the mountain at a much more leisurely grade. In practice, the bottom third and top third of the ski runs are most open, while the middle is choked tight with scrub oak. Link the open sections with a brief stint on the road for the most enjoyable ascent and descent. Either way, finish your approach after about 3 miles, arriving at the top of the slope and just below the runs of

Looking down on Glenwood Springs from the ski run on Red Mountain

Glenwood Park, the second ski area which today sits on private land adjacent to the public open space owned by the City of Glenwood Springs.

THE DESCENTS

First, it's worth noting that, because of its very low elevation, the descent requires the right snow conditions. Even then, leave your fat powder skis at home. Come with a lightweight backcountry setup. Anything more would be overkill.

For the descent, as with the approach, a combination of the **old ski run** and the **road/trail** will probably yield the most enjoyable way down. Use the old ski run for the upper and lower thirds of the mountain. For the middle third, where the run is tightly overgrown, stick to the road until you can continue the descent on the ski run.

The "Buzz"

If you want a lost ski area you can do from town, this is it. The approach basically starts downtown, and goes up Red Mountain from there. The skiing won't blow your mind, but the views down into Glenwood Springs and Glenwood Canyon just might.

—Kelli B.

THE APRÈS SKI

Glenwood Springs offers oodles of dining options . . . more than 60, to be exact. Visit www.glenwoodchamber.com/restaurants.

A personal favorite and regular stop every time I'm in town is:

Glenwood Canyon Brewing Company, 402 7th Street, (970) 945-1276, www.glenwoodcanyon.com

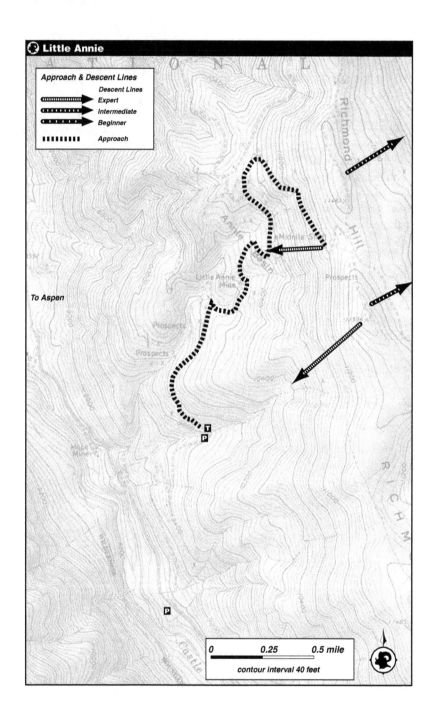

Little Annie

Approach & Descent Lines

Descent Lines
- Expert
- Intermediate
- Beginner

Approach

To Aspen

0   0.25   0.5 mile

contour interval 40 feet

LITTLE ANNIE

THE ESSENTIALS

Nearest Town Aspen
Distance 2.5 miles
Vertical 1500'
Season December to April
Elevation Range 9650' to 11,150'
Difficulty Rating Easy
Skiing Rating ❷ ❷ ❷

SNOTEL Station Independence Pass (542)
Forest Zone White River National Forest, Aspen Ranger District
CAIC Zone Aspen Area
USGS Quad Aspen
Weather COZ010

THE HISTORY

The proximate history of Little Annie dates back to 1960. However, the ski area has earlier ties to Elizabeth Paepcke—one of Aspen's founding mothers. She, in turn, fits into an even broader tapestry of the history of skiing in Aspen.

The story begins prior to 1879, when the Roaring Fork Valley was frequented by Ute Indians during summers. Then, in 1879, the first prospectors arrived from Leadville, having come over the mountains via Independence Pass. Thirteen of those men spent the winter at a town site they called Ute City. The next year, 1880, B. Clark Wheeler and others came over from Leadville to inspect their mining claims. They established a new town site, and named it Aspen.

By 1885, the town of Aspen had hydroelectric power; by 1887, the Denver & Rio Grande Railroad reached town; and by 1889, the Hotel Jerome and Wheeler Opera House were open. One year later, Aspen's population had blossomed to 8000, and the passage of the Sherman Silver Act ushered in a boom era of mining. In 1891, Aspen was the largest silver-producing region in the nation, providing one-sixth of the nation's silver, and one-sixteenth of the world's. The town's population ballooned to more than 12,000.

Just one year after that, in 1893, the Silver Act was repealed, and Aspen's economy—and population—began a long, slow downward spiral. By the 1930s, Aspen's population had contracted to just 700. Then, in 1936, a new "ore" was discovered: snow. Andre Roch, a Swiss skier, had visions of building a ski area on Hayden Peak (see Montezuma Basin on page 143). Hayden never happened, but Roch helped to plan and cut the first ski trail on Aspen Mountain—later named Roch Run—which used a 10-passenger boat tow.

Finally, in 1939, Elizabeth Paepcke came to town. Elizabeth was the wife of Walter Paepcke, a Chicago businessman, philanthropist,

The "Buzz"

Once you make the easy ascent to Little Annie Basin, doing lap after lap is easy. The main slope is great for farming the powder—start on one side and slowly move across the slope, lap after lap. The snowmobile traffic at times can be busy, but in general everyone is considerate and out to enjoy the snow.

—Kelli B.

and chairman of the Container Corporation of America. Elizabeth was staying at a ranch when the plumbing broke. Looking to divert her guests from the problem, she and her friends planned a ski outing near the bleak mining town of Aspen. They hitched a ride part of the way up the backside of Aspen Mountain in the back of a truck filled with some of the region's last miners. Then, the group hopped out, put skins on their skis, and headed uphill. "At the top, we halted in frozen admiration," Elizabeth later recalled in her memoir. They were standing atop Little Annie Basin. The views into the heart of the Elk Mountains, and what would ultimately become the Maroon Bells-Snowmass Wilderness, were stunning.

Elizabeth's inspiration at Little Annie would ultimately vault Aspen into the spotlight of ski megastardom. In 1941, Aspen and the Roch Run hosted the first national championships for downhill and slalom skiing. That same year, Austrian Friedl Pfeifer—a former ski instructor at Sun Valley—became a member of the 10th Mountain Division, and skied Aspen while on breaks from his service. When he left for the war, he vowed to return and make Aspen a world-class ski resort.

By 1945, Elizabeth Paepcke convinced her husband, Walter, to come to Aspen to see the natural beauty that had inspired her six years earlier. Walter was equally taken, and together with Pfeifer, who had returned from World War II, planned Aspen's first chairlift. By 1946, the Aspen Skiing Corporation had come into existence. Aspen Mountain officially opened one year later, although skiing had been continuous there since the days of the Roch Run. In 1950, Aspen hosted the first World Alpine Championships on North American soil. Then, in 1958, both Buttermilk and Aspen Highlands opened. Snowmass would soon follow in 1967, completing the quartet. In addition, the Paepckes also founded both the Aspen Institute and the Aspen Center for Environmental Studies.

Finally, in 1960, Little Annie crept back into the skiing scene, having been overlooked in the 20 years since Elizabeth's first introduction to the area in 1939. Waddill "Waddy" Catchings of Aspen was the man with the idea—a new ski area that spanned Little Annie and Hurricane basins, running from the floor of the Castle Creek Valley up to the ridge crest of Richmond Hill, which extended south from the summit of the Aspen Mountain ski area. Catchings spent time negotiating the acquisition of various mining patents near the Little Annie and Midnite mines, and envisioned a gondola lift from the Castle Creek Road up into Little Annie Basin, and then a chairlift that would carry guests the rest of the way to the top of the ridge. At last, on December 12, 1960, he filed for a special use permit with the U.S. Forest Service.

Yet neither Catchings nor succeeding developers could get enough financial investors to back the project. By October 1972, Little Annie was considered a "case closed."

And so Little Annie remains undeveloped to this day. Presently, the Little Annie Basin is a snow-lover's paradise, shared between backcountry skiers, snowmobilers, and snowcat operators like Aspen Mountain Powder Tours.

THE TRAILHEAD

Begin at the winter road closure of the Little Annie Road, at the Little Annie/Lower Hurricane Road fork **(UTM: 13 341941 4331522)**. From Aspen, travel west on Highway 82 to the roundabout. From the roundabout, go south on Castle Creek Road for 6.7 miles. Turn left onto Little Annie Road. Pass a small parking area after 0.1 mile, and arrive at the

The author on the main slope at Little Annie

Unfolding views along the approach to Little Annie Basin

main parking area (72-hour parking) and trailhead after 1.3 miles. If the trailhead parking area is full, you'll need to park in a lot on the west side of Castle Creek Road directly across from the base of Little Annie Road. This will add 2.6 miles to your roundtrip distance.

THE APPROACH

From the Little Annie parking area, continue on the Little Annie Road. The first several hundred yards you head southwest across an open slope, with stunning views to the west of the Elk Mountains and the edge of the Aspen Highlands ski area. At 0.3 mile, the road turns northeast into the trees and begins a gradual ascent into Little Annie Basin. At 1.1 miles, you'll emerge from the trees into the bottom of Little Annie Basin, and the site of the old Little Annie Mine. Although you're on Forest Service land, the lower basin is dotted with small private cabins. Please respect private property.

Continue for another 0.2 mile on Little Annie Road. Here, the road makes a hard switchback to the right before cutting back across the slope above you. However, it's likely that the basin's heavy snowmobile traffic has blazed a shortcut straight up the slope to your left. Technically, snowmobiles here are restricted to the road. If you're on skis, take your pick of routes. The options merge back into one another at mile 1.6, just north of the Midnite Mineshaft.

From here, continue uphill on the Little Annie Road until mile 1.8, where you turn due north and climb a short steep slope to a tailings pile on an open, broad, flat stretch of Richmond Hill. Just north of the tailings pile, turn right (southeast) onto a connector road that links the Little Annie/Midnite roads with the Richmond Hill Road. The road does a gently rising traverse above Little Annie Basin, heading in and out of the trees. Arrive at your destination at mile 2.4, above a large open snow slope perched at 27–30 degrees. From here it's 600-plus vertical feet down to the Little Annie Road below you—perfect for doing laps **(UTM: 13 342859 4332958)**.

THE DESCENTS

The primary descent at Little Annie is on the broad, open **snow slope above the Midnite Shaft**. It's about 600 to 700 feet of vertical, depending on your particular line. The slope is perched at 27–30 degrees, and it's worth digging a pit to analyze the snow's stability before you drop in. There are subtle differences in the slope aspect across the bowl—ski what's best on your particular day.

EXTRA CREDIT

You can also continue to the top of Richmond Hill, where you have two options: drop down the east side of the ridge into the Roaring Fork drainage, or go south to Point 11,534 and ski the southwest slopes.

THE APRÈS SKI

The après ski scene doesn't get any better than in Aspen. Check out the Dining and Nightlife section of the Business Directory on the Aspen Chamber of Commerce website: www.aspenchamber.org.22.

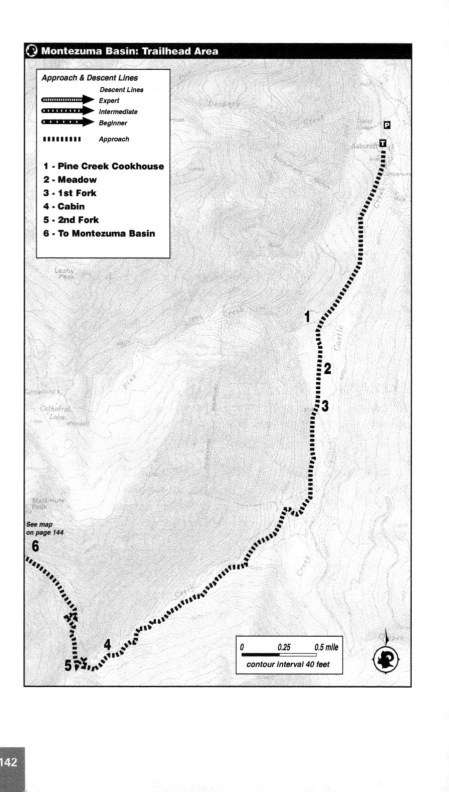

Montezuma Basin: Trailhead Area

Approach & Descent Lines

Descent Lines
- Expert
- Intermediate
- Beginner

Approach

1 - Pine Creek Cookhouse
2 - Meadow
3 - 1st Fork
4 - Cabin
5 - 2nd Fork
6 - To Montezuma Basin

See map
on page 144

0   0.25   0.5 mile
contour interval 40 feet

MONTEZUMA BASIN

THE ESSENTIALS

Nearest Town Aspen
Distance 7.2 miles
Vertical 4400'
Season December to September
Elevation Range 9400' to 13,800'
Difficulty Rating Strenuous
Skiing Rating 😊😊😊

SNOTEL Station Independence Pass (542)
Forest Zone White River National Forest, Aspen Ranger District
CAIC Zone Aspen Area Mountains
USGS Quad Hayden Peak
Weather COZ010

THE HISTORY

In a roundabout way, the history of the old Montezuma Basin ski area begins with the history of another area that was never built. In the summer of 1936 a trio of men, Ted Ryan, Billy Fiske, and T. J. Flynn, who dreamed of a Highland Bavarian ski resort, built the Highland Bavarian Lodge near the junction of Castle and Conundrum creeks. They had the grand ambition of an aerial tram that would reach all the way to the 13,300-foot saddle south of Hayden Peak's summit.

In November 1936, Flynn secured a special use permit to conduct a survey and study for the placement of chairlifts and ski trails. That winter—1936/1937—Andre Roch and Italian Gunther Langes surveyed the east slopes of Hayden Peak. The following year Flynn's company obtained title to the ghost town of Ashcroft in the Castle Creek Valley. One year later, the route of the aerial tram was surveyed. It climbed an amazing 4000 feet of vertical, from the ghost town at 9400 feet all the way to 13,400 feet on Hayden Peak. A 1939 promotional brochure sought endorsements and investors for the project, which was estimated to cost $1.25 million, including the construction of the ski trails.

With the high price tag, in March 1939 Flynn advocated for federal funds to support the project. He revised the estimated price tag, citing the cost of constructing New Hampshire's aerial tram in Franconia Notch. That gambit failed. By February 1940, there was still no movement on the plan.

Then, in 1941, the Colorado State Legislature passed Senate Bill 224, which was subsequently approved by the governor. The state would borrow $650,000 and build the aerial tram and ski area. But as was the case with more than one lost ski area, World War II got in the way. Aside from the blunt impact of the war, one of the project's main partners—Billy Fiske—became the first American in the Royal Air Force

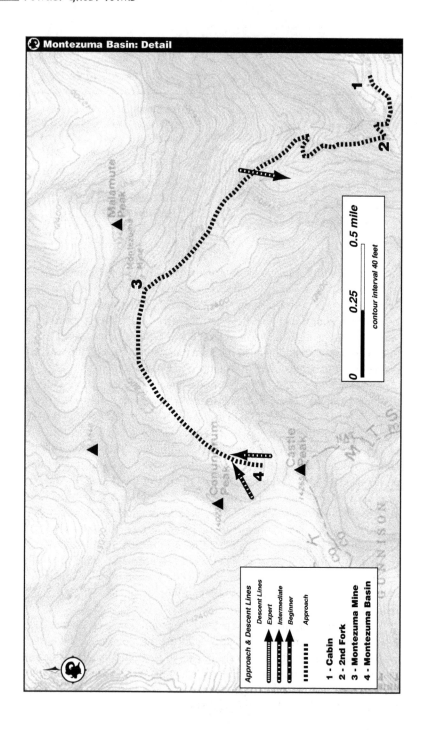

Montezuma Basin: Detail

0.25   0.5 mile

contour interval 40 feet

0

Approach & Descent Lines

Descent Lines
Expert
Intermediate
Beginner

Approach

1 - Cabin
2 - 2nd Fork
3 - Montezuma Mine
4 - Montezuma Basin

to lose his life in the Battle of Britain. The war, Fiske's death, and financing problems combined to sabotage the project.

In 1961, the project took on a new life. One of the remaining partners, Ted Ryan, claimed to have $25 million in available funds, and envisioned the possibility of a new tram location to the top of Electric Peak, south of Hayden. Between the years of 1965 and 1967, a variety of helicopter surveys were conducted. Those surveys included Ryan and Roche, as well as U.S. Forest Service "snow ranger" Paul Hauk, Darcy Brown (president of Aspen Skiing Corporation), and Max Marolt (an Aspen ski racer).

The federal Roadless Area Study of 1972 and interest in expanding the boundaries of the Maroon Bells-Snowmass Wilderness Area eventually squashed the Highland Bavarian Ski Resort for good, but Marolt had already acted on a different idea: Montezuma Basin.

Marolt and local Dick Milstein wanted to install a rope tow, shelter hut, and toilet facilities, and to extend the mining road for the Montezuma Mine to the base of the ski area. They planned to build the base facilities on two existing mining patents, and they argued that skiers already used the snowfields—both a snowfield on the north face of Castle Peak (later dubbed "Maxie's Glacier"), and another, lower snowfield between Castle and Conundrum peaks. Forest Service rangers had surveyed the area, and despite what they described as "marginal access and income problems," approved a special use permit. Marolt signed on the dotted line on November 16, 1966 for a flat rate of $25 per year for the permit.

By July 25, 1967, the road had been extended, a parking area was complete, and most of the rope tow equipment was on-site. In March 1968, however, Marolt decided to get out of the game. He sold Montezuma Basin to John Hollingsworth, who started a new proposal and permit process that included a Doppelmayr double chairlift that would be permanently installed on the lower snowfield.

Hollingsworth's Montezuma Skiing Corporation operated from late summer until early fall of 1969. (Montezuma always had the most unique ski season of any area in Colorado—mid- to late summer until October or so.) One year later, Montezuma failed to open due to money problems.

Tumultuous times followed. The ski area sometimes operated, sometimes didn't. The Forest Service argued that the lifts had to be inspected and certified by the state Tramway Board, and threatened to revoke the permit. Hollingsworth said he planned to open for the 1973 season, but a February 1973 ad in *Aspen Today* listed a lift, snowcat, generator, and 9.5 acres of deeded land for $100,000. Montezuma Basin was up for sale.

By August 1975, the Aspen Ski Club owned and operated the ski area. But Montezuma Basin failed to operate in 1977 and 1978, and the mountains have since reclaimed their snowfields. You can still visit Maxie's Glacier and the other permanent snowfields of Montezuma Basin, and earn all the backcountry turns you can handle in this stunning high-altitude mountain basin.

THE TRAILHEAD

Begin at the Ashcroft ghost town trailhead located at the Pine Creek Cookhouse—Ashcroft Ski Touring center south of Aspen. From Aspen, drive west on Highway 82. At the roundabout, turn south onto the Castle Creek Road. Continue to the literal end of the road—the winter road closure of the Castle Creek Road. Park in the free public lot just shy of the King Cabin at the Ashcroft Touring Center (**UTM: 13 344293 4324573**).

THE APPROACH

The Ashcroft Touring Center operates under a special use permit with White River National Forest, and maintains 35 kilometers of groomed Nordic trails that are reserved for paying clientele. A public right of way heads south on the extension of the Castle Creek Road providing access to the national forest lands beyond the touring center. This will be your route.

From the trailhead at the Ashcroft Touring Center, head south on the Castle Creek Road extension. At mile 1.3, pass the Pine Creek Cookhouse on your right, and just beyond, Pine Creek itself. From here the route continues south through a broad, wet meadow until mile 2.0, when you reach a fork (**UTM: 13 343517 4321576**). Take the right fork, which is well-signed for Pearl Pass and Montezuma Basin (the left fork leads to Cooper Creek).

For the next 0.7 mile, the road hugs the west edge of the valley and passes beneath several avalanche chute runouts. Be cautious. At mile 2.7, the route turns southwest following Castle Creek beneath the rugged, steep slopes of Malamute Peak. At mile 3.3, the road—now a trail—crosses Castle Creek to the southern shoreline, and continues up the valley. Pass a small cabin on your right at mile 4.6. At mile 4.8, cross back to the north side of Castle Creek, and follow the widened trail (which feels more like a road again) up a series of short switchbacks to a trail junction at mile 4.9 (**UTM: 13 340825 4318949**). The left fork climbs to Pearl Pass. Take the right fork for Montezuma Basin.

From here you'll quickly leave the trees behind as you ascend into a giant, snow-filled cirque. Following the road will become increasingly difficult, but doing so also becomes increasingly less important. Follow the path of least resistance north-northwest into the stunningly scenic valley formed by Malamute Peak, Conundrum Peak, and Castle Peak. At mile 5.5 and an elevation of 11,800 feet, the route squeezes through a constriction before the valley/cirque opens up again.

You'll pass beneath the Montezuma Mine at mile 6.2, and then turn west and then southwest following the valley floor to a point beneath the Conundrum-Castle saddle. From here, head south aiming in line with the summit of Castle Peak, ascending the permanent snowfield on its north face that was once the Montezuma Basin ski area. Your end point, depending on snowfall and avalanche danger, will be mile 7.0 and an elevation of 13,800 feet (**UTM: 13 338874 4319705**).

The "Buzz"

The approach is long, with lots of vertical, but the skiing on the snow slopes of Montezuma Basin is great. Staying at one of the high mountain huts below Pearl Pass for the weekend would make the approach much more manageable.

—Kelli B.

Note: If you ski Montezuma Basin during winter, expect a much longer approach and the possibility that you won't reach the ski area proper due to avalanche hazard. If you ski Montezuma Basin during late spring and throughout summer, you may be able to drive a high-clearance 4WD vehicle all the way to Montezuma Mine at 13,000 feet and shorten your approach dramatically.

THE DESCENTS

There are three primary descents at Montezuma Basin. First, you can ski **the permanent snowfield** on the north face of Castle Peak. Or you can ski a **second permanent snowfield** closer to the saddle between Castle and Conundrum peaks. Lastly, early in the season, you can also ski the **many open slopes** in the basin beneath Malamute Peak. See the topo map for additional information about specific locations.

THE APRÈS SKI

Check out the dining and nightlife section of the Business Directory on the Aspen Chamber of Commerce website: www.aspenchamber.org.

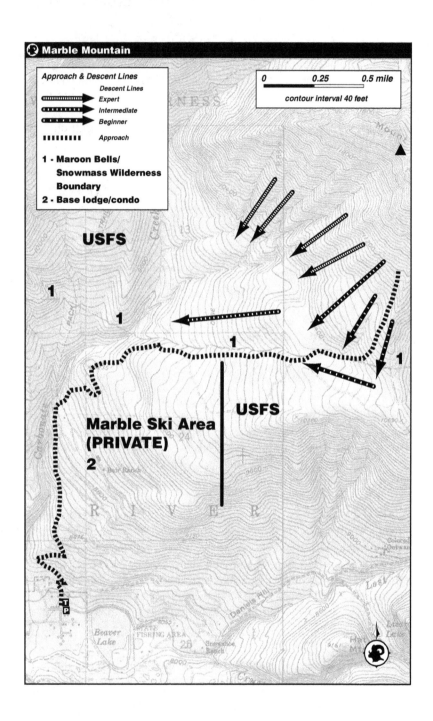

Marble Mountain

Approach & Descent Lines

Descent Lines
Expert
Intermediate
Beginner

Approach

1 - Maroon Bells/
Snowmass Wilderness
Boundary
2 - Base lodge/condo

0   0.25   0.5 mile

contour interval 40 feet

USFS

USFS

Marble Ski Area
(PRIVATE)

1

2

MARBLE MOUNTAIN

THE ESSENTIALS

Nearest Town Marble
Distance 3.6 miles
Vertical 3200'
Season December to May
Elevation Range 8000' to 11,200'
Difficulty Rating Strenuous
Skiing Rating 🎿 🎿 🎿

SNOTEL Station North Lost Trail (669)
Forest Zone White River National Forest, Sopris Ranger District
CAIC Zone Aspen Area Mountains
USGS Quad Marble
Weather COZ010

THE HISTORY

The town of Marble and the small population of the Crystal River valley started sometime in the 1870s, when prospectors came over Schofield Pass from Crested Butte looking for gold and silver. They didn't find a ton of either, but they did find the world's largest marble deposit. Marble went through a series of mining booms and busts, its population never exceeding 1500, and more often hovering around 150. While the town remained small, the marble that came from it went into big projects: the Capitol building in Denver, the Lincoln Memorial, the Tomb of the Unknown Soldier.

Slowly, Marble faded away. In 1972, however, it reincorporated to fight the development of a massive new ski area on the southwest-facing slopes of Mt. Daly just outside of town. (Residents also formed the Crystal Valley Environmental Protection Association to fight the project.) From the outset, the Marble ski area became Colorado's most scandalous and controversial proposed, partially built, and lost ski area. It has been called the "Marble bubble," and a "land speculation boondoggle."

Murmurings of a ski area surfaced in the media in 1970, when a developer proposed a new ski area that would exist partly on private land above Carbonate Creek, and partly on U.S. Forest Service land. It also included plans for a residential subdivision that would house as many as 25,000 people. (By comparison, the populations of Marble and the greater Crystal River valley today are just 125 and 200, respectively.)

The developers wanted to designate a 4600-acre area a Winter Sports Site, and build the ski area somewhere within it. The project took its first suspect turn in 1971, however, when the Forest Service refused to grant the developer a special use permit pending further environmental review.

A pair of Wyoming congressmen requested a meeting with Forest Service officials in Washington, D.C., to discuss the Marble ski area. As it turns out, the father of the Marble ski area's spokesman was a politically-connected sheriff in Wyoming. Not much came of the Washington meeting. In the meantime, a ski lift was built, tested, and opened for business in December 1971 on 200 acres of private land.

Marble ski area finally received its Winter Sports Site designation in 1972 for a 624-acre area, and during that summer and fall, developers built the main access road as well as a number of subdivision roads. Bulldozers "groomed" the cleared ski trails. Both the Forest Service and the ski area's consultants warned that spring snowmelt and runoff would cause excessive erosion. But the ski area took no action. The 1972/1973 winter dropped above-average levels of snow. Come spring, things turned disastrous. Trails and roads washed out. Debris piled up. Marble became an acute political, environmental, and financial nightmare.

From 1973 into 1974, rumors of illegal land sales at the Marble ski area floated to the surface. Then, in July 1974, the ski area surrendered its real estate license. By September it filed for bankruptcy, which the courts granted in October. The saga wasn't quite over yet, however. On October 31, 1975, the Forest Service issued a final denial of a special use permit, citing many significant concerns—water quality, wildlife habitat, air quality, aesthetics, high-density growth, geologic hazards (landslides), and sewage treatment. Then, in February 1976, some of the major players on the developer's side were charged with fraud and Securities and Exchange Commission violations. Finally, the expansion of the Maroon Bells-Snowmass Wilderness area boundary as a result of the Forest Service's Roadless Area Review and Evaluation pounded a final resounding nail into a coffin that had already been sealed shut. The Marble ski area was dead.

In the end, Marble operated for only two seasons: 1970/1971 with snowcats, and 1971/1972 with a double-chairlift. It isn't clear whether anyone actually skied during those seasons, or if the ski area simply had the capability to operate. Almost all of the attention was focused on the surrounding scandal.

Two other potential ski areas were investigated in the Marble/ Crystal River area—one in Bear Basin on Treasure and Treasury mountains, and another on Chair and Elk mountains. Both areas had marginal potential, but the designation of the Ragged Mountains wilderness area and the expansion of the Maroon Bells-Snowmass Wilderness squashed them for good.

The upper ridges and slopes of Mount Daly

From the late 1970s into the early 1980s, Colorado First Tracks operated out of the Beaver Lake Lodge, using a leased high-altitude Lama helicopter to carry skiers. It had the capacity for seven skiers plus one guide. For the 1980/1981 season First Tracks operated in a 32-square mile area. The venture cost clients $245 per person per day, and skiers logged 2400 to 4000 feet of vertical per run. Craig Hall, a former Crested Butte ski patroller and search and rescue team member, served as the guide. But Colorado First Tracks didn't last, and lift-served skiing—helicopter, snowcat, chairlift, or otherwise—left the Marble area for good. (Today, Telluride Helitrax operates Colorado's only heli-skiing service.)

Marble today stands as a community removed from time; old log cabins in a quaint valley far removed from anything but the soaring mountains that surround it.

THE TRAILHEAD

Begin at the Carbonate Creek Trailhead adjacent to Beaver Lake Lodge in the town of Marble (**UTM: 13 311048 4327130**). From Redstone, drive south on Highway 133 for 5 miles. Turn left (east) onto County Road 3 at the base of McClure Pass, following signs for Marble. Follow Route 3 east through the beautiful Crystal River valley for 6 miles to the town of Marble. In town, Route 3 locally becomes West Park Street. Continue to the end, where you're forced to turn left onto West 2nd Street. Make your first right onto West State Street (which becomes East State St.). Turn left onto East Second Street, and continue to the intersection with East Silver Street and Beaver Lake Lodge. Park adjacent to the lodge on a small, plowed dead-end road. This is the winter trailhead for the Carbonate Creek Trail (Forest Service Trail #1971).

THE APPROACH

From the Carbonate Creek Trailhead, the route crosses private property on a Forest Service right of way for the first 1.5 miles. Please respect private property and remain on the route. Start out heading north on the snow-covered road for the first few hundred yards. The trail here passes almost uncomfortably close to a large log home and several snowed-in vehicles. This is in fact the proper way to go, and the homeowner, Vince, has posted a large, hand-painted sign that reads NOT A PRIVATE ROAD to reassure you that you are indeed allowed to pass by.

Shortly beyond "Vince's place," you'll reach the summer trailhead of the Carbonate Creek Trail. From here, the route heads northwest, gently climbing across an open, shrub-filled slope with unfolding views of the town of Marble below you. Around mile 0.4, the trail makes a series of brief switchbacks above Carbonate Creek before turning to the northeast. At mile 0.5 the trail intersects the apex of the curve on a private road, before heading north into the forest again. From here you'll have good views of Gallo Hill to the northwest, a prominent local landmark where the gentle mountainside suddenly falls away in a series of striated cliff bands.

The **"Buzz"**

Marble feels like a mountain town removed from time. The snow slopes above the old Marble ski area are phenomenal. The ski area itself looks like the owners just walked away—the lift towers are still standing, with chairs hanging from the cable. It's wild.

—Kelli B.

At mile 1.0, you'll arrive beneath the base of the old Marble ski area. The ski area is divided into two portions: a smaller section of private property and a much larger area of proposed expansion on national forest land. Here, you're immediately below the private portion of the resort, and are tantalizingly close to the base lodge, old condos with their windows missing, and the lift line. Incredibly, the lift towers are still standing, with the cable strung and chairs still hanging on the cables. Despite the fact that Marble closed more than 30 years ago, it almost looks as if you could start up the lift engine and hop on a chair tomorrow. Resist the temptation to explore the infrastructure—it's on private property, and although the land is the property of an absentee owner from Texas who would likely never know, respect and good etiquette (and the law) dictate that you stick to the Forest Service right of way. And anyways, you're about to get plenty close.

At mile 1.25 (**UTM: 13 311048 4328699**), the route intersects the bottom of the northernmost ski runs of the old Marble ski area, next to an old horse stable. Leave the Carbonate Creek Trail here and turn east onto the Arkansas Mountain Trail (Forest Service Trail #1965). In summer this trail can be hard to follow. Don't expect to see it in winter. Trust your navigation and the route description. The trail climbs along the climber's left edge of the ski run on an old 4WD road. Continue to mile 1.5 and 9200 feet in elevation. Then turn left (north) and contour to Point 9235.

If you continue farther north from here, you'll drop steeply down to Carbonate Creek. Instead, turn right (east) and ascend through the forest on the south side of an unnamed creek drainage, following the boundary line of the Maroon Bells-Snowmass Wilderness Area. Continue ascending due east to mile 2.75, where the trail intersects an old Jeep road. Here, the trees become more sparse, with open slopes of fresh powder between. The snow-clad slopes of 12,610-foot Mt. Daly are visible to your north. Had Marble ski area remained open and eventually expanded onto national forest land according to the proposal, the ski area would have continued as high as 11,200 feet on Mt. Daly.

Turn northeast, aiming for the south and southwest slopes and subtle ridges of Mt. Daly. The skiing possibilities here are almost limitless, from the steep ridges above to the trees and meadows below. Don't forget to look behind you—the views south into the Raggeds Wilderness are stunning.

THE DESCENTS

Unfortunately, the ski runs of the old Marble ski area are located on private property. (At least the primary runs that were cut in the trees.) However, the proposed expansion terrain on Mt. Daly is deliciously on national forest land. There are tons of possibilities. Try these:

From the gentle **saddle between Mt. Daly and Point 10,690,** there are numerous stands of trees interspersed with open snow slopes. Enjoy.

From the saddle, continue north up the **south ridge of Mt. Daly.** When you've gotten as high as you want to go, rip the skins and start your descent.

The **southwest face of Mt. Daly** is streaked with ridges and gullies. The proposed expansion of Marble ski area would have gone up to 11,200 feet in elevation on this face. Ascend your chosen line and ski it. All the lines here funnel into Carbonate Creek drainage, which you could follow back to the trail at the base of the ski area.

THE APRÈS SKI

The town of Marble, small and remote, has a few small lodging facilities, but no nightlife or dining opportunities. Drive into nearby Redstone (www.redstonecolorado.com/dining/), or better, Carbondale (www.carbondale.com/sitepages/pid83.php).

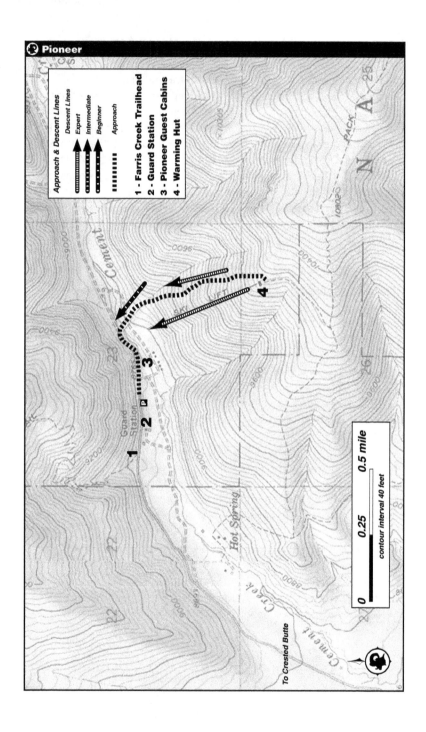

PIONEER

THE ESSENTIALS

Nearest Town Crested Butte
Distance 1.1 miles
Vertical 1400'
Season December to April
Elevation Range 8800' to 10,200'
Difficulty Rating Moderate
Skiing Rating ✪ ✪

SNOTEL Station Butte (380)
Forest Zone Gunnison National Forest, Gunnison Ranger District
CAIC Zone Gunnison Area Mountains
USGS Quad Cement Mountain
Weather COZ012

THE HISTORY

The documented history of skiing in and around Crested Butte and Gunnison dates all the way back to 1857, when guide Jim Baker used self-made skis in the mountains east of Gunnison. By 1886, both Crested Butte and Gunnison were hosting competitive downhill ski races. Throughout the early 20th century, most of the skiing took place on short, crowded slopes. By 1936, skiers wanted a larger ski area with good snow and longer, steeper slopes. In early 1937, skiers caught wind of Sun Valley's chairlift, and then thought of an old tram up at the Blistered Horn Mine on Cumberland Pass.

The Gunnison Valley Ski Club bought the tram for $50 and dismantled its wooden towers, which were constructed of 12-inch by 12-inch timbers. They then transported the entire setup to the Cement Creek Valley, a few miles south of Crested Butte, in an old 4WD World War I army truck. The towers were reassembled, and 6100 feet of cable were strung. Chairs were made from the harnesses for the ore buckets. A steel frame was welded to the harness, and a wooden seat was then attached to the frame. The contraption held 30 single chairs, and was completed in the fall of 1939. Skiers dubbed it "The Comet." It was Colorado's first overhead chairlift.

From the outset, though, it was plagued with problems. First, the U.S. Forest Service dubbed it too dangerous. The chairs, at a height of 10 to 12 feet, were deemed too far off the ground. The Forest Service wanted the chairs lowered, so that they hung less than three feet from the ground. Skiers complied, but once the snows started falling, a new problem became clear. The chairs were too close to the surface of the snow! A new danger emerged—catching one's ski tips on the ground. The Forest Service reversed its directive and demanded the chairs be raised back to their original height. Skiers once again complied, and on December 3, 1939, the state's first chairlift came into service.

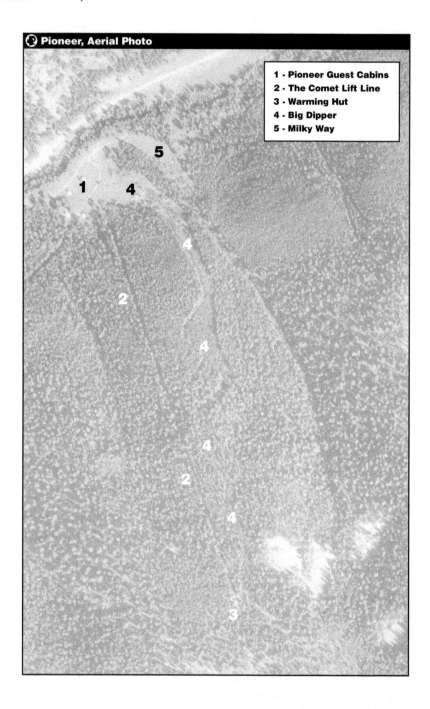

⊙ Pioneer, Aerial Photo

1 - **Pioneer Guest Cabins**
2 - **The Comet Lift Line**
3 - **Warming Hut**
4 - **Big Dipper**
5 - **Milky Way**

Ellen Fordham was the first to ride and test the chairlift. "Bail out if it gets too wild," people told her. That's exactly what she did. Apparently, bailing out was fairly common, particularly when the cable would slip and the chairs would start to go backwards. By March 1940, the folks at Pioneer got the bugs worked out of the system, and the ski area officially opened to the public with rave reviews. There was the Milky Way, a beginner slope, and the Little Dipper. One run, though, quickly earned a notorious reputation: the Big Dipper.

The Big Dipper dropped 1320 feet at a 53 percent grade. Many skiers thought it was insanely steep, and later on, an additional 1500 feet of length was added, extending the run onto a more gentle slope with a forgiving runout. The intention was to make it longer for use as a downhill course, and the extension did make it strikingly similar to the original race trail cut at Hidden Valley, in Rocky Mountain National Park (cut in the 1930s and used for the national downhill championship in 1934).

Steep or not, the Big Dipper and Pioneer remained wildly popular, and operated continuously until World War II. It closed during the war, but reopened in 1946 and stayed in operation until 1952, when it closed its doors for good. By then, the runs didn't meet the standards for collegiate downhill skiing (a requirement for the skiers at Western State College in Gunnison).

The same year that Pioneer closed, talks began for what would become Crested Butte Mountain Resort. The Town of Crested Butte, Western State College skiers, and the Gunnison Chamber of Commerce all wanted a new ski area, not only for the skiing, but also for the stimulus it could bring to the area's winter economy. They had watched the success of other mining towns, such as Breckenridge and Telluride, and wanted to emulate the pattern. The Forest Service conducted a reconnaissance of the Crested Butte area. Many sites were surveyed, but eventually, the present-day location of Crested Butte Mountain Resort was chosen, and the ski area opened to the public for the 1961/1962 season.

Since that time, Crested Butte Mountain Resort has earned a reputation for being "steep and deep." Pioneer, although gone, has

The "Buzz"

The snowpack here is great, and so is the skiing. But best of all is to ski at an area with amazing history—to think that Pioneer had the first chairlift in the state, dating back to 1939. And that you can skin up that same lift line, and ski down the Big Dipper run, trying to imagine all the skiers that have before you, on ancient equipment by today's standards. It's just wild.

—The author

At the base of the Pioneer ski area, in the Cement Creek drainage near Crested Butte

not been forgotten. A group of local ski volunteers still maintain the warming hut at the top of the Comet, which you can visit to this day in winter or summer. And at the base of the old ski area, the Pioneer Guest Cabins stand as a testament to the early pioneers who built the ski area. The cabins have retained their rustic charm, and are available for rent. And the Big Dipper, though partially overgrown, is still there for you to see and ski. In fresh powder on modern skis, it's not as fearsome as it once was, but it's still a joy to ski where Colorado's first chairlift came into service.

THE TRAILHEAD

Begin at a parking pullout on the side of Cement Creek Road 0.2 mile from the Pioneer Guest Cabins (**UTM: 13 338169 4298583**). From downtown Crested Butte, head southeast out of town on Highway 135 for 6.7 miles. Turn left (northeast) onto Cement Creek Road (County Road 740) and continue for 2.1 miles to a pullout parking lot on the right side of the road (0.3 mile beyond Farris Creek Trailhead, 0.2 mile beyond the unmanned Forest Service guard station, and 0.2 mile before the turnoff for the Pioneer Guest Cabins). Park here.

THE APPROACH

From the parking area, start out heading east-northeast on Cement Creek Road. After 0.2 mile, pass the turnoff on your right for the Pioneer Guest Cabins. Continue for another 0.2 miles to the southern edge of the flat area immediately before a 25 MPH road sign. This flat area was once parking for the ski area. Leave the road here, turn right, and descend to and cross Cement Creek. Continue south into an open meadow. To the right (west) are the cabins. Follow the meadow up and left. This is the Milky Way, the beginner ski slope of Pioneer. At the apex of the slope, cut right through the trees and emerge near the base of another ski run—the Big Dipper, Pioneer's largest and most infamous. From here it's all uphill. Follow the Big Dipper to its merger with the lift line—the Comet—at roughly 10,400 feet, where the warming hut still stands (**UTM: 13 338857 4297793**). The higher you ascend on the Big Dipper, the more difficult the run can be to follow. Trees are beginning to grow in. If you have difficulty following the run higher up on the mountain, you can always contour to climber's right until you intersect the unmistakable lift line. However, the lift line is fairly narrow, and in order to preserve its powder for your descent, I recommend trying to stay in the trees next to it.

THE DESCENTS

If you're just looking for a warm-up, ski the **Milky Way,** the beginner slope at Pioneer's base. Otherwise, if you're ready to tackle the infamous **Big Dipper,** drop in. Trees have grown back in the Big Dipper, but it never gets so tight that you can't link turns and enjoy the skiing, and it always opens back up into nice, treeless slopes. Lastly, you can also ski **the lift line of the Comet,** which follows the fall line at an almost perfectly constant 28 degrees.

THE APRÈS SKI

Head into nearby Crested Butte for great pub and grub. Visit www.visitcrestedbutte.com or www.cbchamber.com.

Try this local favorite:

Crested Butte Brewery, 226 Elk Avenue, (970) 349-7496

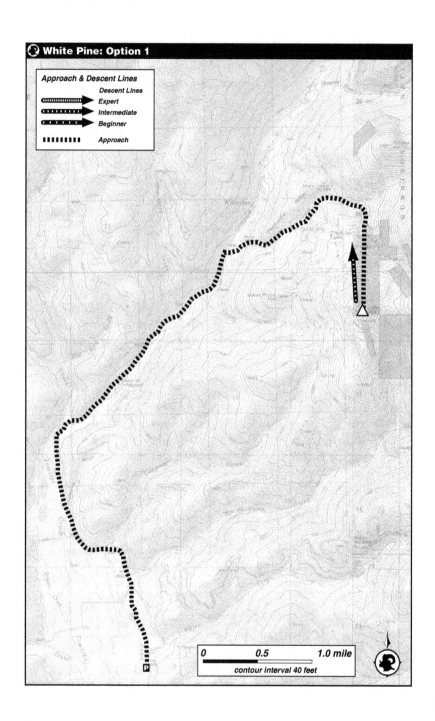

Approach & Descent Lines

Descent Lines

Expert

Intermediate

Beginner

Approach

0   0.5   1.0 mile

contour interval 40 feet

WHITE PINE

THE ESSENTIALS

Nearest Town Salida	**SNOTEL Station** Porphyry Creek (701)
Distance 12 to 15 miles	**Forest Zone** Gunnison National Forest, Gunnison Ranger District
Vertical 2600' to 4200'	
Season December to May	**CAIC Zone** Sawatch Range
Elevation Range 8900' to 12,200'	
Difficulty Rating Strenuous	**USGS Quad** Garfield
Skiing Rating ⟁ ⟁ ⟁	**Weather** COZ060

THE HISTORY

The present-day ghost town and lost ski area of White Pine, near Monarch Pass, got its start on May 25, 1879. The first prospectors came over Old Monarch Pass and dropped down into the Tomichi Creek Valley. There they opened the Parole and Iron Duke mines on Contact Hill, just west of Bald Mountain, mining for silver and lead. The rush for silver in particular was on, and soon, the North Star, Carbonate King, Eureka, and May Mazeppa mines were open on Lake Hill, just south of Contact.

By 1880, White Pine held its first elections. They added the votes from Tomichi, a mining camp just up the valley, and sent the results down to Gunnison, the county seat. As of early 1884, White Pine boasted a population of more than 1000, and had five stores, three saloons, two livery stables, three hotels, a barbershop, meat market, and a photo gallery. A "circuit preacher," Reverend Isaac Whicker (a Methodist minister), served the community from Leadville and Salida (an incredibly long distance away!).

The spring of 1884 was a bad year for avalanches, which miners called "runs." They destroyed mines, homes, and lives. When tensions arose within the community, quarrels were settled with fists, not guns. Typically, those fistfights took place at a spot called Battle Park, just outside of town. The fights took place before breakfast, so workers could be at the mines for the start of their shifts at 8 AM.

The miners also, it turns out, were fond of skiing. "Rookie" miners were known as *tenderfoots.* In one particularly amusing story, A. F. Nathan, a tenderfoot, was receiving some particularly harsh hazing from the "old timer" miners. Much of the hazing centered around Nathan's skiing ability, or lack thereof. Ashamed, he practiced determinedly at night, when no one could see him. Then, sometime later, Nathan and

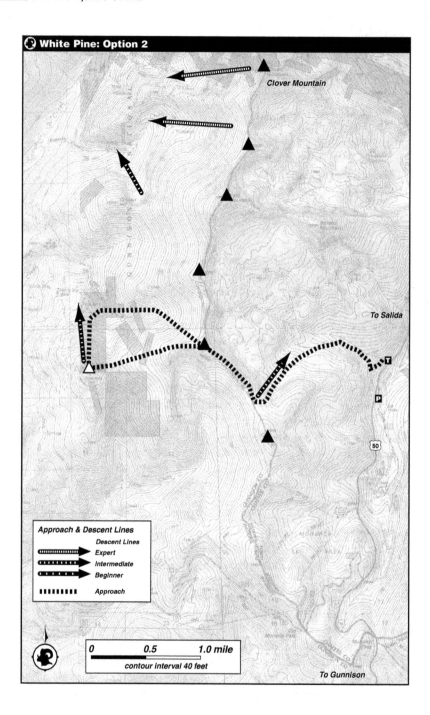

White Pine: Option 2

Clover Mountain

To Salida

To Gunnison

Approach & Descent Lines

Descent Lines
Expert
Intermediate
Beginner

Approach

0   0.5   1.0 mile
contour interval 40 feet

A skier gets first tracks on a descent at White Pine.

the other miners were high on Clover Mountain, north of White Pine, when the old-timers challenged him to a race. The winner of the wager stood to gain oysters and a box of cigars. The old-timers considered it a can't-lose bet. But to everyone's amazement, Nathan won the race.

In 1893, the price of silver crashed and panic ensued. By 1894, White Pine was deserted. But it rose up again in 1900. 1902 proved an even better year, when the Akron Mines Company drilled the Akron Tunnel 4000 into the side of Lake Hill and mined for lead, zinc, and copper, all much needed during the first and second world wars.

As early as the 1930s, the mining company erected a 200-yard-long rope tow on the north face of Lake Hill for the amusement of the miners. Then, in 1946, a more substantial ski area took shape on those same slopes. By 1952, however, the ski area was closed. Zinc prices crashed, the mine shut down, and the lifts were transferred over to Cranor Hill near Gunnison.

Skiing wasn't completely dead in the Monarch Pass area, though. The present-day Monarch Ski Area was in its infancy. In December 1939, the U.S. Forest Service issued the Salida Winter Sports Club (founded in 1936) a permit to start building the beginnings of Monarch. The first run ever cut on the mountain was Gunbarrel, a 300-foot-long run that dropped 150 feet of vertical at a 30 percent grade. It was an expert run then, and retains its black diamond rating today.

For the first season—1939/1940—a season pass cost $1, and 64 were sold. If you didn't have a season pass, use of the rope tow cost just 25 cents for a day, and accounted for $52.80 in receipts by the end of the season. In February 1940, Monarch logged 77 skiers in a single day. The City of Salida leased 10 percent of Monarch's profit until 1951, when the Monarch Ski Area was sold to the Berry family for $100.

By 1961, the price of a lift ticket had increased to $5, but the terrain and facilities had also improved. In 1967, Monarch saw 35,000 skier days. Twenty years after that, the number had increased to 160,000 skier days. Today, Monarch remains one of Colorado's best "mom and pop"-sized ski areas, known for its deep snowpack and fresh powder.

White Pine, meanwhile, has drifted into obscurity. It is remote and hard to get to, especially in winter. Its powder and lost ski area are reserved for the hearty souls that dare to venture where pioneering miners once skied more than a century before.

THE TRAILHEAD

When it comes down to it, there's no easy way to get to White Pine. It's remote and difficult to access. You have to want to ski here. Weigh the options, and embrace the challenge.

Surveying the Continental Divide near Monarch Pass on the approach to White Pine

Option 1

Lots of vertical, shorter mileage

Begin at a parking pullout at the winter road closure for Monarch Park (Forest Road 237, County Road 231). From the Monarch Ski Area on Highway 50, drive northeast for 1 mile to the pullout.

Option 2

Less vertical, more mileage

Begin at the winter road closure of Valley Road (County Road 888) at its intersection with the Old Monarch Pass Road. From the town of Sargents, drive northeast on Highway 50 and turn left onto Valley Road. Information signs prominently list White Pine as 10 miles away. Continue north on Valley Road for 4.5 miles to the winter road closure.

The "Buzz"

My slogan for this area is, "White Pine—the ski area that should remain lost." It's hard to get to—there's no easy way in and out. But the snowpack in the Monarch Pass area is deep and light, and the region has some of the best backcountry skiing in the state. Breaking trail can be tough, but even if you don't make it all the way to White Pine, you'll still earn some great turns.

—Tom H.

THE APPROACH

Option 1

From the parking pullout at the winter road closure for Monarch Park, walk northeast along Highway 50 for 0.2 mile to a tight, treed gully on the uphill side. This gully is just west of a sign in the westbound lanes for Monarch Park. The gully is the creek drainage that flows down from Waterdog Lakes. Ascend this drainage for 0.1 mile, until you intersect a faint trail that contours across your path. Turn left onto this trail, and follow it southwest for 0.15 mile. Here, the trail turns sharply to the north. Continue to follow the trail, which ascends through a forest blanketed in one of the deepest snowpacks in the state. There's a good chance you'll be breaking trail—if someone has broken trail for you, buy them dinner.

Around mile 0.4, you'll intersect power lines. The trail merges with the power line right of way until mile 0.5. When the power lines and trail diverge, do not follow the trail. It leads to Waterdog Lakes, not your destination. Instead, follow the power line's clear slot through the trees west until mile 1.2 and about 11,200 feet in elevation. Here the power lines make an improbable ascent over a steep portion of the Continental Divide. Instead, turn south and aim for the saddle between

Tons of fresh snow blankets the trees on the approach.

points 11,942 and 12,134, arriving at mile 1.7. Here you will be on the Continental Divide, the Continental Divide Trail, and within the operating area of Monarch Powdercat Tours.

Turn northwest and follow the ridgeline to the summit of Point 12,134. From here, you can peer down into the Tomichi Creek valley and the ghost town of White Pine. You have two options to reach the old ski area: Descend a bowl to the northwest until you intersect the continuation of the power line, and follow it to the base of Lake Hill and the North Star Mine. Or descend directly west down a ridgeline to the saddle with Lake Hill. The distance is roughly the same, totaling 3.5 miles from the trailhead.

Option 2

From the winter road closure of Valley Road and Old Monarch Pass Road, continue on Valley Road (County Road 888) heading north. At mile 1.1 the road swings hard to the left (west), before resuming its northward trend around mile 1.5. At mile 2.5 the road turns northeast, following Tomichi Creek, and at mile 3.5 reaches the Snowblind Campground. Two miles beyond Snowblind, you'll reach the ghost town of White Pine (5.5 miles from the trailhead).

From here, turn east into the Galena Creek drainage, following a 4WD road that squeezes between Porcupine Ridge and West Point Hill. Follow that road and creek for 2 miles to the base of Lake Hill, and ascend directly up the north face of Lake Hill to its summit, arriving at mile 7.0 (**UTM: 13 380249 4265595**).

Using this approach with a snowmobile would make reaching White Pine in a day a much more manageable proposition. Area snowmobile rental companies will often trailer the sleds to the trailhead of your choice with a half day or longer rental. Keep this in mind. Unless you have legs of steel, this may be the preferred way to go.

THE DESCENTS

The primary descent at White Pine is the **north slope of Lake Hill,** which offers about 800 feet of vertical. However, if you use the approach from Monarch, you'll also earn several more descents on the way in and out (the northwest face of Point 12,134 on the approach; the descent northeast off the saddle between points 12,134 and 11,942 on the way out).

EXTRA CREDIT

If you're keen on recreating your own version of the ski race involving A. F. Nathan, head farther up the Tomichi Creek valley and follow 4WD roads up onto Clover Mountain.

THE APRÈS SKI

Salida, east of Monarch Pass, is your best bet. For more information, visit www.centralcolorado.com/salida/dining/dining.htm, http://coloradoheadwaters.com/dining/index.cfm, and www.salidachamber.org/bizdirectory/viewtopic.php?TopicID=10.

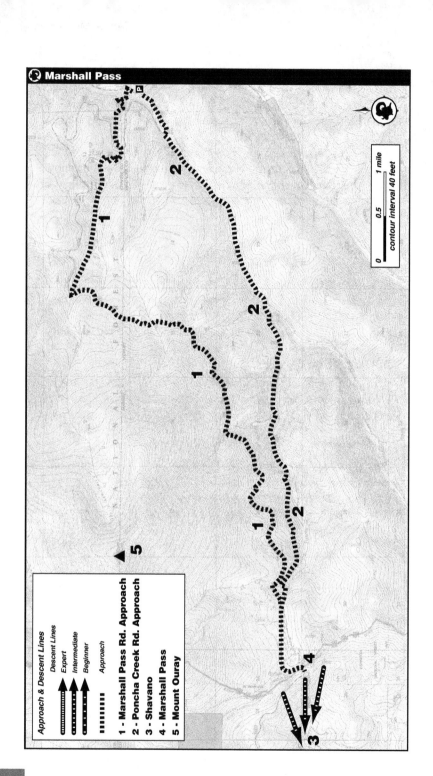

contour interval 40 feet

0   0.5   1 mile

Approach & Descent Lines

Descent Lines

Expert
Intermediate
Beginner
Approach

1 - Marshall Pass Rd. Approach
2 - Poncha Creek Rd. Approach
3 - Shavano
4 - Marshall Pass
5 - Mount Ouray

MARSHALL PASS

THE ESSENTIALS

Nearest Towns	Salida, Poncha Springs	**SNOTEL Station**	Porphyry Creek (701)
Distance	8 to 10 miles	**Forest Zone**	San Isabel National Forest, Salida Ranger District
Vertical	2200'		
Season	December to April		
Elevation Range	8600' to 10,800'	**CAIC Zone**	Sawatch Range
Difficulty Rating	Strenuous	**USGS Quad**	Mount Ouray
Skiing Rating 🎿 🎿		**Weather**	COZ060

THE HISTORY

arshall Pass was an important transportation route between Salida on the east and Gunnison on the west. (For a more detailed history of skiing at Salida, see the chapter on White Pine. For a more detailed history of skiing at Gunnison, see the chapter on skiing at Pioneer.) The pass was also home to a unique ski area. Today, the ski train from Denver to Winter Park is both popular and well-known as a way to get from the Front Range to the ski area. But in earlier years at Marshall Pass, a train served not only as the way to get *to* the ski area, it also served as the lift *at* the ski area.

In 1873, Lieutenant William L. Marshall became the first white man to "discover" and traverse Marshall Pass, which was later named after him. As the story goes, Marshall was conducting a survey in the San Juan Mountains. Wanting to return to Denver before heavy winter snows clamped down on the mountains, he and his party struck out eastward. But a nasty toothache caused Marshall to separate from the group to seek a more direct route through the mountains that would get him to Denver and a dentist sooner. His subsequent exploration took him over Marshall Pass.

Not long after the discovery of the pass, a wagon road was constructed and operated as a toll road under the auspices of the Marshall Pass Toll Road Company. In 1880, the road was pressed into different service. The Denver & Rio Grande Railroad was extending its narrow gauge transcontinental line that connected Denver and Salt Lake City. It chose Marshall Pass for its route, and used the wagon road for the track line. The railroad began laying track in 1880, and by 1881, the line over the pass was complete. The "baby railroad," as it was called, was 3 feet wide and climbed at a steep 4 percent grade.

By the early 1920s, a new town had grown up alongside the railroad tracks at the base of the east side of the pass. Shirley was a mining town that served the Kerber Creek Mining District and the mines at Bonanza, where there was a 7.5-mile aerial tramway. The Denver & Rio Grande Railroad then shipped the ore to smelters in Salida, Leadville, and even Salt Lake City via Marshall Pass. But in 1930, the area's largest mine—the Rawley Mine and Mill—closed, and Shirley slowly faded out of existence.

In the 1930s, though, the trains served a new purpose: transporting skiers. By the winter of 1937/1938, two ski trains were running. One came up the west side of the pass from Gunnison, the other up the east side of the pass from Salida. The Salida train left the station at 7 AM, and returned at 10:05 PM.

Up on Marshall Pass, skiers tackled a slope with 700 feet of vertical on the west side. The runs started at the height of the pass, and dropped down to a hairpin turn in the railroad far below. That hairpin turn was the location of a section house and water tower, and was known as Shavano. The railroad renovated the section house to serve as a warming hut for skiers. If there were too many skiers to fit in the hut, heated coach cars from the trains were used for the overflow crowd. A dedicated train shuttled skiers from the bottom of the run back to the top of the pass. At one point in time, Thor Groswold (a Denverite prominent in so many aspects of Colorado's skiing history), T. J. Flynn (of Aspen's Highland Bavarian Resort proposal), and Count Phillipe de Pret taught skiing at Marshall Pass, and the Gunnison Ski Club organized regular outings to Marshall.

As narrow-gauge railroad lost out in popularity to standard gauge, the D&RG eventually stopped its trains that went over Marshall Pass. The tracks were pulled out, and with them, the skiing of Marshall. The rail line reverted to a gravel road. Today, an old railroad bridge is still visible near the Shirley townsite, and at the height of the pass, at least one old wooden snowshed still stands. But Marshall Pass is no longer maintained in winter, except for grooming on the Marshall Pass Road that allows relatively easy snowmobile access. For skiers on foot, the mileage is long, and the destination a lot more remote than it once was. But as you stand atop Marshall Pass, peering 700 feet down to the hairpin turn below, try to imagine that old locomotive chugging back up the hill and unloading cars full of skiers, ready to drop in for more turns.

THE TRAILHEAD

Begin at the Shirley Site Trailhead (**UTM: 13 401381 4253048**) near Poncha Pass. From Poncha Springs, drive south on Highway 285. Roughly 2.5

The Poncha Creek Road route

miles below the summit of the pass, turn right (west) onto Marshall Pass Road (Forest Road 200). Continue for 2.4 miles to the Shirley Site Trailhead, with a large parking area on the left side of the dirt road. Park here.

THE APPROACH

The old Marshall Pass ski area has the longest approach of any in this book. Consider yourself warned. There are two ways to do the approach: sane, and insane. The sane way is to come armed with a snowmobile (rental locations in Salida, Poncha Springs, and Monarch will trailer a sled to the trailhead of your choice with a half-day or longer rental). The insane way is to skin the entire route on skis.

You have two options for the approach:

Option 1

This option is several miles longer than option 2, but is groomed. The benefit of not having to break trail may outweigh the added miles, especially if heavy snow has recently fallen. From the trailhead, backtrack along the road for several hundred yards and turn west onto Marshall Pass Road, now Forest Road 200. (Although you drove in on Marshall Pass Road, the road changes names as you passed this turnoff, and the trailhead parking lot is actually located on Forest Road 47YY.)

After 0.7 mile, you'll reach a four-way junction. Turning left leads to Poncha Creek. Turning right is the continuation of the Marshall Pass Road. Continue straight ahead, following signs for O'Haver Lake. As you climb, the road will switchback several times before coming to another junction. This junction is located at the southeast edge of O'Haver Lake. The right fork leads to campsites. Follow the left fork along the southern edge of the lake, until the road terminates at the southwestern corner.

From the southwestern corner of O'Haver Lake, continue due west, now following the Grays Creek Trail. At mile 2.6, the Grays Creek Trail intersects the Marshall Pass Road, having shaved off several miles of unnecessary meandering. Turn left (south) and follow the well-defined Marshall Pass Road for 5.5 more miles as you climb toward Marshall Pass and traverse the southern slopes of Mt. Ouray. At mile 8.1, you'll break out into a broad, high-alpine meadow just shy of Marshall Pass. Views of Mt. Ouray to the north will open up.

At the west end of the meadow, you'll find the Marshall Pass Trailhead, Continental Divide Trail, map kiosk, toilet facilities, and an old snow shelter from earlier days. You're almost to the ski runs now. The road makes a hard left turn to the south briefly, before turning west again and squeezing through a tight rock cut. Just on the western side of that rock cut is Marshall Pass **(UTM: 13 391064 4250035)** and the top of the ski runs.

> ## The "Buzz"
>
> Marshall Pass is so far from roads and trailheads, there's a good chance you'll have a solitary day in the mountains. But it's also far enough that, if you don't use a snowmobile or do the trip as an overnight, you might be too tired to enjoy the backcountry skiing once you've finished the approach.
>
> —The author

Option 2

This option is several miles shorter than option 1, and although it offers solitude and quiet away from snowmobiles, isn't groomed. From the trailhead, do not backtrack to the Marshall Pass Road. Instead, head due west, following signs for Marshall Pass and Poncha Creek. After 0.6 mile, cross from the south side to the north side of Poncha Creek on an old railroad bridge. Here the route immediately terminates in a T intersection. Turning right (east) leads up to the four-way junction below O'Haver Lake. Instead, turn left onto Forest Road 203 (Poncha Creek Road).

Up until mile 3.0, the route gains relatively little elevation as you head west up the Poncha Creek valley. At mile 3.0, you'll pass the Starvation Creek Trailhead. From here, the route becomes considerably steeper, and the road becomes more and more drifted under in deep pillows of snow. Around mile 6.0, the route emerges into a small meadow with a view north of the upper slopes of Mt. Ouray.

From that meadow and creek drainage, the route turns left (south) and rounds a subtle, forested ridge before coming upon a second, very similar meadow and creek drainage. This time, instead of turning left again with the Poncha Creek Road, head northwest up the creek drainage. Maintaining this track will deposit you in the southeastern corner of the expansive meadow immediately below the summit of the pass. Trend north-northwest until you intersect the Marshall Pass Road. When you do, turn left (west) and continue as for approach option 1 to the summit of Marshall Pass.

Ascending option 2 and descending option 1 also makes a reasonable combination.

THE DESCENTS

There are three main descents at Marshall Pass. All three descents end at the hairpin turn in the road 700 feet below.

- From the pass, continue north a short way on the road, then drop west off the road and ski **a combination of glades and open slopes.**

- From the pass, find a gas pipeline right of way directly to the west. The start of the right of way is marked with a buck-and-rail wooden fence and a sign. **Ski the right of way.**

- From the pass, continue south until you're above a small basin mostly free of trees. **Ski the basin** and follow the drainage and fall line to meet up with the other two runs near the base.

THE APRÈS SKI

Salida, east of Monarch Pass, is your best bet. For more information, visit www.centralcolorado.com/salida/dining/dining.htm, http://coloradoheadwaters.com/dining/index.cfm, and www.salidachamber.org/bizdirectory/viewtopic.php?TopicID=10.

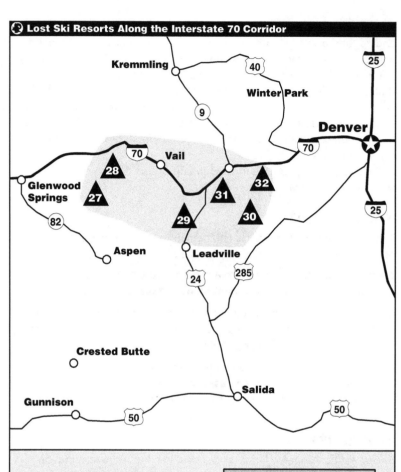

Lost Ski Resorts Along the Interstate 70 Corridor

27. Adam's Rib
28. Meadow Mountain
29. Climax
30. Hoosier Pass
31. Peak One
32. Porcupine Gulch

Legend

Large Cities
Medium Cities
Small Cities

◣ Lost Ski Area
🛡25 Interstate Highway
🛡285 U.S./State Highway
⑧ State Highway
✪ State Capital
○ City

Lost Ski Resorts Along the
Interstate 70 Corridor

The Interstate 70 Corridor describes the region spanning Eagle and Summit counties, including the Vail Valley. Practically speaking, it begins at Loveland Pass and the Eisenhower Tunnel, and stretches west to the beginning of Glenwood Canyon. This section of the guide includes six lost ski areas. With Denver and the Front Range population an easy highway drive away, this region is home to some of Colorado's most popular and visited ski resorts: Arapahoe Basin, Keystone, Breckenridge, Copper Mountain, Vail, Beaver Creek, Arrowhead, and Ski Cooper. All the more reason to leave the lifts behind and head into the backcountry! The lost areas are listed from west to east.

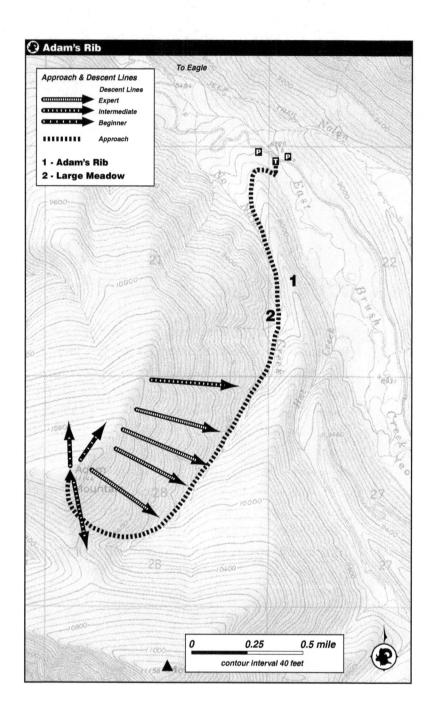

ADAM'S RIB

THE ESSENTIALS

Nearest Town	Eagle	**SNOTEL Station**	Kiln (556) or McCoy Park (1040)
Distance	2.5 miles		
Vertical	2200'	**Forest Zone**	White River National Forest, Eagle Ranger District
Season	December to April		
Elevation Range	8900' to 11,100'		
Difficulty Rating	Moderate	**CAIC Zone**	Aspen Area Mountains
Skiing Rating	😀 😀 😀	**USGS Quad**	Fulford
		Weather	COZ010

THE HISTORY

Although skiing in Eagle County is today synonymous with Beaver Creek and Vail just to the east of the town of Eagle, it wasn't always so. As recently as the early 1940s, there was very little skiing to speak of in the area at all. That was until the 1945/1946 season, when Whittaker Ridge opened. It was located off of Bruce Creek south of Eagle, and wasn't much to look at, or ski. It had one rope tow, and one single run, called "South Side," that was several hundred feet long and dropped about 300 feet of vertical. It had a small shack that sold hamburgers, and that was it. Even so, it successfully operated for a full decade through the 1955/1956 season, when it finally shut down, bowing to the growing popularity of Ski Cooper. (Vail and Beaver Creek would subsequently open, and would have been definitive nails in the coffin of Whittaker Ridge, even if Ski Cooper hadn't already played that role.)

But then, in the late 1960s, a site not far from Whittaker Ridge caught the eye of the U.S. Forest Service. The agency was conducting one of its inventories of potential ski areas that could be developed on national forest land, and Adam's Rib made the list (rated as "good"). Adam's Rib is a long, curving ridge—possibly a moraine—that extends off the east side of Mt. Eve and Adam Mountain. The ridge separates No Name and Hat creeks, and would have been the centerpiece of a large ski resort on the his-and-hers mountains just above.

The first potential developers of the area came to the table in March 1970. From 1970 through 1973, there were many talks, and many interested players. Ultimately, nothing came of it. Or so it seemed.

Fred Kummer, a St. Louis–based businessman who made his money in hospitals and luxury hotels, vacationed at Vail in the late 1960s. During that trip he surveyed the Forest Service's list of potential ski area sites. A new addition to the list—Adam's Rib—got his attention.

The author enjoying the light powder on a descent of one of Adam Mountain's avalanche chutes

In 1972, he applied for a special use permit to start the project. It was slow to get off the ground, however, due in part to a series of approvals the project required first: Forest Service, Eagle County, and Army Corps of Engineers. Locals in Eagle, for their part, didn't want to the ski area built.

There were many concerns: environmental and wetland impacts, traffic congestion, the character of the rural valley, the presence of other large ski areas nearby. Kummer didn't help his own case—each time he came to meetings seeking approvals, he had changed the development plans. In addition to the massive ski resort on the north slopes of Adam Mountain, his plan eventually called for thousands of acres of hotels, condos, golf courses, and more. When one of his plans was squashed due to unacceptable wetland impacts in the valley, Kummer offered an even more unpalatable approach: literally slice off the top of Adam's Rib to create a flat bench on which he could build his hotels and condos.

Still, in 1983 the Forest Service granted a special use permit for a ski area that would have had similar capacity to Beaver Creek. Eagle County granted tentative approval for a golf course, housing units, and a resort complex. By the mid-1990s, however, Kummer still hadn't succeeded in securing all the required approvals. Meanwhile, the Forest Service and town officials decided that the shifting sands of Kummer's proposal, coupled with its heavy environmental and community impacts, amounted to nothing more than an elaborate scheme to sell real estate. It wasn't about the skiing.

Permits were revoked, and Kummer eventually threw in the towel, having invested $30 million in a project that was never built. He was down, but not totally out. Adam's Rib Ranch recently opened just outside the town of Eagle. The *Denver Business Journal* called it a "leaner Adam's Rib." The more than 1,000-acre development consists of Adam's Mountain Country Club, surrounded by home sites in an upscale gated community. Thankfully, Adam's Mountain, Mt. Eve, and the real Adam's Rib remain untouched, and the character of the valley unchanged. Instead, backcountry skiers can enjoy an unparalleled day in a spectacular wilderness, with fresh powder, stunning views of the Gore and Elk ranges, and an experience altogether removed from the warped vision of a St. Louis businessman.

THE TRAILHEAD

Begin at a small parking area (room for two or three vehicles) and Sylvan Lake State Park kiosk and self-service pay station 0.1 mile shy of the yurts on East Brush Creek Road south of Eagle (**UTM: 13 354498 4376368**). This trailhead requires a $6 day pass per vehicle. From Interstate 70 in the town of Eagle, drive south on Eby Creek Road. At the roundabout, turn right (west) onto Highway 6 (Grand Avenue). At the next roundabout, turn left (south) onto Sylvan Lake Road. Continue on Sylvan Lake until it intersects with Brush Creek Road. Turn right onto Brush Creek. Travel south for approximately 10 miles, crossing into White River National Forest and passing the Sylvan Lake State Park visitor center on the left. Very shortly after the visitor center, the road forks. Bear left at the fork onto East Brush Creek Road. The pavement ends here. Expect the road to be snow-covered. Continue for approximately 4.25 miles (passing the Elk Crossing and Aspen Grove parking areas en route, as well as a pair of switchbacks on the road). If you reach the Old Fulford trailhead or the yurts, you've gone too far. Park on the right side of the road at a state park kiosk with room for only two or three vehicles.

THE APPROACH

From the trailhead, continue southeast on East Brush Creek Road for just 100 yards. Look for a truck weight limit sign and gated old road on the right. This is immediately before the road crosses Brush Creek, and approximately 25 yards before the Old Fulford Trailhead. The gated old road is the start of the route. Turn right (south) and follow the road grade along the west edge of the East Brush Creek/Yeoman Park meadow. Continue south for only 0.1 mile.

Before you've truly committed yourself to the Yeoman Park meadow, turn right (west) and contour around and over the gentle ridge in front of you. This is the terminus of Adam's Rib. Note: from this point onward and upward, if you're careful setting your skin track, when you're done skiing for the day you can cruise out to the car almost exclusively downhill.

As you crest Adam's Rib, turn south, now entering the No Name Creek drainage. Adam Mountain is on your right (east and north), while Adam's Rib—an extension of Mt. Eve—is to your left (west and south). As you continue up the valley following No Name Creek, try to imagine this peaceful spot swarming with skiers, the aspen-covered top of Adam's Rib literally chopped off to make room for condos.

An old forest road may be evident here. Follow it, or No Name Creek, south until you arrive in a large, open meadow at mile 0.75. Skin across the meadow to its far southern end, and continue your ascent of the No Name Creek valley, which now makes a slow, gradual turn from south to west as it steadily climbs up to the saddle between Adam and Eve. During your climb, stay on the right (north) side of the creek. The route here passes beneath numerous glades as well as avalanche runouts that—if conditions are stable—may offer the best skiing of the day.

Around 10,200 feet in elevation and mile 2.0, No Name Creek makes a sharp and sudden turn to the northwest. Instead of continuing west to the true saddle between Adam and Eve, turn northwest with the creek, and begin a steadily steep northwesterly ascent of Adam Mountain's southern slopes. If you navigate your way perfectly up through the trees, you'll pop out of the forest at the base of Adam's south ridge at 10,900 feet in elevation and mile 2.4.

From here, it's a short, steep, treeless pitch to the summit. However, if the snow isn't stable, you're safer turning around and skiing the glades below you, or traversing north into open shots through the trees, rather than tempting this final pitch to slide. On the other hand, if the snow is stable (a good bet, since the slope is south-facing), head to the 11,144-foot summit of Adam's Mountain at mile 2.5 (**UTM: 13 353019 4374154**).

The "Buzz"

You'll be setting your own skin track, but once it's in, you're good to go. From the summit of Adam Mountain, there are incredible views of the Elk and Gore mountains. The northern slope of the mountain is mellow, but gullies and avalanche chutes on the southeast face offer amazing descents. As long as the snowpack is stable, drop in and carve your way to the bottom. You won't be disappointed.

—Kelli B.

THE DESCENTS

Adam's Rib has a number of possible descents. I'll describe them starting at the summit and continuing down the mountain's northeast ridge.

- From the summit, ski **the south face** back to treeline and the aspen, trending toward the Adam-Eve saddle.

- From the summit, ski the gentle **north slopes** for several hundred vertical feet until the trees close in.

- From the summit, ski **the northeast ridge** (primarily as a way to access the following runs).

All smiles with lots of vertical left to go

Five gullies and avalanche chutes are located on the face of Adam Mountain that curves from south-facing to southeast to east-facing. As long as snow conditions are stable, any of these runs provide the best skiing on the mountain—great slope angle, great snow, choice of aspect, lots of vertical, and open runs. See the topo map for specific locations of each. For the runs that don't continue all the way to the bottom and meet up with No Name Creek and your skin track, the trees below stay nice and open, providing great glade skiing.

THE APRÈS SKI

Nearby Eagle has a good selection of restaurants. Visit www.eagle valley.org for a list of options.

Definitely check out:

Eagle Diner, 112 West Chambers Avenue, (970) 328-1919, a classic diner with the typically diverse menu of basic American fare

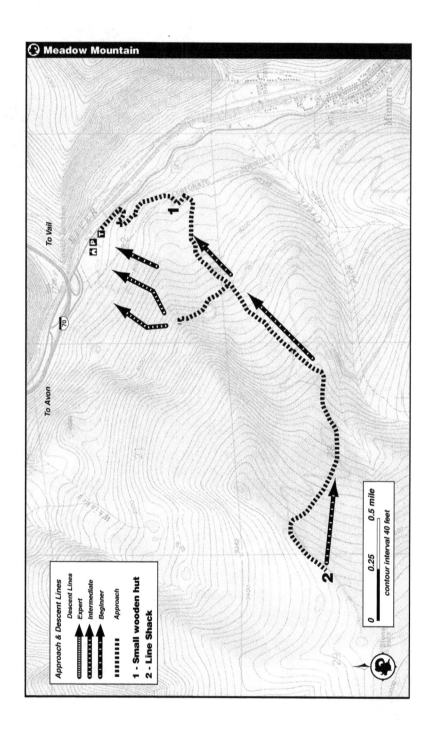

Approach & Descent Lines

Descent Lines
Expert
Intermediate
Beginner
Approach

1 - Small wooden hut
2 - Line Shack

To Vail

To Avon

0   0.25   0.5 mile
contour interval 40 feet

MEADOW MOUNTAIN

THE ESSENTIALS

Nearest Towns Minturn, Vail
Distance 3 miles
Vertical 2000'
Season December to April
Elevation Range 7750' to 9750'
Difficulty Rating Moderate
Skiing Rating ☻ ☻

SNOTEL Station Beaver Creek Village (1041)
Forest Zone White River National Forest, Holy Cross Ranger District
CAIC Zone Vail & Summit County Area
USGS Quad Minturn
Weather COZ010

THE HISTORY

The history of the old Meadow Mountain ski area property dates back to the 1920s, when the land was used by Evercrisp Lettuce for farming. When the company realized they could grow lettuce year-round in California, they packed up and moved on, leaving the land idle. In 1960, the U.S. Forest Service took the first survey pictures of the area, probably associated with its review of Vail Associates' application to build the Vail ski area nearby. Vail officially opened in 1962, and two years later, in 1964, Jack Oleson (a cattle rancher from Avon) bought an immense swath of land encompassing Meadow Mountain and Grouse Creek directly to its south.

Two years later, in September 1966, Oleson applied for a study permit to examine 12,600 acres of land on and around his property, with the idea of possibly building a ski area there. The Forest Service happily granted the permit, motivated largely by the idea that the permit would protect the area from Gulf & Western Industries, which had recently acquired the New Jersey Zinc Company in Minturn.

The Meadow Mountain ski area opened for the 1966/1967 season. The *Denver Post* called it an "encouraging, if unspectacular" start. The main ski area—110 acres—was served by a Poma lift and a 3200-foot-long double-chairlift, and had 900 feet of vertical. The following season—1967/1968—was described as "near disastrous" for reasons I've been unable to pin down. Then, in 1968/1969, Meadow Mountain saw a 10 percent decline in skier attendance compared to its opening season numbers.

A new manager, Frank Doll, had a clever marketing idea—he repositioned Meadow Mountain as a "learn to ski" mountain, rather than trying to compete directly with places like Vail. A small "boomlet" in skier attendance ensued. As of January 1969, any teacher in Colorado could buy a season pass to Meadow Mountain for $10. Any school child in Eagle or Lake counties could do the same for $15.

By then, Vail had set its sights on Meadow Mountain. Later in 1969, Vail acquired the purchase options for 3900 acres plus the assets of the ski area for $850,000. Residents in the town of Minturn opposed the sale, but it went through one year later for the price of $3 million. Later that year, Vail shut down the Meadow Mountain ski area after the end of the 1969/1970 season.

Some people say it was because Vail didn't like the competition. Others argue, convincingly, that Vail was thinking about participating in the bid for the 1976 winter Olympics, and Meadow Mountain was a potential venue. Eventually, Vail also purchased the "Nottingham property" west of Meadow Mountain in 1971, and built Beaver Creek instead (it was approved in 1975). Also in 1971, the Forest Service successfully negotiated to buy the Meadow Mountain / Oleson property.

Today, Meadow Mountain remains a part of national forest land. A small rope tow and tubing hill sit at the base, and the open ski runs are visible directly above. Meadow Mountain is a popular destination for backcountry skiers, snowshoers, and snowmobilers alike, who are all helping to write the next chapter in the mountain's history.

> ## The "Buzz"
>
> *The lower runs are easy to access and great for doing laps. If you go all the way to the Line Shack, the approach is longer, but still mellow. Once you reach the Line Shack, take off your skis, step inside, warm up, have a snack, chat with other skiers and snowmobilers that may be there. A wood-burning stove may already be lit, or you can fire it up. Once you're ready, reverse your route for a great and fast descent back to the trailhead.*
> —The author

THE TRAILHEAD

Begin at the Meadow Mountain Trailhead (**UTM: 13 375958 4385093**) in Minturn south of Interstate 70. From I-70, take exit 171 and go south on Highway 24. Continue for one quarter mile, and turn right into the parking lot at the base of the old Meadow Mountain ski area. The parking lot is located adjacent to a winter tubing area and the Holy Cross Ranger Station. Many of the runs of the old ski area are visible from the parking lot directly uphill on the northeast slope of Meadow Mountain.

THE APPROACH

From the Meadow Mountain Trailhead, follow Forest Road 748 southeast as it parallels Highway 24 directly below the tubing hill. At mile

0.25, the road makes a pair of switchbacks before resuming its south-easterly trend. Around mile 0.6, you'll arrive below a short slope with an old, wooden shack at the top. Follow the road as it skirts the slope below the shack, then turns and climbs up to a point even with the old building.

Beyond the old building, the route heads west up a broad, open meadow. The northeast ridge of Meadow Mountain is visible to your right. In summer, the road switchbacks up this meadow, but in winter, a snowmobile-ski-snowshoe track heads straight up it to mile 1.3. Here **(UTM: 13 375636 4383954)** you have a choice. To ski the runs on the northeast face of Meadow Mountain, turn north and intersect the northeast ridge/shoulder at 8600 feet in elevation. From there, choose your run and enjoy. For a longer outing that ends on a spectacular ridge with an old log cabin, continue west-southwest.

At mile 1.8, the winter route intersects a road junction. Turning left (south) leads into the Grouse Creek drainage. Turning right (west-north-west) leads to the summer route road switchback. Instead, stay straight (southwest) and to the left of the trees, continuing up to a point on a mellow ridge above Grouse Creek at mile 2.0. Here you've regained the road but skipped the added mileage of the switchback below.

A skier is ready to begin the descent from the open ridge top near Line Shack.

A small wooden hut below Meadow Mountain's northeast face

The Line Shack

Follow the road now west to mile 2.25, first crossing an open snow slope, and then entering the forest. From here, you can continue on the road as it makes a short switchback, or take a more direct route west through the trees. When you exit the forest into another open run, you should be back on the road (assuming you took the shortcut) and at mile 2.4.

From here, leave the road and turn straight up the open slope (north), following the fall line all the way to the top of the ridge above. Reach the ridgetop at mile 2.9 and 9700 feet in elevation. Turn left (west) and continue for 0.1 mile, arriving at the Line Shack at mile 3.0 **(UTM: 13 373355 4383182)**. From your vantage on this ridge, you have incredible views of the Grouse Creek and Whiskey Creek valleys, as well as the upper ski runs of Beaver Creek Ski Resort less than 2 miles away.

THE DESCENTS

The primary descents are the ski runs on **the northeast slope** of Meadow Mountain, visible from the parking lot. In addition, if you go as far as the **Line Shack,** there are plenty of opportunities to leave the trail on your descent and make turns in the untracked snow on either side. Enjoy.

THE APRÈS SKI

When you're done on the slopes for the day, head into Minturn, Vail, or Avon. All are equally close. For more information, visit www.minturn.org/VisitMinturn/index.html, www.vailvalleydiningguide.com, www.vailchamber.org/restaurants.php, and http://co-avon.civicplus.com.

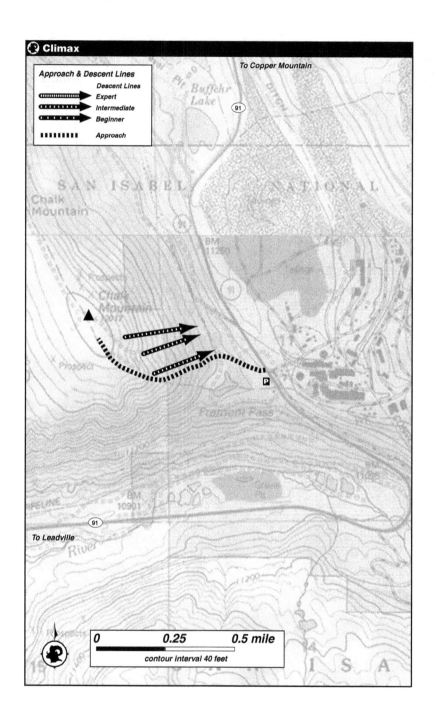

CLIMAX

THE ESSENTIALS

Nearest Towns Leadville, Copper/
Frisco
Distance 0.75 mile
Vertical 700'
Season December to May
Elevation Range 11,300' to 12,000'
Difficulty Rating Easy
Skiing Rating ❷ ❷

SNOTEL Station Fremont Pass (485)
Forest Zone San Isabel Na-
tional Forest, Leadville
Ranger District
CAIC Zone Sawatch Range
USGS Quad Climax
Weather COZ058

THE HISTORY

The year was 1879 when Leadville prospector Charles Senter discovered an outcrop of molybdenite near the summit of Fremont Pass. Senter didn't know what it was, and it took until 1895 for a chemist to identify the deposit. There wasn't a market for the material at first, but steelmakers soon discovered molybdenum's usefulness in producing hard steel alloys. By 1915, the first ore shipments began, and by 1918, a mine known as Climax was in full-blown operation. However, the end of World War I also saw a drop in ore prices, and the mine shut down in 1919.

Then, in 1924, the Climax Molybdenum Company reopened the mine, which operated continuously into the 1980s. Over time, a community sprang up next to the mine, and that "town" eventually became the highest settlement in the United States, and home to the highest post office and highest railroad station in the country. (All three claims have since been relinquished now that Climax no longer exists.)

At its height, that mining town atop Fremont Pass had 500 houses that were home to 1600 people. In the fall of 1936, mine employees John Petty and Scott "Jack" Gorsuch asked resident manager Tex Romig for permission to cut runs in the trees on the east slope of Chalk Mountain for a downhill ski area. The mining company thought it was a great idea, an improvement that would make life on the pass more bearable for the miners and their families.

Using a book, *The Art of Skiing,* as their guide, and lights and wires borrowed from the mine, Petty, Gorsuch, and numerous volunteers worked nights—91 straight evenings and weekends in all—to clear trees and to burn and blast out tree stumps. The Climax Ski Area opened in January 1937, with no lift service. Skiers hiked to the top and skied down, squeezing in three runs per day. Nevertheless, Climax grew in popularity, and on April 25, 1937, held the first Climax Ski Meet, which drew a crowd of 300 people. The following year, the race was sanctioned by the Southern Rocky Mountain Ski Association, and 70 racers arrived for the slalom course on Chalk Mountain—1400 feet long with 600 feet of vertical.

In 1941, Climax skiers founded the Continental Ski Club. Under the club's direction, the ski area shifted from a private affair for the miners to a publicly available ski area. The club also undertook some significant upgrades. Skiers installed a rope tow, powering it with a diesel engine salvaged from a wrecked dump truck. They also added night lighting, using thousands of bulbs from the mine strung along three runs on the mountain. It was Colorado's first night skiing. The improved area opened in December 1941, and had night skiing from 7 PM to 10 PM on Wednesdays and Fridays, and day skiing from 10 AM to 4 PM on weekends.

In addition to slalom races on Chalk Mountain during that 1941/1942 ski season, Climax started holding downhill ski races on 13,555-foot Bartlett Mountain, on the east side of the pass above the mine and Glory Hole, its massive open pit. The race course was 1.25 miles long, and had over 2000 feet of vertical. Six sets of flags guided skiers the safest way down the mountain, skirting the edge of the Glory Hole, negotiating a gully called the Chimney, and ending near the Philipson Tunnel Portal. Spectators could watch the whole thing from Chalk Mountain across the pass. Slalom races on Chalk, meanwhile, were marked using 100 flags to mark 35–40 gates.

Although the ski area averaged 28 skiers per day, during World War II Climax became very popular, attracting hundreds of skiers (up to 500 on a weekend day, including soldiers from the 10th Mountain Division, who trained at nearby Camp Hale). It has also been reported that, owing to its night skiing and proximity to Camp Hale, Climax was the only ski area in the world with its own dedicated air defense blackout warden, a man responsible for cutting the night lights in the event of a blackout alert.

After the war, in 1946, Climax hosted a downhill race that has become the stuff of legend. The details of the account are consistent, although the date of the race is debated as having happened either in April, or on May 6. Regardless, the day was cloudy, with snow falling. Racers, who had to climb Bartlett Mountain to the top of the race course, carried pine boughs with them and dropped the branches along the course to better mark the route in the poor visibility. Racers started the downhill course at half-minute intervals. Immediately, several problems became evident. The radios allowing the start and finish lines to communicate stopped working. Also, thanks to the poor visibility, some racers finished the course, but others did not. One racer reportedly finished 5 miles below the pass! Organizers cancelled the race, and everyone retired to the local tavern instead. The slalom race, held the next day, was infinitely more successful.

In 1947, the Climax mine funded a major renovation for the ski area. A new, steel, 300-skier per hour T-bar was installed, 2600 feet long (other sources say it carried 600 skiers per hour, and was 2800 feet long). It extended lift service to the top of Chalk Mountain, adding to the vertical drop to make a total of 720 feet. The mine leased the new lift back to the Continental Ski Club for $75. Four ski runs were fully lit for night skiing. Climax employees paid $10 for a season pass. Their families skied for free.

The "Buzz"

This mountain is great because it's basically roadside. There's a super-short approach, and gentle slopes with generally low avalanche danger. However, the gentle slope makes it too low angle to enjoyably ski in deep powder. Spring skiing on firm snow would be best, though turns in midwinter can be great, too, as long as the fresh snow's not too deep.

—Andrew J.

Into the 1950s, Climax remained a popular destination, officially operating from November 15 through April 15. Amenities included a warming hut, snack bar, ski patrol and first aid station, and ski equipment rental shop. The Fremont Trading Post, near the parking lot, had a ski shop, general store, food market, service station, garage, restaurant, and paid ski patrollers. Season passes then cost $17.50 per person, which also paid your membership in the Continental Ski Club. A one-day lift ticket was just $2.

The runs on Chalk Mountain were eventually named for Jack Gorsuch, one of the original men to cut the trails, and his family. There was "Zella Intermediate," "Jackie Beginners," "Davey's Cutoff," "Billy Bash," and "Scott Downhill." Jack's son, Dave Gorsuch, went on to become a U.S. Olympian, skiing in the 1960 Olympics at Squaw Valley.

Two years later, in 1962, the Climax ski area shut down. The mining company got out of the business of providing homes and amenities for its employees, to focus exclusively on the mining. The residential houses were transported down to Leadville in 1965, and the ski area was no more.

Today, the runs are still visible on the east slope of Chalk Mountain, as is an old wooden hut near their base. Otherwise, little remains of the ski area that hosted Colorado's first night skiing. The Climax mine, meanwhile, plans to reopen in 2010.

THE TRAILHEAD

Begin at the Fremont Pass Trailhead (**UTM: 13 397653 4358228**) between Copper Mountain and Leadville on Highway 91. From Leadville, drive north on Highway 91 for 13 miles to the 11,318-foot summit of Fremont Pass. Park on the west side of the pass across from the Climax Mine. From Copper Mountain, drive south on Highway 91 for 11 miles to the summit of the pass.

THE APPROACH

From the trailhead on the west side of Fremont Pass, Chalk Mountain and the old Climax Ski Area are visible directly to the west above the trees. Walk north on the shoulder of Highway 91 for 50 yards or so, and then start skinning west up a 4WD road. Although Chalk Mountain above is on national forest land, the immediate area of the Fremont

Chalk Mountain viewed from the summit of Fremont Pass

Pass summit is private property and patented mining claims. Stick to the road and respect the private property around it.

Around mile 0.15, the road forks. The right fork turns north and contours across the lower east face of Chalk Mountain. Stay left, aiming for the base of the leftmost ski run. At mile 0.2, you'll be there. Leave the road behind, and head west directly up the ski run. At mile 0.5, you should reach treeline and arrive at the southeast shoulder of the mountain. Gradually turn northwest, following the path of least resistance to the 12,017-foot summit of Chalk Mountain (**UTM: 13 396619 4358573**), which is reached at mile 0.75.

THE DESCENTS

There are three primary descents on Chalk Mountain: one on **skier's right** (also used for the ascent); **the east face** directly below the summit (which continues down into a shallow gully); and one to **skier's left** on a mellow ridge. If skiing from the summit, beware of an avalanche-prone slope just below the convex rollover from the summit plateau to the east face. During a visit here in early December, I saw this slope slide naturally. It can be safely skirted to skier's right or left. Immediately below the avalanche-prone area, an old 4WD road cuts across the face. This is a good point from which to start your descent for the middle run and the run to skier's left. For the run to skier's right, start where you like and have fun.

THE APRÈS SKI

At the end of the day, descend off Fremont Pass into Leadville. Visit www.centralcolorado.com/leadville/dining/dining.htm or www.skicooper.com/leadville/restaurants.html.

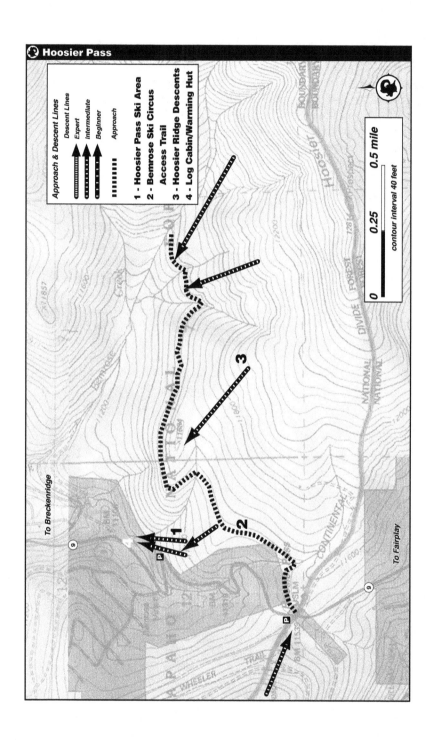

HOOSIER PASS

THE ESSENTIALS

Nearest Town	Breckenridge	**SNOTEL Station**	Hoosier Pass (531)
Distance	2.5 miles	**Forest Zone**	White River National Forest, Dillon Ranger District
Vertical	1000' max.		
Season	December to April		
Elevation Range	11,100' to 12,200'	**CAIC Zone**	Vail & Summit County Area
Difficulty Rating	Easy		
Skiing Rating	⚡⚡	**USGS Quad**	Alma
		Weather	COZ034

THE HISTORY

The history of skiing at Hoosier Pass and Breckenridge, as with many other lost Colorado ski areas, begins with the history of gold and other such objects of miners' affections. During the summer of 1859, gold was discovered along the Blue River. Miners established a base camp that would ultimately become the Breckenridge we know today. In November 1859, General George Spencer formally created the Town of "Breckinridge." Looking to gain the favor of the federal government (and a post office), Spencer named the town after John Cabell Breckinridge, vice president to James Buchanan. It worked, and in 1860, Breck had its post office.

With the onset of the Civil War, however, Breck had egg on its face. John Cabell Breckinridge sided with the South, was made a Confederate Brigadier General, and was kicked out of the U.S. government for treason. Embarrassed, the Colorado town altered the spelling of its name to *Breckenridge*.

By 1879, Breckenridge and Hoosier Pass had their earliest and most famous skier: Father John Dyer. Dyer was known as the "Snowshoe Itinerant," a Methodist minister who carried mail and the gospel throughout the surrounding high country. He built Breck's first church in 1880 (it still stands on Wellington Avenue). He also skied enormous distances—to Alma, Fairplay, and South Park—using 12-foot-long wooden skis.

Lift service finally became a part of the equation in January 1938, when the South Park Lions Club first investigated the idea of building a ski area on the north side of Hoosier Pass. One year later, in January 1939, it was a reality. They had a lift-served downhill ski area with several runs, as well as a 200-foot jump and a toboggan slide. There was a large restaurant with a bar, dancing area, and restrooms, and a separate log cabin used as a warming hut. The restaurant no longer stands, but the warming hut does.

The "Buzz"

Because the old ski area is road-side, and there's tons of below- and above-treeline terrain nearby, you can basically have as big or small a day as you want. It's super accessible from either side of the pass.

—The author

The Hoosier Pass ski area operated through the 1940s, and reportedly even had lights for night skiing. It shut down in 1951 at the end of the 1950/1951 ski season and never re-opened. Just a decade later, however, the Breckenridge Ski Area opened in December 1961. It would grow to become one of the most visited ski resorts in all of the United States, logging more than 1.4 million skier visits during the 1999/2000 season.

Today, in addition to the warming hut, two of the runs of the old Hoosier Pass ski area are plainly visible. Above the old ski area is the Bemrose Ski Circus, named for the nearby Bemrose mine. The Forest Service named the area borrowing a European term used for alpine areas connected by a network of lifts and trails. Lifts there are not, but trails and the backcountry skiing, absolutely. And then there's Hoosier Pass itself, historic stomping grounds of Father Dyer, the Snowshoe Itinerant Preacher.

THE TRAILHEAD

There are two trailhead possibilities for Hoosier Pass: the lower ski area, and the summit of Hoosier Pass.

The Lower Ski Area Trailhead provides immediate access to the old runs of the Hoosier Pass ski area. From downtown Breckenridge, drive south on Route 9 for 9 miles. At the apex of the road switchback at 11,240 feet, there is a small parking pullout with room for just one vehicle. Park here, if the space is available. Otherwise, continue to the summit of Hoosier Pass.

The Hoosier Pass Summit Trailhead provides access to the old ski area, the Bemrose Creek Ski Circus, Hoosier Ridge, Father Dyer's historic ski route, and other backcountry skiing destinations. From Breckenridge, drive south on Highway 9 for 10 miles to the summit of Hoosier Pass. Park in a large lot on the west side of the pass. From downtown Fairplay, drive north on Highway 9 for 11 miles to the Hoosier Pass summit.

THE APPROACH

If approaching from the lower trailhead, head east into the trees. Almost immediately you'll intersect the middle of the ski run to skier's left. Yes, you're already there. It's that easy.

If approaching from the Hoosier Pass Summit Trailhead, carefully cross to the east side of Highway 9, and ascend the snowbank for 25 yards to the trailhead sign for the Bemrose Creek Ski Circus. From the trailhead sign, turn north and follow the trail. It soon turns east, and at mile 0.25 crosses a small creek drainage. The route turns north again into the forest, and slowly turns east as the trail rounds a subtle ridge. At mile 0.8 you'll intersect another creek drainage. Following (and skiing) this drainage downhill leads to the old ski run on skier's right. Following (and skinning) this drainage uphill (a trail may or may not be visible, depending on conditions) leads to the upper north-facing slopes of Hoosier Ridge.

Continue on the main trail until mile 2.0, at which point you'll intersect the main drainage that feeds Bemrose Creek. Multiple gullies and snow-covered slopes are above you on Hoosier Ridge. Choose your line.

THE DESCENTS

At the old Hoosier Pass ski area, there are **two open slopes** still visible. Ski either one. You can also continue up into the Bemrose Ski Circus, where there are other downhill skiing opportunities. Above treeline, numerous **gullies** and **slopes** are prime for skiing on Hoosier Ridge. The upper portions of the ridge get blown clean by wind, but the lower portions and areas down into the trees are great. Focus on staying in the trees in midwinter, and venture higher in spring when the wind slab has turned to spring corn.

EXTRA CREDIT

Close by on the west side of the pass is an obvious snow slope popular with skiers and snowboarders. Take your turn on it.

THE APRÈS SKI

At the end of the day, descend the north side of the pass into Breckenridge, where you'll have more than enough options for dining and drinks. Visit www.breckenridgediningguide.com and www.gobreck.com/page.php?pname=winter/about/dining.

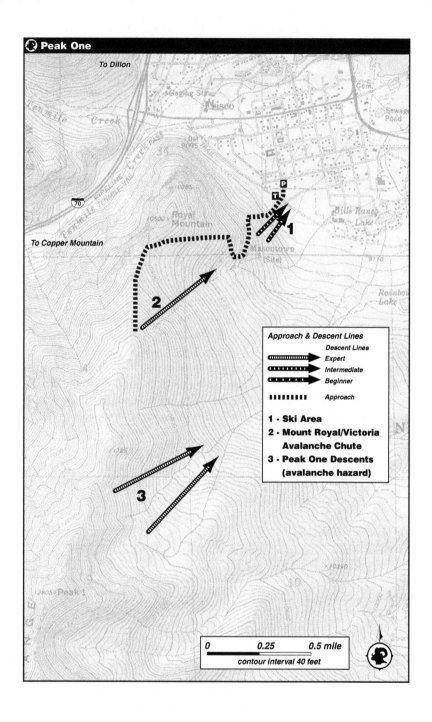

Peak One

To Dillon

To Copper Mountain

Approach & Descent Lines

	Descent Lines
▬▬▶	Expert
▬▬▶	Intermediate
▬▬▶	Beginner
▮▮▮▮▮	Approach

1 - Ski Area
2 - Mount Royal/Victoria
    Avalanche Chute
3 - Peak One Descents
    (avalanche hazard)

0   0.25   0.5 mile

contour interval 40 feet

PEAK ONE

THE ESSENTIALS

Nearest Town Frisco
Distance 1.7 miles
Vertical 2100'
Season December to April
Elevation Range 9100' to 11,200'
Difficulty Rating Easy
Skiing Rating 🌀 🌀

SNOTEL Station Copper Mountain (415)
Forest Zone White River National Forest, Dillon Ranger District
CAIC Zone Vail & Summit County Area
USGS Quad Frisco
Weather COZ034

THE HISTORY

Peak One, Mount Royal, and Frisco's skiing history dates to 1910, when Peter Prestrud built a ski jump north of Interstate 70 near the entrance to Tenmile Canyon. The ski jump was located on the tailings pile of the Excelsior Mine. Nine years later, another jumping hill was built—this one near Dillon—where the world record was temporarily set by Anders Haugen. That ski area was later inundated when the dam was built and Dillon Reservoir flooded the valley. Beginning in the 1920s, the Arapahoe Basin Ski Club organized "snow carnivals" in the Frisco area.

Then, in 1967, Art Brookstrum developed the ski runs you can see today. They were used primarily by local high schools for ski-jumping competitions, although backcountry skiers currently use the old runs to make turns in fresh backcountry powder a stone's throw from downtown. By 1979, the Colorado High School Activities Association discontinued jumping at high school ski meets, and the area went into a period of disuse. It reopened briefly in February 1989, when the ski area was used for a Junior Olympic qualifying tournament. Summit High School retained the U.S. Forest Service special use permit for a while, though no additional skiing took place there.

Around the same time that Brookstrum developed the small ski area just outside of Frisco on the lower slopes of Mt. Royal, another developer had a much grander plan for the northeast slopes of Peak One. Jim Temple and Peak One Limited envisioned a base area a half mile south of Frisco, with several large lifts that would whisk skiers to the upper slopes of Peak One. An earlier and similar proposal in 1954 never got off the ground because the key landowner at the base—Dan Mogee—wasn't interested. However, Temple's Peak One ski area proposal reportedly had the support of the Town of Frisco. However, the Forest

The "Buzz"

Like Red Mountain in Glenwood Springs, this ski area can almost be done from downtown. The views are great, and the skiing's good. And nothing's better than ending your day in a town with a good microbrewery.

—The author

Service ultimately determined that the preexisting Breckenridge and Keystone ski areas, the scenic impacts of developing Peak One, and the preferability of Copper Mountain as a site for ski area development, were too much to justify the Peak One ski area, and the project was never built.

The Forest Service did consider a ski area on the north slope of Ophir Mountain, a comparatively small hill just south of Frisco exclusively on Forest Service land, but it, too, was never built.

Today, Peak One and Mt. Royal are a combination of what was and what almost was. The slopes of Peak One are highly avalanche-prone in winter, but provide great spring skiing once the snowpack stabilizes. The ski runs on Mount Royal make a great winter destination, as does the Masontown site above the ski area. An avalanche chute above the Masontown site, when stable, also provides a great ski.

THE TRAILHEAD

Begin at the Mt. Royal Trailhead in Frisco. From Main Street in Frisco, turn south onto 2nd Avenue. Drive four blocks to the intersection of 2nd and Pitkin Street. Just beyond that intersection is the winter road closure for the trailhead. Park here.

THE APPROACH

From the Mt. Royal winter trailhead, continue south on the extension of 2nd Avenue. After less than 0.1 mile, cross the Summit County Recreation Path, which links Breckenridge and Copper Mountain. Continue to the base of the mountain and a day-use area. Here you have two options. A split-rail fence marks the base of one of the ski runs. Go to it, pick your run, and start skinning up. Or, to preserve the powder on the runs, you could use a connector trail that leaves from the northwest corner of the day-use area and links with the Mt. Royal Trail after 0.2 mile. Then turn left on the Mt. Royal Trail, arriving at the top of the ski runs after 0.4 mile. Start skiing laps.

To add more vertical to your day, and to see some more history, continue to the old Masontown site, and then upward to the north ridge of Peak One, where old log cabins sit hidden in the woods. From the Mt. Royal Trail atop the old ski runs, continue west on the Mt. Royal Trail to the Masontown site at mile 0.5. Stay with the trail, which will switchback once before making a long, ascending traverse to the 10,400-foot saddle between Mt. Royal and Peak One. From the saddle, turn south and tackle the North Ridge of Peak One directly. En route you'll pass the remains of several old log cabins. At mile 1.5, you should be on the shoulder of the North Ridge at an elevation of 11,200 feet. From here, contour east around the ridge until you intersect the top of an avalanche chute. Decades ago, this chute had a large treeless starting zone that loaded with snow. In the years since, the starting zone has filled in somewhat, but the chute remains clear of trees, making for a phenomenal ski run. It is, however, perched at 37 degrees—prime angle to slide. Study the snow stability carefully before committing to it. Otherwise, stay to skier's left in open trees and gentler slopes.

THE DESCENTS

There are three main areas to ski—the **old ski area**, the **avalanche chute** above Masontown, and the **east slopes of Peak One**. The old ski area has two main runs still visible and very skiable. Pick either one.

If you're looking for more vertical per run, continue up the shoulder of Peak One (the shoulder is also known as Mt. Victoria) to the top of the avalanche chute. Make sure the snow is stable. If it is, enjoy the long run perched at 37 degrees. You can also stay to skier's left in a section of open trees.

EXTRA CREDIT

For extra credit, you can ski the east slopes of Peak One. These slopes are very avalanche-prone in midwinter. Wait for spring for the snow to consolidate, and make sure it's stable before you take any risks.

THE APRÈS SKI

Frisco is your obvious choice. Visit www.townoffrisco.com/business/ directory/directory.php?sort=Dining.

Try this local favorite:

Backcountry Brewery, 710 Main Street, (970) 668-2337, www.backcountrybrewery.com

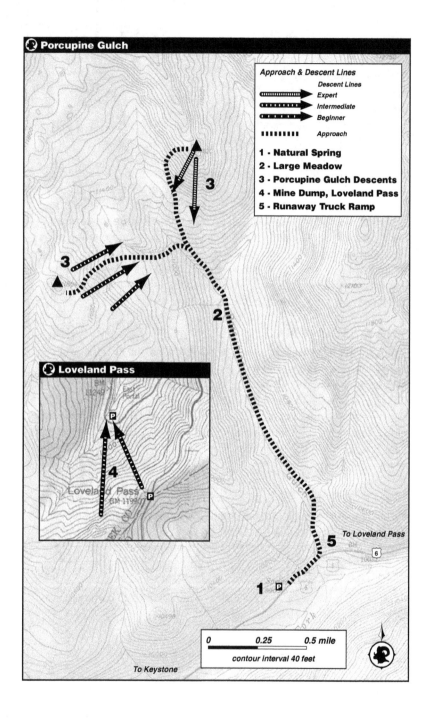

Porcupine Gulch

Approach & Descent Lines

Descent Lines
- Expert
- Intermediate
- Beginner

Approach

1 - Natural Spring
2 - Large Meadow
3 - Porcupine Gulch Descents
4 - Mine Dump, Loveland Pass
5 - Runaway Truck Ramp

Loveland Pass

To Loveland Pass

To Keystone

0   0.25   0.5 mile

contour interval 40 feet

PORCUPINE GULCH

THE ESSENTIALS

Nearest Towns Keystone, Dillon	**SNOTEL Station** Loveland Basin (602)
Distance 2.5 miles	**Forest Zone** White River National Forest, Dillon Ranger District
Vertical 1850'	
Season December to May	
Elevation Range 9950' to 11,800'	**CAIC Zone** Vail & Summit County Area
Difficulty Rating Moderate	**USGS Quad** Loveland Pass
Skiing Rating ❄ ❄ ❄	**Weather** COZ034

THE HISTORY

During the 1910s, ski clubs were forming with increasing frequency throughout the state, including in Denver, where the Denver Winter Sports Club took shape (an early predecessor to today's Colorado Mountain Club). By the 1930s, several Denver skiers had established themselves as prominent fixtures in the state's skiing community: J. C. Blickensderfer, Dick Tompkins, and Thor Groswald, a Norwegian who started a ski factory in Denver at 12th and Shoshone streets. The men formed a new club: the Ski Club Zipfelberger. Loveland Pass was its base of operations.

Leading up to the mid-1930s, Loveland Pass was popular among backcountry skiers, who would drive or hike to the top of the pass and then ski down. The most popular run was called Mine Dump (it still exists today), which ended at a switchback in the road below the east side of the pass. Between 1936 and 1938, Loveland Pass closed for repairs and improvements. When the pass reopened for the winter of 1938, Groswold and Blickensderfer set up a portable rope tow in a snowy basin on the east side of the pass. It was powered by a 4.5-horsepower engine mounted on a toboggan, and they left the setup in place for several weeks. On December 12, 1938, the *Rocky Mountain News* published an article about the new and improved road over the pass, which the state planned to keep open throughout winter in order to allow access for skiing on both sides of Loveland.

Inspired by the ski area at Sun Valley, Idaho, clubs like the Zipfelbergers wanted their own ski lodges. In 1939, the Zipfelbergers made their lodge a reality. They built it in the trees just below treeline on the east side of the pass. That December, the U.S. Forest Service built two ski runs (near the present-day Loveland Valley ski area), and by Thanksgiving 1940, the Zipfelbergers completed a second cabin near the first.

Soon, the beginnings of today's Loveland ski area were in operation on the east side.

However, despite their cabin's location on the east side, the Zipfelbergers' favorite ski run was Porcupine Gulch, on the west side of Loveland Pass halfway between Arapahoe Basin and Keystone. Groswold and others would bring their portable rope tow—including the toboggan-mounted engine—along with 1000 feet of rope on a pulley system. They'd anchor the setup to trees and snow anchors, and ski Porcupine Gulch to their hearts' content. They called it the Little Sweden Freezer Company. Sometimes, rather than ride the tow up into Porcupine Gulch, they'd start out atop Loveland Pass and drop into Porcupine Gulch from above, schussing for several miles before popping out low on the Loveland Pass Road.

As the Loveland ski area (and then Arapahoe Basin and then Keystone) grew and became more popular with better infrastructure, Porcupine Gulch fell out of use. Today it is a wild and untouched place. There are no trails, no people, just snow and the basins of Loveland Pass' west side, and the memory of the Zipfelbergers that once schussed those very slopes.

THE TRAILHEAD

Begin at a parking pullout for a natural spring halfway between Arapahoe Basin and Keystone Resort on the north side of Highway 6 (**UTM**:

A skier chest-deep in crust on dust during a descent at Porcupine Gulch

13 421205 4386484). From Arapahoe Basin, drive west on Highway 6 for 3 miles to the parking area, which is located less than a third of a mile west of a prominent runaway truck ramp. From Keystone, drive east on Highway 6 for 3 miles to the trailhead.

THE APPROACH

From the parking area, walk east along the shoulder of Highway 6 for 0.2 mile. Before reaching the runaway truck ramp, you'll arrive at Porcupine Gulch, where a creek meets the road from the north. This is your ticket. Click in to your skis here.

Start out heading north up Porcupine Gulch, keeping to the east side of the drainage. Up until mile 0.5, there is a subtle trail. It will guide you past the west end of the truck ramp. However, be cautious of staying too far to climber's right in the drainage. Don't get lured up a side drainage below Point 12,103. Stay with the main creek of Porcupine Gulch. Doing so will guide you through a series of meadows with stands of forest in between. Finally, at mile 1.6, you'll arrive in a large meadow (**UTM: 13 420679 4388660**) with views of Point 11,830 to your north.

From the meadow, Porcupine Gulch splits. Take the left fork. However, as you ascend, stay on the slopes above the creek drainage. Following the creek too closely can get you caught in a steep-walled gully that is miserable to climb out of. Save yourself that trouble and stay above the creek. Three-tenths of a mile above the meadow, you have a choice. Cross the creek and head west up to the northeast face of Point 11,804. Or continue northwest, and then north, and then northeast, up the south- and southwest-facing slopes of Point 11,830. Your choice of destination will depend on snow conditions, time of year, and which slope aspect holds the best snow. Either option results in a total distance of 2.5 miles one way from the parking lot.

THE DESCENTS

Porcupine Gulch offers many opportunities for great descents. Try these options:

The "*Buzz*"

Access is convenient, even if the approach is arduous. Once you're in there, it's worth it. The terrain is friendly, and has great runs. Plus, it's cool to see Arapahoe Basin and Keystone so close in the background while you're skiing. The only downside is that you could get stuck in skier traffic, even though you were in the backcountry and never at the resorts!
—Jeff B.

Point 11,830: Ski the southwest-facing slopes, which offer about 600 feet of vertical per lap perched at 37 degrees.

Point 11,804: Ski the northeast and east-facing slopes. Also about 600 feet of vertical per lap, with varying slope angles.

EXTRA CREDIT

Park at Loveland Pass and take your turn on Mine Dump. Drop down the east side of the pass and follow the fall line (or hordes of backcountry skiers) to the hairpin turn 600 feet below. Use a shuttle car, or hitch a ride back to the top. (Or park at the hairpin turn below, reverse the order of operations, and ski back down to your vehicle.)

THE APRÈS SKI

Keystone and Dillon offer your best bets. Visit http://keystone.snow.com/info/din.asp, www.summitchamber.org/dining.cfm, and www.townofdillon.com/Business%20Directory/Restaurants.

Try this local favorite:

Dillon Dam Brewery, 754 Anemone Trail, (970) 262-7777, www.dambrewery.com

Looking up one of many possible runs at Porcupine Gulch

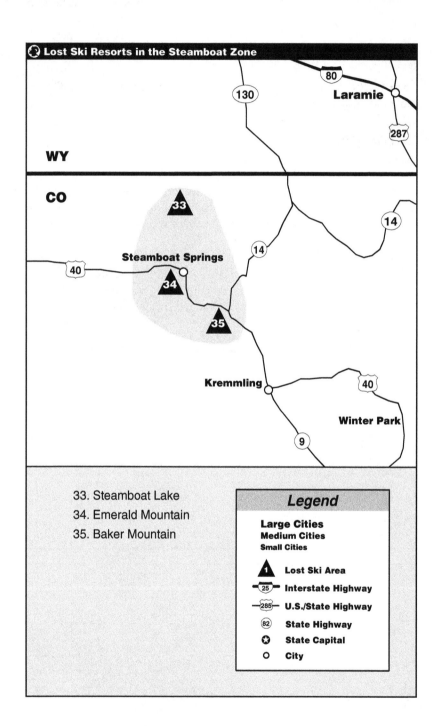

WY

CO

80

130

Laramie

287

33

14

Steamboat Springs

14

40

34

35

Kremmling

40

Winter Park

9

33. Steamboat Lake
34. Emerald Mountain
35. Baker Mountain

Legend

Large Cities
Medium Cities
Small Cities

1   Lost Ski Area
25   Interstate Highway
285   U.S./State Highway
82   State Highway
✪   State Capital
○   City

Lost Ski Resorts in the
Steamboat Zone

he Steamboat zone describes the region in
northwestern Colorado surrounding the town
of Steamboat Springs. It stretches from Kremmling
west to Yampa, and north to the village of Hahn's
Peak. This section of the guide includes three lost
ski areas. The Steamboat zone has earned a rightful
reputation for some of the lightest powder in the
state, as well as for some of the deepest snowpack,
second only perhaps behind Wolf Creek Pass in the
southern San Juans. The zone is home to the famed
Steamboat Springs (Mount Werner) ski area, as well
as some of the largest lost resorts in the whole state
(Stagecoach, south of Steamboat, may be the largest). The lost areas are listed from north to south.

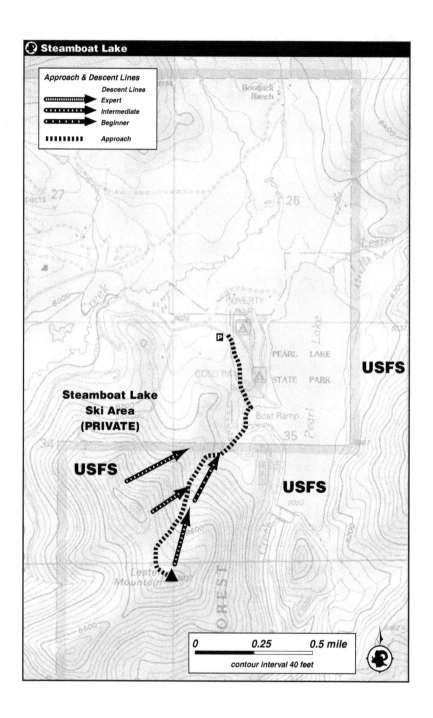

Steamboat Lake

Approach & Descent Lines

Descent Lines
━━━━━▶ Expert
━━━━━▶ Intermediate
━━━━━▶ Beginner

▪▪▪▪▪▪▪▪ Approach

Steamboat Lake
Ski Area
(PRIVATE)

USFS

USFS

USFS

PEARL LAKE
STATE PARK

Boat Ramp

Lester
Mountain

0   0.25   0.5 mile

contour interval 40 feet

STEAMBOAT LAKE

THE ESSENTIALS

Nearest Towns Clark, Steamboat
Springs
Distance 1.3 miles
Vertical 800'
Season December to April
Elevation Range 8000' to 8827'
Difficulty Rating Easy
Skiing Rating ❷ ❷

SNOTEL Station Elk River (467)
Forest Zone Pearl Lake State Park;
Routt National Forest,
Hahn's Peak/Bears
Ears Ranger District
CAIC Zone Steamboat/Park Range
Area
USGS Quad Hahn's Peak
Weather COZ004

THE HISTORY

The old Steamboat Lake ski area and the peak and town of Hahn's Peak feel far removed from the relative hustle and bustle of Steamboat Springs just 20 miles to their south. Skiing in the area dates to the 1900s, when miners would ski on Hahn's Peak (the mountain), as well as on the tailings piles of mines around Hahn's Peak (the town). The community hosted winter carnivals as early as 1912. Tales are told of a skier who "leapt clear over the courthouse." It's been assumed that the story is a tall tale, but a February 2, 1912, *Routt County Sentinel* article references the feat. A log cabin at the base of a hill on the south end of town served as the courthouse from 1880 to 1900, and it seems very possible that someone could in fact have jumped over it. According to the article, the Norwegian (they're ubiquitous in the stories of Colorado's skiing past) climbed 400 yards up a 40-degree hill before turning around for the courthouse-leaping jump.

Numerous small rope tows on area ranches were the only lift service in the region for many decades until the old Steamboat Lake ski area came into existence. The Steamboat Lake ski area is not at all near the actual Steamboat Lake. It is just west of Pearl Lake, several miles away. The ski area was built on 318 acres of private land on the north side of Lester Mountain. The original developers were the Middle Park Land & Cattle Company and the Steamboat Lake Development Corporation. However, Lifetime Communities, a Florida-based real estate investment trust, foreclosed on the developers and assumed control of the development. The plan was to build a ski area in conjunction with a golf course and $1 million country club; the area was to have possibly as many as 10,000 residents.

Only the ski area was ever built. It had several runs and two double-chairlifts. Gordy Wren managed the area, but it only operated for one season: January through April 1973, weekends only. The development folded. The base lodge was relocated to Mt. Werner (the Steamboat Springs ski area) in 1979, where it became part of the Norwegian Log Condominiums. The chairlifts were removed in 1989, and one was relocated to Howelsen Hill in downtown Steamboat.

The *"Buzz"*

Lester Mountain is home to some great tree skiing at a mellow angle. You can be sure you'll be the only skier on the mountain, and you're not far from the legendary "champagne powder" of Steamboat.
—The author

Today, the old Steamboat Lake ski area is still on private property, with a new, massive log home at the base where the lodge once stood. The ski runs and lift lines are growing in, though still plainly visible. And above, the national forest slopes of Lester Mountain, on which Steamboat Lake was built, remain an enticing destination for the backcountry skier.

As a side note, the Steamboat Springs area is home as well to one of Colorado's largest lost ski areas, also located on private property. Known as Stagecoach, if fully realized, it would have included five base areas, 22 chairlifts, 34 subdivisions, a golf course, and a reservoir. The project lost funding in 1973, and only some of the trails, three lifts, and 22 partial subdivisions were completed. The current owner has run sporadic snowcat operations at the area in the past, but presently has no plans to reopen the ski area.

THE TRAILHEAD

Begin at the entrance to Pearl Lake State Park (the winter road closure) between Glen Eden and Hahn's Peak north of Steamboat Springs. From Steamboat Springs, drive north on Elk River Road (which becomes Route 129) and continue through the tiny towns of Clark, Glen Eden, and Willow Creek Pass. Turn right onto Forest Road 209, and continue for 2 miles to the winter road closure of Pearl Lake State Park (open in winter). Park on the right side of the road just before the information kiosk **(UTM: 13 340237 4517126)**. En route to the trailhead, watch for the old ski runs of the Steamboat Lake ski area to the south, on the north slope of Lester Mountain. The runs and lift line are plainly visible.

THE APPROACH

Alas, the old ski runs, which are on the lower slopes of Lester Mountain's north side, are on private property, just outside the boundaries of both Pearl Lake State Park and Routt National Forest. Fortunately, the

Typical glade terrain—open stands of aspen—
on Lester Mountain above the old Steamboat Lake ski area

The extra-credit "mystery ski area" in Routt National Forest, northeast of Pearl Lake

upper slopes of Lester Mountain have skiing just as good, if not better, and are fully public.

From the trailhead, continue on the road, heading east and then south. At mile 0.3, the road forks. The left fork leads to campsites, the picnic area, and the observation deck. Take the right fork, which descends to the boat ramp on the lakeshore. From here you're on the shore of a small cove on Pearl Lake's west side. Follow the shoreline south to the southwest corner of the cove. Do not continue on the Pearl Lake Connector Trail. Instead, turn west and follow a subtle creek drainage. This drainage provides the easiest route to the summit of Lester Mountain.

At mile 0.6, your route up the creek drainage will be crossed by a snow-covered road, Forest Road 405 (**UTM: 13 340270 4516403**). Continue following the drainage, which is primarily filled with old-growth aspen, and higher up, evergreens. The trees graciously remain wide open and a joy to ski both on the way up and on the way down. Following the creek, your route will slowly veer from west to south. Simply trust that once you're in the drainage, it will lead you to where you want to go. Around mile 1.2, you'll arrive at the saddle between Lester Mountain's summit and a sub-summit (**UTM: 13 339717 4515693**). From here, turn left (west) and follow the rounded ridge to Lester Mountain's 8827-foot summit (**UTM: 13 339834 4515550**).

THE DESCENTS

From the summit of Lester Mountain, drop off the north side and follow your skin track back down the **unnamed creek drainage**. Don't forget to take the time to enjoy turns through untracked snow and wide-open stands of old-growth aspen.

Alternatively, from the saddle below the summit, turn right (north) instead of left (southeast). Continue over a false summit and ski **the next drainage**. Toward the bottom, stay hard to skier's right to stay on national forest and state park lands.

EXTRA CREDIT

Northeast of Pearl Lake is a slope within the bounds of Routt National Forest that looks suspiciously like an old ski area if I've ever seen one. No one knows anything about it. Nevertheless, the slopes are eminently skiable. If the lake is safely frozen, cross Pearl Lake to its northeast shore (otherwise, skirt the shoreline), and ascend the Lester Creek drainage to the base of the slopes. Then climb the area and ski!

THE APRÈS SKI

The closest food can be found in Clark:

Glen Eden Resort, (970) 879-3907, www.glenedenresort.com/tavern. htm

Otherwise, Steamboat Springs has tons of options. Visit www.steamboat-dining.com.

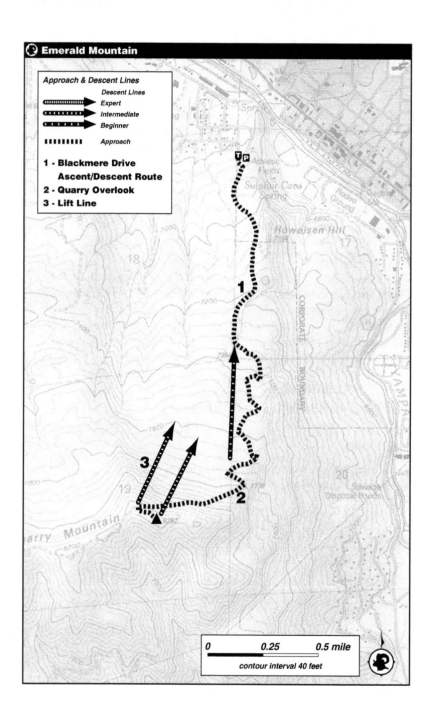

Emerald Mountain

Approach & Descent Lines

Descent Lines
Expert
Intermediate
Beginner

Approach

1 - Blackmere Drive
   Ascent/Descent Route
2 - Quarry Overlook
3 - Lift Line

0   0.25   0.5 mile

contour interval 40 feet

EMERALD MOUNTAIN

THE ESSENTIALS

Nearest Town	Steamboat Springs	**SNOTEL Station**	Dry Lake (457)
Distance	2.6 miles	**Forest Zone**	City of Steamboat Springs
Vertical	1400′		
Season	December to April	**CAIC Zone**	Steamboat/Park Range Area
Elevation Range	6800′ to 8200′		
Difficulty Rating	Easy	**USGS Quad**	Steamboat Springs
Skiing Rating	⊘	**Weather**	COZ005

THE HISTORY

The history of Emerald Mountain is intimately connected to that of Howelsen Hill, Carl Howelsen, and Steamboat Springs. They combine to form one of the richest skiing heritages anywhere in the United States, just one reason Steamboat has successfully branded itself as "Ski Town USA."

The miners around Steamboat had already started skiing the 28-plus feet of snow that fell in an average winter on the mountains' slopes when Norwegian Carl Howelsen arrived in town in 1912. Soon after, he started ski jumping at Strawberry Park. Howelsen organized Steamboat's first Winter Carnival in 1914. There was a ski jump on Woodchuck Hill, men's and women's downhill ski races, and skijoring with horses. Howelsen, nicknamed the Flying Norseman, won the first ski jump competition.

In 1917, the ski slope in town was renamed in Carl's honor: Howelsen Hill. It wasn't until sometime between 1936 and 1938 that Rabbit Ears Pass was kept open in winter. The U.S. Forest Service cut new downhill ski trails, and the popularity of the sport took off. The Emerald Mountain ski area was built to meet that new demand. The ski area was built on its namesake peak, also known as Quarry Mountain on some maps, directly behind Howelsen Hill. Some sources say its first year of operation was the 1947/1948 season, but I've also seen a trail map published in 1939. The mountain had a combination T-bar and single chair to get you up the mountain. The T-bar carried you up the face of Howelsen Hill, from which you'd ski down its backside and re-load onto a chair that carried you to the summit of Emerald. From there you had your choice of many trails, including one that brought you to the Quarry Overlook. There was also the Memorial Run, a 1.5-mile-long trail. And there were two open fields for "free skiing."

In 1943, Steamboat Springs became the first town in the state to have a public school ski program. Then, in 1954, Emerald Mountain shut down. The next year, however, Jim Temple (the same Temple who proposed the Peak One ski area near Frisco) spearheaded the development of what would become today's Steamboat Ski Resort. The new ski area—at first quite modest—opened in 1961 on Storm Mountain. It closed for the following season (1961/1962), but reopened in January 1963 with upgrades and new terrain. One year later, Storm Mountain was renamed Mount Werner, in honor of local Olympic skier Buddy Werner, who was killed in an avalanche in Switzerland. Ownership of Steamboat changed many times, until present-day owner Intrawest took the helm. Steamboat Ski Resort now includes nearly 3000 acres of terrain, 20 lifts, and 165 trails. The town, for its part, has produced more winter Olympians that any other in North America.

Today, thanks to a land exchange between private landowners, the City of Steamboat Springs, and the Bureau of Land Management, much of Emerald Mountain is now public land (part of Steamboat's Parks and Recreation Department), laced with ski trails that you can take all the way to the Quarry Overlook and the mountain's summit. In addition, a 712-acre conservation easement held by the Yampa Valley Land Trust on land owned by the Orton family allows nonmotorized access to the meadows that were once part of the ski area as well. These

The Blackmere Trail leading to the summit of Emerald Mountain

days, the lift line is still evident, but instead of the lift, a power line runs up to the summit of the mountain. Similarly, the summit, which once had lift towers, now has cell and radio towers.

THE TRAILHEAD

Begin at the Blackmere Drive Trailhead of the Howelsen Hill trail system in Steamboat Springs. From downtown Steamboat, drive north on Lincoln Avenue (Highway 40). Turn left onto 13th Street, and then left again onto Gilpin Street (some maps also list this as 2nd Avenue). At the top of Gilpin, turn left onto Saratoga Avenue, and right onto Routt Street. The trailhead is at the top of Routt Street where it meets with Fairview Drive. Park here.

The "Buzz"

Leave your fat boards at home, take your light gear, and have fun. Expect to see lots of people—hikers, dogs, Nordic skiers, a few backcountry skiers, snowshoers. You can chug uphill for a good aerobic workout, then cruise downhill at a relaxed pace, casual enough to hold a conversation with your ski partners.

—The author

THE APPROACH

From the trailhead, follow the Blackmere Drive Trail all the way to the summit of Emerald Mountain (also identified as Quarry Mountain on some maps). A variety of other trails weave a network across the north and east slopes of Emerald Mountain. Blackmere Drive is the largest and most obvious of the trails.

At mile 0.5, you'll pass directly behind the top of Howelsen Hill, which is still in operation. As you pass beneath power lines, take time to pause and look up at Emerald Mountain. That power line was once the old lift line of the ski area, and the lift towers that once stood on top of the mountain have been replaced by cell phone and radio transmission towers. But it's easy to see where the ski area once existed.

Continue on Blackmere to mile 1.9. Here you'll be at the quarry overlook, with great views of downtown Steamboat Springs below, and of the Mt. Werner ski area directly across the valley. From here, turn sharply west on a steeper trail that ascends across the upper north slopes of Emerald Mountain. At mile 2.5, you'll reach the summit ridge and the top of the lift line. The view down the steep lift line to the open snow of Emerald Meadows is grand. To reach the true summit of Emerald Mountain, turn east on the road and follow the summit ridge for 0.1 mile to the top.

THE DESCENTS

Emerald Mountain has a variety of possible descents:

Blackmere: Follow the Blackmere Trail from the summit all the way back to the trailhead. From the summit down to the Quarry Overlook, it's like an easy, narrow intermediate trail at a ski resort. From the Quarry down to the trailhead, it's like a chill green groomer.

Lift Line: Ski the old lift line, which today has a power line in place of lift towers. At the base of the hill, cut to skier's right across a large meadow (part of the conservation easement) and intersect Blackmere.

Glades: From the summit, instead of retracing your steps on the trail, drop straight north into the trees. It starts out tight, but then opens up and is great. When you intersect the trail below, turn right and follow as for Blackmere, or continue down the north slopes in the trees, coming out in the meadow at the base of the hill.

THE APRÈS SKI

Steamboat Springs has tons of options. Visit www.steamboat-dining. com.

Looking down the lift line, home to a power line that serves the radio towers atop Emerald Mountain

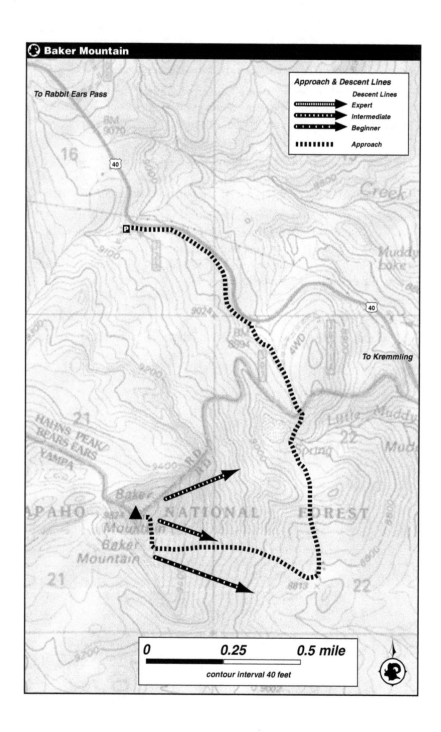

Baker Mountain

To Rabbit Ears Pass

Approach & Descent Lines

Descent Lines
Expert
Intermediate
Beginner

Approach

To Kremmling

HAHNS PEAK/
REARS EARS
YAMPA

Baker
Mountain
Baker
Mountain

APAHO   NATIONAL   FOREST

0   0.25   0.5 mile

contour interval 40 feet

BAKER MOUNTAIN

THE ESSENTIALS

Nearest Town	Kremmling	**SNOTEL Station**	Rabbit Ears (709)
Distance	1.6 miles	**Forest Zone**	Routt National Forest, Parks Ranger District (Kremmling)
Vertical	900'		
Season	December to April		
Elevation Range	8900' to 9800'	**CAIC Zone**	Steamboat/Park Range Area
Difficulty Rating	Easy		
Skiing Rating	⚫ ⚫	**USGS Quad**	Rabbit Ears Peak
		Weather	COZ031, COZ004

THE HISTORY

The Baker Mountain ski area got its start thanks to two ranchers from Kremmling, Joe McElroy and Willard Taussig. (McElroy was later credited as the source of the term "Champagne Powder," used today by Steamboat Springs and the Steamboat Ski Resort.) As the story goes, McElroy and Taussig got tired of driving the 50 miles to Winter Park in order to ski, often with their combined 12 kids in tow. (This sounds awfully reminiscent of the owners of Geneva Basin, who had a similar complaint with their 15 kids!)

Baker Mountain opened in 1950 with three downhill ski runs, a 500-foot rope tow powered with an electric engine, and a second lift to carry skiers higher onto the mountain. Aside from a small avalanche-prone area near the summit, the area was described as having "aspen, open parks, ample snow, and no wind." There was a warming hut at the base heated with a wood stove, and an Army surplus truck fitted with a rotary snow plow was used to try and keep the access road open.

A lifetime membership to the ski area cost $70, and several dozen Middle Park and North Park families became regulars. The Steamboat Springs High School ski team also reportedly trained here occasionally. Alas, after three seasons, Baker Mountain closed in 1953. It may be one of the only ski areas to close because of receiving too much snow. Typically, McElroy or Taussig would plow all day on Saturday to get the road open. But by Sunday, the road and the rope tow were often buried under snow again. The Army truck simply couldn't cope with the quantity of snowfall, and the 75 skiers per day who visited on a busy weekend weren't enough to pack out the road.

Baker Mountain shut its doors, but the same aspen and open snow slopes that lured Kremmling and Middle Park skiers in the first place remain. The lift lines are still visible, cutting an arrow-straight slot through the trees. And perhaps best of all, Baker Mountain stands tall as a proud tribute to Grand County's love of skiing. While other areas of Colorado have earned the accolades in more recent years, Grand County is, in many ways, where it all began. Hot Sulphur Springs, the county seat, hosted the first Winter Carnival west of the Mississippi in February 1912, years before Steamboat had its carnival, Berthoud and Glen Cove had their rope tows, Pioneer had its chairlift, or Climax had its night skiing.

The "Buzz"

Baker Mountain is tons of fun. The approach is easy, the summit is exhilarating with its cliffs off the backside, and the skiing is great. While Rabbit Ears Pass is swarmed with skiers and snowmobiles, chances are you'll have Baker to yourself.

—Kelli B.

THE TRAILHEAD

Begin at the intersection of Forest Road 325 and Highway 40 above Muddy Pass Lake, and between Muddy Pass and Rabbit Ears Pass (**UTM: 13 364085 4472177**). If coming from Kremmling and points east, measure from the junction of Highways 40 and 14 immediately above Muddy Pass. From the junction, drive west on Highway 40, passing Muddy Pass Lake at mile 0.6, and arriving at a large parking area on the left (south) side of the road at mile 1.5. Park here. If coming from Steamboat Springs and points west, measure from the east summit of Rabbit Ears Pass and drive east on Highway 40 for 1.6 miles to the parking area.

THE APPROACH

From the trailhead, start out heading east along Highway 40, skinning on the south side of the road. At mile 0.5, you'll reach a pronounced curve in the road above Muddy Pass Lake. From this curve, look carefully for old Forest Road 307, which heads south up a meadow. The meadow funnels down at its upper end, at which point you'll intersect the road if you haven't found it already. Continue south on Forest Road 307. At mile 1.0 you'll pass a small lake on your right. This unnamed lake is a spring that feeds Little Muddy Creek.

Continue to mile 1.1. Here, the road makes a sharp left turn to contour around a low ridge. Instead of following the road, leave the road here and continue south, climbing a short, open slope to a saddle in the ridge. From the saddle, you have a clear view down to the meadow that was once the base of the old ski area. Descend straight south to the meadow, arriving at mile 1.4 (**UTM: 13 365055 4470428**).

From the meadow, the runs of the old ski area are all to your west. A brief stand of aspen now separates the base from the runs above. Head west uphill through the aspen, popping out onto an open slope at mile 1.6. From the upper right end (northwest corner) of this open slope, find an arrow-straight slot through the trees—this was one of the old lift lines. Follow it until you once again emerge onto open slopes. From here, make a rising traverse to the left (west-southwest), staying on open slopes and skirting the edge of a stand of evergreens.

At mile 2.0, and the 9500-foot elevation, you'll be near the crest of Baker Mountain's southeast ridge. The other side of the ridge falls away in a series of steep cliffs, and following the ridge above is impractical due to the presence of several bands of rock. Instead, turn north-northwest, and contour across the upper east face of the mountain directly beneath the last stand of trees that separates you from the summit. Once beyond those trees, nothing but snow lies between you and the top. Switchback up the east face and arrive at the 9824-foot summit at mile 2.2 (**UTM: 13 364107 4470711**).

THE DESCENTS

From the summit of Baker Mountain, you have several general descent options, with some overlap between them.

Baker Mountain, with the runs in full view, seen during the drive to the trailhead from Kremmling

A skier makes turns on Baker Mountain.

Looking down a run from below Baker Mountain's summit

Follow the **northeast ridge** downhill, and then break off to skier's right (east), descending open slopes to treeline. Continue east through the trees until you intersect the approach road.

Drop directly east from **the summit,** watching for a small avalanche-starting zone and a few rock outcrops. Below those, continue straight down the fall line until you're past the highest stand of trees. Then angle to skier's right toward large, open snow slopes. From those slopes:

Follow the **fall line** straight downhill. At the bottom of the slope, duck into the trees and pop out again quickly into another open area.

Angle hard right around some trees and onto the **southeast shoulder** of the mountain. Ski wide-open slopes to your heart's content. At the next treeline, cut hard to skier's left to intersect the previous run and the lift line, or follow the fall line directly east toward the base area.

THE APRÈS SKI

Kremmling, to the east, is your best bet. Visit www.kremmling chamber.com/restaurants.htm.

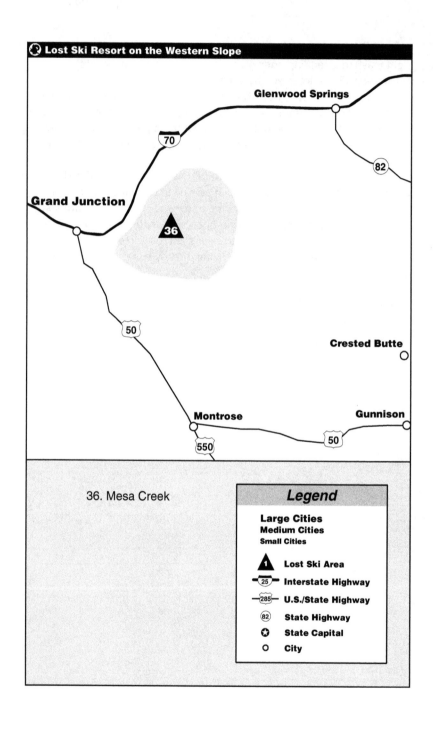

Glenwood Springs

70

82

Grand Junction

36

50

Crested Butte

Montrose

Gunnison

550

50

36. Mesa Creek

Legend

Large Cities
Medium Cities
Small Cities

1   Lost Ski Area
25   Interstate Highway
285   U.S./State Highway
82   State Highway
✪   State Capital
○   City

Lost Ski Resort on the
Western Slope

The Western Slope essentially describes the Grand Mesa. It stretches from Glenwood Springs west to Grand Junction, and south to Paonia. This section of the guide includes just one lost ski area—Mesa Creek. The Western Slope is also home to Powderhorn, the only major ski area within a short drive of Grand Junction and Colorado's canyon country. But what the region lacks in terms of quantity of ski areas (lost or not), it more than makes up for in quality.

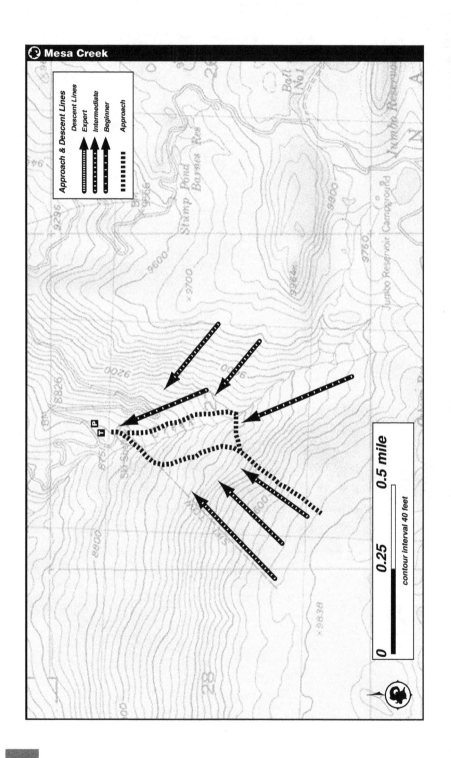

MESA CREEK

THE ESSENTIALS

Nearest Towns Mesa, Cedaredge, Parachute
Distance 1.0 mile max.
Vertical 1000'
Season December to April
Elevation Range 8750' to 9750'
Difficulty Rating Easy
Skiing Rating 🔄 🔄 🔄

SNOTEL Station Mesa Lakes (622)
Forest Zone Grand Mesa National Forest, Grand Valley Ranger District at Grand Junction
CAIC Zone Grand Mesa
USGS Quad Mesa Lakes
Weather COZ009

THE HISTORY

Skiing arrived on Colorado's Western Slope sometime during the 1930s. Even so, it was a hit or miss proposition at first. Yet, as the population grew, so did the popularity of the emerging sport. The first lift-served skiing in the region took place during that same decade atop the Grand Mesa at a place known as Land's End, on the southwest edge of the mesa. Skiers packed out the snow on foot, and used a crude rope tow. When it didn't work, they simply herring-boned uphill. There was also a rope tow called Rimrock on the south side of the mesa near Island Lake. It had great snow, but not much vertical. Throughout the 1930s, the active ski population in the area numbered only about 50.

In 1940, local skiers from the Grand Junction Ski Club built a new ski area "where the wagon road crosses Mesa Creek." It was humble, but unlike earlier areas, it succeeded. Then, following World War II, the U.S. Forest Service issued a permit in 1950 for Mesa Creek, a nonprofit community venture that would expand the small area. There were two ski runs, and two rope tows, each serving 500 feet of vertical.

Throughout the 1950s, local skiers continued to vastly upgrade Mesa Creek, adding a 1300-foot Poma lift and a 2600-foot Poma lift. Many new runs were cut, and the vertical of the ski area was greatly extended. An abandoned Civilian Conservation Corps building at the base became Mesa Creek's warming hut.

By the 1965/1966 season, Mesa Creek logged more than 14,000 skier days per year consistently. But discontented skiers had already begun calling for a larger ski area. They wanted more terrain, more vertical, and more challenging runs. Back in 1958, the Grand Mesa Winter Sports Group had studied a nearby site in Beaver Creek Bowl, where the organization envisioned just such a new ski area to meet skier demands. In 1964, the Forest Service gave its blessing, and the Colorado Grand Mesa Ski Corporation formed to head the venture. It bought the

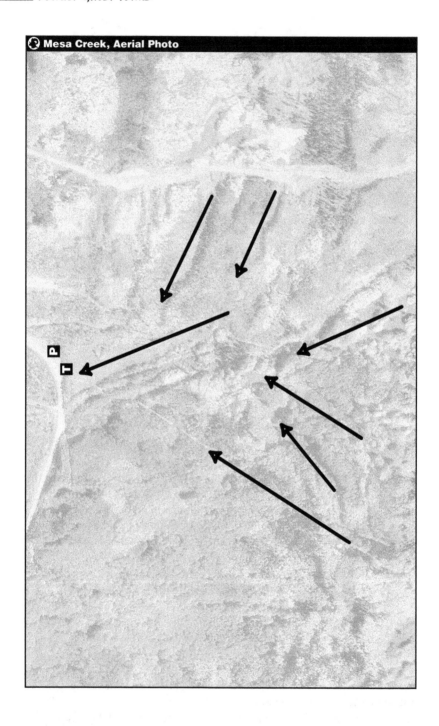

Mesa Creek, Aerial Photo

lifts from Mesa Creek, and in 1966, built the first runs of Powderhorn ski resort.

With Powderhorn up and running, skier activity shifted from Mesa Creek to the new area. Powderhorn was popular, but not enough to keep it out of bankruptcy, which it filed in 1990. Despite such challenges, Powderhorn recovered financially and reopened as a semi-destination resort. Today it has 600 acres of skiable terrain, 1650 feet of vertical, and 250 inches of snow in an average season.

Mesa Creek, meanwhile, is closed but far from forgotten. A Forest Service information kiosk marks the old base area. The runs are still wide open, and Mesa Creek remains a popular backcountry ski destination for skiers on the Western Slope.

The "Buzz"

Access and approach couldn't be easier, and there's tons of great terrain at Mesa Creek. This is simply a phenomenal area.

—Kelli B.

THE TRAILHEAD

Begin at the Mesa Creek parking area at the base of the old ski area (**UTM: 12 750382 4328244**). From the turnoff for Powderhorn ski area on Highway 65, continue east for 2.25 miles. Park on the right side of the road at the obvious base of the old Mesa Creek ski area.

THE APPROACH

Mesa Creek (the stream) divides Mesa Creek (the ski area) in two halves. Where you decide to ski will depend in part on your desired slope angle, and on your desired slope aspect. Since you're already standing at the base of the runs, choose your desired run and skin up it. However, keep in mind that much of Mesa Creek is bound within a steep-walled ravine, and the creek itself doesn't always have enough snow coverage to safely cross in all places. You're left with three choices—cross immediately to the west side at the bottom, cross on a small wooden bridge partway up, or wait until you've climbed nearly to the top and cross above.

If crossing near the bottom, from the base make a beeline for the lift line. It will bring you to a reasonable spot to cross the creek. Once across the creek, begin ascending the lift line, but before you've gained more than 100 feet or so, begin an ascending traverse to climber's left, until you intersect the bottom of the ski runs. If crossing on the wooden bridge, ascend the main beginner run for 100 to 200 yards, and then locate the bridge across the ravine in the trees to climber's right. Once

The author earns his turns on one of Mesa Creek's many ski runs.

across, immediately turn left and continue to follow the ravine on an open slope until you intersect the obvious bottom of the ski runs. Alternatively, if crossing near the top, follow the ski area's main central run straight up the drainage until you've reached the top of the run and the trees. Cut to climber's right, and find a safe spot to cross the creek. Once across, make a rising traverse to climber's right until you intersect a ski run. Once on the run, turn left (uphill) and skin to the top of the mesa.

THE DESCENTS

There are good descents on the **eastern half** of the ski area, and great descents on the **western half**. Refer to the topo map and aerial photo for more detailed location information.

THE APRÈS SKI

Powderhorn ski area offers the closest dining. Otherwise, Mesa, Palisade, and Parachute on the north side of the mesa, and Cedaredge on the south side are the next nearest options. Visit www.powderhorn.com/content/view/74/88/, www.parachutechamber.org/PCC/directory.php?CATEGORY=131, www.palisadecoc.com/dining.html, and www.cedaredgecolorado.com/businessdirectoryii.asp.

RESOURCES

Agencies

Arapaho National Forest
www.fs.fed.us/r2/arnf/

Clear Creek Ranger District
101 Chicago Creek Road
Idaho Springs, CO 80452
(303) 567-3000

Sulphur Range District
9 Ten Mile Drive
Granby, CO 80446
(970) 887-4100

City of Glenwood Springs
www.ci.glenwood-springs.co.us/

101 West 8th Street
Glenwood Springs, CO 81601
(970) 384-6400

City of Steamboat Springs
http://steamboatsprings.net/index.
php?id=250

245 Howelsen Parkway
Steamboat Springs, CO 80477
(970) 879-4300

Colorado State Forest
http://parks.state.co.us/Parks/
StateForest/

56750 Highway 14
Walden, CO 80480
(970) 723-8366

Grand Mesa National Forest
www.fs.fed.us/r2/gmug/

Grand Valley Ranger District at
Grand Junction
2777 Crossroads Boulevard,
Suite 1
Grand Junction, CO 81506
(970) 242-8211

Gunnison National Forest
www.fs.fed.us/r2/gmug/

Gunnison Ranger District
2250 Highway 50
Delta, CO 81416
(970) 874-6600

Jefferson County Open Space
www.co.jefferson.co.us/openspace

700 Jefferson County Parkway,
Suite 100
Golden, Colorado 80401
(303) 271-5925

Medicine Bow National Forest
www.fs.fed.us/r2/mbr/

Brush Creek/Hayden Ranger
District
South Highway 130/230
Saratoga, WY 82331
(307) 326-5258

Laramie Ranger District
2468 Jackson Street
Laramie, WY 82070
(307) 745-2300

Pearl Lake State Park
http://parks.state.co.us/Parks/
pearllake

PO Box 750
Clark, CO 80428
(970) 879-3922

Pike National Forest
www.fs.fed.us/r2/psicc/

Pikes Peak Ranger District
601 South Weber
Colorado Springs, CO 80903
(719) 636-1602

South Platte Ranger District
19316 Goddard Ranch Court
Morrison, CO 80465
(303) 275-5610

Rio Grande National Forest
www.fs.fed.us/r2/riogrande/

Divide Ranger District
13308 West Highway 160
Del Norte, CO 81132
(719) 657-3321

Rocky Mountain National Park
www.nps.gov/romo/

1000 Highway 36
Estes Park, CO 80517
(970) 586-1206

Roosevelt National Forest
www.fs.fed.us/r2/arnf/

Boulder Ranger District
2140 Yarmouth Avenue
Boulder, CO 80301
(303) 541-2500

Routt National Forest
www.fs.fed.us/r2/mbr/

Hahn's Peak/Bear Ears
Ranger District
925 Weiss Drive
Steamboat Springs, CO 80487
(970) 879-1870

Parks Ranger District
2103 East Park Avenue
Kremmling, CO 80459
(970) 724-3000

San Isabel National Forest
www.fs.fed.us/r2/psicc/

Leadville Ranger District
810 Front Street
Leadville, CO 80461
(719) 486-0749

Salida Ranger District
325 West Rainbow Boulevard
Salida, CO 81201
(719) 539-3591

San Carlos Ranger District
3028 East Main Street
Canon City, CO 81212
(719) 269-8500

San Juan National Forest
www.fs.fed.us/r2/sanjuan/

Dolores Ranger District
29211 Highway 184
Dolores, CO 81323
(970) 882-7296

Durango Ranger District
15 Burnett Court
Durango, CO 81301
(970) 247-4874

Uncompahgre National Forest
www.fs.fed.us/r2/gmug/

Ouray Ranger District
2505 South Townsend Street
Montrose, CO 81401
(970) 240-5300

White River
National Forest
www.fs.fed.us/r2/whiteriver/

Aspen Ranger District
806 West Hallam
Aspen, CO 81611
(970) 925-3445

Dillon Ranger District
680 Blue River Parkway
Silverthorne, CO 80498
(970) 468-5400

Eagle Ranger District
125 West 5th Street
Eagle, CO 81631
(970) 328-6388

Holy Cross Ranger District
24747 U.S. Highway 24
Minturn, CO 81645
(970) 827-5715

Sopris Ranger District
620 Main Street
Carbondale, CO 81623
(970) 963-2266

History

WEBSITES

Colorado Ski History Information about lost ski resorts in Colorado and elsewhere. www.coloradoskihistory.com/lostresorts.html

The Colorado Ski Museum www.skimuseum.net/

New England Lost Ski Areas Project www.nelsap.org/

Snow Safety

BOOKS

Daffern, Tony. *Avalanche Safety for Skiers, Climbers, and Snowboarders*. Calgary, Alberta, Canada: Rocky Mountain Books, 1999.

McClung, David, and Peter Shaerer. *The Avalanche Handbook*. Seattle: The Mountaineers, 1993.

Tremper, Bruce. *Staying Alive in Avalanche Terrain*. Seattle: The Mountaineers, 2001.

WEBSITES

Colorado Avalanche Information Center http://avalanche.state.co.us

National Snow and Ice Data Center http://nsidc.org

U.S. Search and Rescue Task Force www.ussartf.org/avalanches.htm

INDEX

ABOUT THE AUTHOR

Peter Bronski (www.peterbronski.com) is a critically acclaimed author and avid backcountry skier. In addition to *Powder Ghost Towns,* he is the author of *At the Mercy of the Mountains: True Stories of Survival and Tragedy in New York's Adirondacks* (The Lyons Press), *Hunting Nature's Fury: A Storm Chaser's Obsession with Tornadoes, Hurricanes, and Other Natural Disasters* (coauthored with Roger Hill, Wilderness Press), and *Artisanal Gluten-Free Cooking* (coauthored with Kelli Bronski, The Experiment).

Bronski's award-winning writing has appeared in more than sixty magazines, including *5280, Denver Magazine, Men's Journal, Rock and Ice, Vermont Sports, Off Piste, AMC Outdoors,* and many others. A member of the North American Snowsports Journalists Association and North American Travel Journalists Association, his work has won awards from the NATJA, Solas Awards for Best Travel Writing, and others.

An amateur ski mountaineering racer during winter, and a nationally competitive Xterra off-road triathlete during summer, Bronski serves as one of the Athletes for Awareness spokespersons for the National Foundation for Celiac Awareness. He lives in Boulder, Colorado with his wife, Kelli, their daughter, Marin, and their dog, Altai.

9 780899 974668